Dazzlingly original but deeply engaged with the philosophical currents of her time, Margaret Cavendish (1623–1673) was one of the most ingenious and exciting philosophers of the seventeenth century. In *Cavendish*, Alison Peterman provides a systematic reading of Cavendish's natural philosophy. While highlighting interpretations of Cavendish that present her as an anthropomorphic thinker, Peterman advocates instead for reading Cavendish in light of her naturalism, materialism, and anti-anthropocentrism, explaining how these themes ramify in Cavendish's metaphysics, philosophy of mind, epistemology, and method. *Cavendish* articulates and explains what is novel and heterodox in Cavendish's views, and also examines her philosophical engagement with other seventeenth-century thinkers like Hobbes, Boyle, Descartes, and Hooke.

An outstanding introduction for newcomers to Cavendish, *Cavendish* is essential reading for students and scholars of Cavendish as well as those taking courses in seventeenth-century philosophy, metaphysics, history of science, philosophy of mind, epistemology, and philosophical methodology.

Alison Peterman is Associate Professor of Philosophy at the University of Rochester, USA. She has written about early modern metaphysics, philosophy of science, philosophy of mind, and epistemology.

The Routledge Philosophers

Edited by Brian Leiter

University of Chicago, USA

Routledge Philosophers is a major series of introductions to the great Western philosophers. Each book places a major philosopher or thinker in historical context, explains and assesses their key arguments, and considers their legacy. Additional features include a chronology of major dates and events, chapter summaries, annotated suggestions for further reading and a glossary of technical terms.

An ideal starting point for those new to philosophy, they are also essential reading for those interested in the subject at any level.

Also available:

For more information about this series, please visit:
https://www.routledge.com/The-Routledge-Philosophers/book-series/ROUTPHIL

Alison Peterman

Cavendish

Routledge
Taylor & Francis Group

LONDON AND NEW YORK

First published 2025
by Routledge
4 Park Square, Milton Park, Abingdon, Oxon OX14 4RN

and by Routledge
605 Third Avenue, New York, NY 10158

Routledge is an imprint of the Taylor & Francis Group, an informa business

British Library Cataloguing-in-Publication Data
A catalogue record for this book is available from the British Library

Library of Congress Cataloging-in-Publication Data
Names: Peterman, Alison, author.
Title: Cavendish/Alison Peterman.
Description: Abingdon, Oxon; New York, NY: Routledge, 2025. |
Series: The Routledge philosophers | Includes bibliographical
references and index.
Identifiers: LCCN 2024045218 (print) | LCCN 2024045219 (ebook) |
ISBN 9780367619565 (hardback) | ISBN 9780367619558 (paperback) |
ISBN 9781003107255 (ebook)
Classification: LCC B1299.N274 P47 2025 (print) | LCC B1299.N274 (ebook) |
DDC 192—dc23/eng/20241213
LC record available at https://lccn.loc.gov/2024045218
LC ebook record available at https://lccn.loc.gov/2024045219

ISBN: 978-0-367-61956-5 (hbk)
ISBN: 978-0-367-61955-8 (pbk)
ISBN: 978-1-003-10725-5 (ebk)

DOI: 10.4324/9781003107255

Typeset in Joanna
by codeMantra

Contents

Acknowledgments

I am deeply grateful for the generosity of so many who provided feedback on the manuscript or just philosophical conversation and inspiration: Paul Audi, Katherine Brading, Deborah Boyle, Tessa Brunnenmeyer, David Cunning, Dante Dauksz, Boris Demarest, Vanessa de Harven, Karolina Hübner, Bryce Huebner, Laura Georgescu, Kevin Lower, Heather McDaniel, Will Miller, James McGrath Morris, Bob Pasnau, Elliot Samuel Paul, Kristin Primus, Lewis Powell, Raul Saucedo, Anat Schechtman, Eric Schliesser, Jonathan Shaheen, Brooke Sharpe, Alison Simmons, Kathryn Tabb, Charles Wolfe. Colin Chamberlain, Keota Fields, and Marcy Lascano deserve extra special thanks for their friendship and tolerating Cavendishian outbursts in the group chat.

I am incredibly lucky to have brilliant and kind mentors and role models, especially Drew Baden, Katherine Brading, Michael Della Rocca, Antonia LoLordo, Miriam McCormick, Yitzhak Melamed, Alyssa Ney, Baron Reed, Eric Schliesser, Alison Simmons, and Rachel Zuckert.

This book has benefited from the support of the editors and the wisdom of three referees, especially Referee #1, who disagreed with almost everything in it but provided extremely generous feedback.

I am grateful for my colleagues and students at the University of Rochester, past and present, in the philosophy department as well as with the Rochester Educational Justice Initiative, the staff and students of which have taught me the meaning of community. Students in a 2023 seminar at Attica CF gave feedback on parts of this manuscript and concluded appropriately that Cavendish was a 'badass'.

I am struck by how many places this manuscript has seen. I am grateful to those in whose company and under whose roofs many parts of this book were written, and especially to my friends at A Bar Above, the Village Tavern, Peppermints, Milka, and Ryce, who kept me focused with encouragement, companionship, coffee, and nourishment.

To my family: thank you for your acceptance and example, and especially to Kelli, for all the owls. To Laura, Chris, Annie, and Luis: thank you for being chosen family. And to my friends: thank you for being you.

Texts and abbreviations

Cavendish's works are in different states of development. All are in the public domain, and most are available online through Early English Books Online and Project Gutenberg. Unfortunately, not all of those are paginated. Some now have excellent critical editions, like the *Observations upon Experimental Philosophy* and the *Grounds of Natural Philosophy*; however, they do not preserve the page references in the original book. Some have online editions developed by scholars, like the 1663 *Philosophical and Physical Opinions*, edited by Marcy Lascano, and *Poems and Fancies*, edited by Liza Blake. A number of critical editions are currently in development, including a 20-volume *Complete Works*, edited by Liza Blake, Shawn Moore, and Jacob Tootalian. Some editions have modernized spelling and capitalization; some do not.

This all makes standardizing references and conventions difficult. With one exception, I have decided to use editions freely available online and, where possible, to cite them by sections, chapters, and the like, rather than by page numbers, to more easily accommodate alternative editions. These editions also have the benefit of being searchable so that passages are easy to find without page numbers. The spelling and capitalization are uncorrected or minimally corrected in these editions.

The one exception is *Observations Upon Experimental Philosophy*. It is one of the most-cited texts in this book, and it is sectioned in a baroque way that makes referencing difficult without page numbers. Moreover, there is an excellent critical edition widely available by Eileen O'Neill. This edition is heavily corrected for spelling and capitalization; other editions are partly corrected or uncorrected.

The citation format for each text is appropriate to that text and given below. Cavendish often has several prefatory sections or appendices. Those will be indicated in the citation on a case-by-case basis (e.g. (GNP Preface) or (GNP To the Reader)).

BW   *Blazing World*
        Cavendish, Margaret. *The description of a new world, called the blazing-world.* Early English Books Online Text Creation Partnership, https://name.umdl.umich.edu/A53044.0001.001.
        Cited as (BW <Page>)
GNP   *Grounds of Natural Philosophy*
        Cavendish, Margaret. *Grounds of Natural Philosophy.* Early English Books Online Text Creation Partnership, http://name.umdl.umich.edu/A53045.0001.001.
        Cited as (GNP <Part> <Chapter>) and (GNP Appendix <Part> <Chapter>)
OEP   *Observations Upon Experimental Philosophy*
        Cavendish, Margaret. *Observations Upon Experimental Philosophy.* Edited by Eileen O'Neill.
        Cited as (OEP <Page>)
P&F   *Poems and Fancies*
        Cavendish, Margaret. Margaret Cavendish's Poems and Fancies: A Digital Critical Edition. Ed. Liza Blake. http://library2.utm.utoronto.ca/poemsandfancies/. Website published May 2019.
        Cited as (P&F <Poem Name>)
PL   *Philosophical Letters*
        Cavendish, Margaret. *Philosophical Letters.* Early English Books Online Text Creation Partnership, https://quod.lib.umich.edu/cgi/t/text/text-idx?c=eebo;idno=A53058.0001.001
        Cited as (PL <Section> <Letter>)
PPO1   *Philosophical and Physical Opinions, 1655 edition*
        Cavendish, Margaret. 1655. *Philosophical and Physical Opinions.* Early English Books Online Text Creation Partnership, http://name.umdl.umich.edu/A53055.0001.001.
        Cited as (PPO1 <Chapter>)
PPO2   *Philosophical and Physical Opinions, 1663 edition*
        Cavendish, Margaret. 1663. *Philosophical and Physical Opinions.* Edited by Marcy P. Lascano. https://cavendish-ppo.ku.edu/.
        Cited as (PPO2 <Part> <Chapter>)

SL   Sociable Letters
         Cavendish, Margaret. 1664. Sociable Letters. Early English Books Online Text Creation Partnership, https://quod.lib.umich.edu/cgi/t/text/text-idx?c=eebo;idno=A53064.0001.001
         Cited as (SL <Letter>)

WO   *World's Olio*
         Cavendish, Margaret. 1655. *Worlds Olio*. Early English Books Online Text Creation Partnership, https://name.umdl.umich.edu/A53065.0001.001.
         Cited as (WO <Section Name>)

Chronology

(Titles are listed the year of publication. If no author is listed, it is a work by Cavendish)

1623	Margaret Lucas is born in Colchester, Essex
1641	Descartes, *Mediations on First Philosophy*
1642	The English civil war begins; the Lucas estate is stormed and the family flees to Oxford
1643	Lucas joins the court of Queen Henrietta Maria
1644	Lucas is exiled with the court to France
	Descartes, *Principles of Philosophy* (in Latin)
	Digby, *Two Treatises*
1645	Lucas marries William Cavendish, then-Marquess of Newcastle, in Paris
1646	William and Charles Cavendish begin to host meetings of the Cavendish Circle, which was visited by Hobbes, Descartes, Charleton, and others
1648	Margaret Cavendish moves with the court and her husband to Holland; houses of Peter Paul Rubens. Charles Lucas executed
1649	King Charles I executed in London
	Descartes, *The Passions of the Soul*
1651	Cavendish travels to London with Charles to plead for the return of William's estate.
	Hobbes, *Leviathan*
1653	Cavendish returns to Antwerp
	Poems, and Fancies

Introduction

My friend Annie recently acquired some land in the Blue Ridge mountains. Giving me a tour of the treasures in her woods, she stopped at a cluster of yellow lady slipper orchids. 'I had no idea orchids grew wild around here', she said, bending over to examine one. 'How does nature do that? People could never in a million years figure out how to make these'.

That kind of wonder at the power of nature—and how far it outstrips, differs from, and determines our own—is at the heart of Cavendish's philosophy. Nature is filled with a huge and magnificent menagerie of 'creatures', as Cavendish calls everything from wildflowers to earthworms to veins of silver. Like all creatures, human beings are infinitesimally tiny parts of an infinite and eternal universe, and our power is an infinitesimally tiny manifestation of nature's power. We will never, Cavendish thinks, engineer an orchid.

This wonder ramifies everywhere in Cavendish's system. It informs her theory of God and of creation, and her metaphysics of self-moving matter. It inspires her account of the human mind, according to which it is just one among the countless ways that creatures have of interacting with their environments. It determines her evaluation of the ways that we can know, be they philosophical, theological, or scientific. And it affirms the value of nature and everything in it, decentering the concerns of human beings, who otherwise love to imagine ourselves not as parts of nature, but as so many 'petty gods' (GNP Appendix 1) dwelling within it.

This book provides an overview of Cavendish's system that takes this wonder at the power of nature as its starting point. I will call it a naturalistic reading of Cavendish's philosophical work, but since

DOI: 10.4324/9781003107255-1

that word is so polysemous and polemical, I should say what I mean by it.

The word 'naturalist', in Cavendish's England, sometimes described an inquirer into nature, which included natural philosophers and what we would today call scientists. One such kind of naturalist is what Francis Bacon called the 'natural historian': someone who makes detailed studies of particular biological species—the bug inspector and leaf collector. Cavendish was a naturalist in both of these senses: she sought the 'principles and causes' of nature as a whole but was also an enthusiastic observer of the activities of ants and varieties of plants.

'Naturalist' was also used to describe philosophers who were thought to be a little *too* interested in nature, especially if that interest distracted them from the contemplation of the divine. Uses from this period describe 'blasphemous truth-opposing...Atheisticall naturalists' who 'explode Christ and Scriptures at last as unnecessary' (OED). Meanwhile, a poem attributed to John Stansby describes Cavendish just after her death as

> The great atheistical philosophaster,
> That owns no God, no devil, lord nor master;
> Vice's epitome and virtue's foe,
> Here lies her body but her soul's below.

Stansby was probably poking fun, at least in part, at the tidal wave of eulogizing flattery dedicated to the duchess. But the always-dead-serious Ralph Cudworth described an unnamed philosopher who is almost certainly Cavendish as a 'bungling Well-Wisher to atheism' (Cudworth, 1678: 137).

'Naturalists' in this sense were often seen as the heirs of certain Presocratic philosophers, including Thales, Heraclitus, and Democritus, and 'naturalist' even served as a translation of 'physikoi', the name given to those philosophers by Aristotle in light of their speculations about the nature of the cosmos. In Cavendish's time, the term was even more closely associated with the post-Socratic Stoics and Epicureans, who were seen as taking up the mantle of Democritus, and especially with several specific positions of theirs, including that everything is material, that whatever happens is fated to happen, that the world is eternal, and that matter moves itself. Cavendish was deeply influenced by both Epicureanism and Stoicism and was more or less sympathetic to all of these views.

Cavendish insists that she was both 'a good Christian, and a good Natural Philosopher' (PL 3 21). But she also denies that God or anything else supernatural is a proper concern of natural philosophy, that scripture and revelation are sources of knowledge, and that God has any influence on nature. Within the polemical context, that was more than enough to undermine her plea that readers 'account me not an Atheist' (PPO1 An Epistle to my Readers). Even today, we might describe Cavendish's opinion that God never acts on the world by answering prayers or performing miracles as a 'naturalistic' one. Cavendish also denies the existence of other supernatural, quasi-natural, or non-natural beings and activities. That includes witches, spirits, ghosts, and other obviously spooky entities, but also 'Hobgoblins': ontological posits by other natural philosophers, like accidents and modes of substances.

One important reason that Cavendish classifies these entities as non-natural is that they are not made of matter. Cavendish holds that everything in nature is matter, but as we will see in Chapter 2, her position is stronger than this slogan makes it sound. As that chapter argues, the limits of nature represent the limits of what we can perceive, conceive, and know—the limits of reality, as far as it concerns us. So in fact, Cavendish holds that—as far as we can sensibly claim—everything that exists is matter. Chapter 2 outlines, in the most general terms, how Cavendish thinks about the concept of nature, and interprets her central claims about nature, which are that it is material, that it contains both variety and coherence, that it changes, and that it is eternal and infinite.

What makes matter especially 'natural'? One answer is that matter was understood by many historical philosophers as what is accessible to our senses, and Cavendish holds that what is natural, and hence real, is what is perceptually accessible to us. Cavendish's materialism also reflects an historical association of materialism with nominalism: among the things that her materialism precludes are abstract entities like universals or ideas. But, as Chapter 3 argues, Cavendish's materialism is different from familiar versions of materialism, both historical and contemporary. It is motivated by Cavendish's attempt to explain the great variety of natural phenomena with minimal metaphysical posits. The fact that nature contains infinite variety and yet is coherent necessitates that there is some metaphysical structure, and Cavendish takes minimal metaphysical structure to be that of parthood and composition, rejecting all other metaphysical posits and distinctions. As Chapter 2 argues, her commitment to materialism is ultimately, at its core, the claim that stuff exists and has compositional structure.

It is not the claim that a certain kind of substance exists and that other kinds do not, as we might conclude if we think of materialism primarily as an intervention into debates over dualism. This is especially true if we imagine that matter is a certain kind of thing because of the kinds of creatures that there are—as Cavendish puts it, it would be to imagine that matter must be clayey in order to make clay. That would restrict matter's ability to explain the infinite variety of things and kinds of things. Instead, to say that everything is the effect of self-moving matter is to say that everything is what it is because of structures.

This contrasts with many interpretations of Cavendishian matter, according to which matter has all kinds of powers and properties, like life, thought, agency, or sympathy. These readings miss an important motivation for Cavendish's materialism and what I take to be a primary interest and significance of her intervention into natural philosophy: Cavendish is, among her European contemporaries, the philosopher most ruthless in her rejection of occult explanations. Cavendish holds that we are almost entirely ignorant of the particular causes of things, and takes most attempts to identify particular causes to involve the illegitimate projection of the features of effects onto causes. While she writes that 'Nature in her self is a Magicianess', she clarifies that this is 'called natural Magick or Witchcraft, merely in respect to our Ignorance; for though Nature is old, yet she is not a Witch, but a grave, wise, methodical Matron' (PL 3 17),

That nature is methodical means that her actions are at least in principle intelligible, and that is reflected in Cavendish's insistence that all natural phenomena are grounded in the structure and activity of self-moving matter. Cavendish describes those natural phenomena in terms of creatures and their actions. As Chapter 4 details, creatures are self-moving, self-organizing composites that change by dividing and composing. That chapter explains how the natures of all those creatures and their actions can be explained in terms of their compositional structures, and argues that doing so does not require appeal to any new metaphysical posits like sympathies or natural kinds.

The generation of creatures, as well as all their infinitely various and surprising behaviours, are just actions of matter, dividing and composing itself, and we do not need to posit any additional qualities or forces to matter to account for it. This means that the fact that matter is self-moving is an extremely important fact about nature for Cavendish. Given all the work that it must do, many readers have been tempted to interpret Cavendishian motion very richly, so that, for example, motions include fundamental changes of colour or other qualitative properties. Others, responsive to Cavendish's seemingly mechanistic rhetoric, assume that motion must be local motion, which is to say change of place. Chapter 5 argues that for Cavendish, motion is fundamentally what we may call 'compositional motion': for matter to move is just for it to divide and compose. Other kinds of motion, including local motion, can be understood as kinds of compositional motion. Chapter 5 also examines Cavendish's reasons for holding that all matter is self-moving, arguing that is arises from Cavendish's denials of the coherence of one thing's acting on another. Finally, the chapter elucidates what might seem to be an abandonment of parsimony at the most fundamental metaphysical level: Cavendish's doctrine of the triumvirate of matter. While matter is homogeneous inasmuch as it is all self-moving, Cavendish is driven by the fact of matter's heterogeneous action to hold that it is ultimately a perfect mixture of what she calls 'sensitive', 'rational', and 'inanimate' matter. I argue that Cavendish does not think that these three different 'degrees' of matter are three distinct substances but rather that homogeneous natural matter contains two 'principles of heterogenity'—the active and the passive—which are manifest by the variety of its actions. Sensitive and rational matter are, as their names suggest, responsible for all sense and reason, but only because self-motion is the 'life and Soul of Nature' and not because they have anything like the sensitive or rational capacities that humans and other animals specifically have.

The argument for that is the start of a broader argument that Cavendish is a deeply anti-anthropomorphic thinker. Less controversially, one of Cavendish's most deeply held principles is her anti-anthropocentrism, according to which human exceptionalism is an absurd and pernicious myth that stands in the way, at every turn, of our understanding of nature. Not only do human beings lack any special power or knowledge, but we also do not have any special value or status in the eyes of God. Our belief that we are 'The flower and chief of all the produce of nature upon this Globe of the Earth' (PL 2 5) is nothing but man's 'conceited prerogative'. This has consequences for how we should live: we should care for animals and plants, respect nature as a whole, and resist interpreting nature in terms of human desires, values, and capacities. While Cavendish certainly sees a role for religion in human life, human beings do not have any special capacity to understand or worship God that the rest of creation does not have. 'I cannot believe', she writes, 'that the Omnipotent Creator has written and engraven his most mysterious designs and counsels only in one sort of creatures; since all parts of nature, their various productions and curious contrivances, do make known the omnipotency of God' (OEP 71). Cavendish sometimes suggests that human beings may be special inasmuch as they have a place in a world beyond this one. But at the same time, she holds that such claims do not lie in the purview of natural philosophy or even of knowledge, and she makes clear that the afterlife mystifies and scares her, as when she laments that life, after passing 'like a Flash of Lightning…Continues not, and for the most part leaves black Oblivion behind it' (SL 90).

Most of Cavendish's interpreters agree that she rejects anti-anthropocentrism, but the majority take this to lead her to some kind of anthropomorphism. The idea is that in denying human exceptionalism, Cavendish means to attribute to other creatures, matter, and nature itself the abilities that we humans jealously guard for ourselves. As Karen Detlefsen, who has provided an early and carefully argued version of this interpretation, articulates it,

> for Cavendish, matter itself embodies traits typically associated with humans: it moves, it senses, it reasons, it is free, and its freedom allows choices to agree or dissent from the good. Cavendish, then, might be called an "anthropomorphic naturalist" who permits significant teleology into her natural philosophy.
> (Detlefsen 2007: 181)

According to readings like this, all activity is thoughtful, goal-directed behaviour; perception is something like the representation that we have of external objects through the senses; and knowledge is objective insight into reality. Nature is responsive to fundamental norms and is structured in a rational way, and matter itself is rich with cognitive and epistemic states. Such readings are bolstered both by Cavendish's frequent claims that all creatures are perceptive and knowing, and by her frequent use of anthropomorphic metaphors. Cavendish's alleged anthropomorphism complements the widespread reading of Cavendish as a panpsychist, who 'takes thinking agents as her basic causal model in explanation' (Duncan 2012: 19), endorses 'a form of panpsychism in the strong sense that every part of nature contains the same rational principle as humans' (Shaheen 2021: 636), and holds that 'mentality is already among [the] immediate properties [of bodies]' (Cunning 2016: 73).

This book argues that Cavendish does not fundamentally explain what happens in nature in anthropomorphic or psychic terms. She does not hold that creatures without brains and sense organs represent the world around them or are guided by thoughtful teleology or are conscious. Neither do Cavendishian natural philosophical explanations appeal to irreducible epistemic states, at least not if epistemic states necessarily involve mental states. While Cavendish describes all creatures, down to stones, as perceptive and knowing, she is not suggesting that they have anything like human epistemic capacities. The argument for this requires understanding Cavendish's metaphysics as well as her natural philosophical project and what she thinks counts as good explanations of phenomena like mentality. It especially requires establishing non-anthropomorphic and non-mentalistic accounts of Cavendishian perception and knowledge, which I do in Chapters 6 and 7.

Chapter 6 argues that Cavendish holds that all creatures have many capacities for acting responsively to the world around them, which she calls perceptions. Kinds of perceptions include, in animals, not only sense perceptions but the ability to digest food and respirate as well as non-animal capacities like photosynthesis and gravitation. Cavendish's account of sense perceptions, as well as what she calls animal rational perceptions, makes clear that other kinds of perception are not cognitive in the sense that they are. At the same time, Cavendish provides a radically naturalistic account of these kinds of perceptions, arguing that they do not give us the kind of special objective access to nature that we think they do. That would be to have a touch of the divine, of which Cavendish provides the following assessment:

> And for the mind, which some say is like gods,
> I do not find 'twixt man and beast such odds.
>
> (P&F Of Humility)

Perception is one species of knowledge, but Chapter 7 examines how Cavendish thinks of knowledge more generally. Again, we discover that Cavendish's claim that all creatures are knowing does not mean that all creatures have anything like mental representations or operations, or consciousness. Instead, creaturely knowledges are the abilities that creatures have, in virtue of the structures of their bodies, to act in certain ways and to respond to the world around them. Some of those kinds of knowledge, in animals with brains, are the ones we classify as cognitive, and Cavendish sometimes describes these as conceptions or thoughts. The human mind, like everything else, is material, and it is just another way that certain creatures regulate themselves and interact with their environments. Thought, to borrow a phrase from Ruth Garrett Millikan, is first and foremost a biological category.

Cavendish's embrace of materialism—which Leibniz would a little later describe as 'the wicked doctrine of those who, following Epicurus and Hobbes, believe that the soul is material' (Leibniz [1716] 2006: 111)—is more radical even than most of today's physicalists. Physicalists hold that cognition and mentality emerge from or are grounded in the physical, while Cavendish holds the much stronger position that cognition and mentality are identical to the material. This means that we can give complete explanations of animal cognition, including human cognition, in terms of the structures of animal bodies. There is no being but the being of matter and no structure but parthood structure, so the structure of mental representation and conscious experience cannot be richer or finer grained than material structure. There are mental parts if and only if there are material parts. To explain everything in terms of fundamental agency or mentality is a kind of mystification that, I believe, Cavendish would reject.

What should we make, then, of Cavendish's liberal use of anthropomorphic metaphors to describe things that are not human? Nature is a 'Wise and Provident Lady' who 'governs her parts very wisely, methodically, and orderly' (OEP 105); rational matter is the 'architect' of Nature (OEP 3); bodies have free will and they consent to follow nature's norms. Cavendish simply tells us not to take these anthropomorphic metaphors literally. We might wonder why she makes such liberal use of them if one of her central philosophical insights is that nature, and the things in it, do not act as humans do. In one place, she explains that she does so 'to make my meaning more intelligible to weaker capacities' (OEP 178). But it is not only those of us with weaker capacities that must rely on anthropomorphism. Cavendish thinks that it is impossible for us to avoid thinking of things in human terms, because we are human. To avoid it would be to transcend our partial and particular human natures and perspectives, and a philosopher who pretends that she can do that will just end up relying on anthropomorphism unawares. In this way, Cavendish can be called an *epistemic* anthropocentrist and anthropomorphist: she recognizes that the ways that we perceive and understand the world are inescapably dependent upon our human natures, and so we inevitably project our own self-understanding onto other things. This does not mean that the self-understanding that we project is correct, and we can, to some extent, improve that self-understanding by understanding our commonalities with other creatures and our place in nature. Our knowledge of ourselves and of nature will always be unstable in this way. By oversaturating her philosophy with obvious—and obviously inadequate—anthropomorphism, Cavendish makes us more sensitive to the widespread and inevitable, but often hidden, reliance on it in natural philosophy.

Cavendish's diagnosis of the conceit that human beings have objective or accurate views of nature as anthropocentrism seems to lead to quite a radical scepticism. As Chapter 8 shows, Cavendish is indeed very critical of many of the methods that human beings have devised for ostensibly discovering truth, and she strictly limits the scope and certainty of our knowledge. This means that Cavendish is not a naturalist in one very important 21st-century sense: she is not a scientific naturalist.[1] According to scientific naturalism, science should guide philosophical inquiry, whether on the basis of an 'ontological thesis that what exists are solely the entities posited by the natural sciences', a 'methodological thesis that philosophical inquiry should take the results of the natural sciences as authoritative', or some nuanced variant or combination of these.[2] Cavendish holds that tools like applied mathematics and experimental techniques like microscopy and chemical analysis, along with other ways that humans have developed of purifying or clarifying inquiry like logic and systematic induction, are human inventions, not discoveries. Like other technologies, they may sometimes help us to live and thrive, and they may sometimes contribute to our knowledge of nature. But Cavendish roundly rejects the idea that they provide human beings with that God's-eye view of nature, especially when they are adopted as unreflectively as she thinks they usually are.

That said, Cavendish does seem to think that we (or at least she) can know quite a bit about nature, like that it is eternal and infinite, that it is material, that there are three kinds of matter, that everything has sense and reason, perception and knowledge, and so on. It is presumably reason that she relies upon to build her metaphysical system. But unlike other great rationalist system builders like Spinoza and Leibniz, her epistemology seems to lack the resources to provide the grounds of these speculations. Chapter 8 explores the grounds that Cavendish takes herself to have for these claims, arguing, first, that Cavendish takes natural philosophical knowledge to be probable rather than certain, second, that Cavendish thinks of natural philosophy as essentially a discursive project, and third, that the limited nature of Cavendish's speculative commitments somewhat eases the tension between her speculative philosophy and her epistemology.

Finally, Chapter 9 asks what it means to hold, as Cavendish does, that nature is orderly. This claim has struck many as an irreducibly

---

1   An interesting comparison may be made here between Cavendish's views and Huw Price's argument that what he calls 'subject naturalism'—the view that 'we humans are natural creatures' and that 'human knowledge is itself a natural phenomenon' (Price 2004:77)—may undermine certain versions of 'object naturalism', according to which the object of our inquiry is the natural world.
2   Spiegel et al. (2023).

normative one, that would require values, norms, wills, or other metaphysical principles beyond those that we have so far developed. That chapter argues that it does not, and that nature is ordered, for Cavendish, just because every part is related to every other part given nature's compositional structure.

The version of Cavendish presented in this book is extremely systematic. In *Observations*, she provides a terse, 13-item statement of the principles of her natural philosophy, whose importance she emphasizes in a preface to the reader. The core of Cavendish's system is contained in and can be articulated out of the first three principles of that statement:

1. There is but one matter, and infinite parts; one self-motion, and infinite actions; one self-knowledge, and infinite particular knowledges and perceptions.
2. All parts of nature are living, knowing, and perceptive, because all are self-moving; for self-motion is the cause of all particular effects, figures, actions, varieties, changes, lives, knowledge, perceptions, etc. in nature, and makes the only difference between animate and inanimate matter.
3. The chief and general actions of nature, are division and composition of parts, both which are done but by one act; for at the same time, when parts separate themselves from such parts, they join to other parts; and this is the cause there can be no vacuum, nor single parts in nature. (OEP 191–192)

There is one nature, which is matter. Matter is self-moving, or acting, which is the cause of everything that happens. Self-motion is the *only* difference between inanimate and animate matter, so while Cavendish describes animate matter as sensitive and rational, these are simply manifestations of self-motion. All parts of nature are living, perceptive, and knowing because of the self-motions of matter. Finally, all of these self-motions—the 'chief and general actions of nature'—are 'division and composition of parts'.

I take the systematicity of this interpretation of Cavendish to be a virtue. Like any (interesting) philosopher, there is no (interesting) interpretation of Cavendish's philosophy that perfectly captures everything she wrote—for that, one should simply read Cavendish. I provide quotations only when they are especially illustrative, but cite texts so that the reader can read the passages for themselves. And I have tried to be explicit about where the texts are ambiguous and when my interpretation is particularly out of the mainstream.

The interpretation developed in this book may be seen as one extreme among interpretations and interpretive lenses; most scholars of Cavendish's philosophy do not detect all the kinds of naturalism that I argue in this book can be found in her system. The most obvious example of this disagreement is my denial that Cavendish is a panpsychist, but it is manifested also in the austere picture of matter presented, with its denial of forms, qualities, and other metaphysical frameworks; in the interpretation of Cavendish's attitude toward God and values; and in Cavendish's account of perceptual representation and inference. Cavendish shows us how deeply a true resistance to anthropocentrism shakes the foundations of philosophy. I hope I have given enough context that the reader can pursue the rich and interesting alternative lines of interpretation provided by others. I also hope I have given enough arguments that the reader finds this interpretation a plausible and interesting one.

I do not say 'the right one'. This is not the place for a long polemic about methodology in the history of philosophy, but maybe it is the place for a short polemic. An interpretation of a historical philosopher may have many different virtues, and not all can be realized by a single interpretation. I am also unsure that it is always best to think of the primary goal of the history of philosophy as providing interpretations—or, at least, only as that. I like to think of it as doing philosophy with past philosophers—as learning from them and pursuing shared philosophical projects with them. One interesting question is whether Cavendish thought X. But another interesting question is whether she thought X but doubted it—especially for Cavendish, who is so open to sharing her competing thoughts. Yet another interesting question is whether Cavendish thought X but could have been convinced of not-X on the basis of her other views. In fact, Cavendish 'entreat[s] the ingenuous reader', in the Preface of her *Observations*, to interpret her opinions 'to the best sense; for they are not so material, but that either by the context or connexion of the whole discourse, or by comparing one place with another, the true meaning therof may be easily understood' (OEP 140).

My goal is to convey what I take to be Cavendish's deepest motivations and most unique and profound insights, and develop what seems to me to be a philosophically motivated and fruitful account of her philosophy. Cavendish's metaphysical system, like any great metaphysical system, is full of insight as well as hubris. To enter and appreciate it requires a certain suspension of disbelief and a willingness to participate in conceptual play. But it is a coherent and beautiful vision of the world and of our cognitive relationship to it, one that distils even as it subverts centuries of philosophical influences. Cavendish's natural philosophy expands conceptual space in the early modern period. At the foundation of her system is the natural, and at the foundation of her conception of the natural is the notion of parthood. To be natural, for Cavendish, means to be part of something bigger than oneself.[3]

---

3 There is some limited overlap between Chapter 3 (especially Section 3.3) and Peterman 2025; between Chapter 4 (especially Section 4.1) and Peterman 2019b; and between Chapter 6 and Peterman 2023.

One
Life

'Who knows but after my honourable burial, I may have a glorious
resurrection in following ages, since time brings strange and unusual
things to passe'
(PPO1 To the Two Universities)

Cavendish's personality is so big and beguiling, and her celebrity
so intense and polarizing, that it is tempting to minimize her biography, lest it distract from her philosophical work. It is especially
tempting to downplay 300 years of takes calling her ridiculous,
a madwoman, a simpleton, and a whore. A wise friend once advised
me: 'Don't self-deprecate. People believe what you say about your-
self.' No need to risk anyone believing much of what has been said
about Cavendish.

But this is exactly why it is important to talk about the takes. It
cannot be said that Cavendish became a great philosopher against
incalculable odds. She had plenty of money, freedom, and leisure
time, and her station afforded her some access to the intellectual world of her time and the support she needed to publish.
But despite these advantages, Cavendish received no significant education—she barely learned how to write—and she was
mocked and dismissed at every turn. The copious front matter of
her work is filled with half-self-deprecating, half-defiant pleas to
be taken seriously. These pleas remind us how difficult it is to do
philosophy when you are not the kind of creature who is thought
to be philosophical.

DOI: 10.4324/9781003107255-2

Recognizing this, some people[1] have cast Cavendish as a great mind who might have been a great philosopher had she only been properly trained. In Cavendish, Edward Jenkins detected 'a genius strong-winged and swift, fertile and comprehensive' but 'without system' (Cavendish et al. [1872] 2016: 8–9). 'Had the mind of this woman been disciplined', he conjectured, 'it would have stood out remarkable among the feminine intellects of our history'. Cavendish's 'fitful and ill-balanced brilliance', wrote B.G. MacCarthy, was 'so productive and so various, her ideas so original and so ill-regulated, her vision so exalted, her ignorance so profound, her style alternately so preposterous and so perfect, that one despairs of ever reducing to the cold canons of criticism the inspired confusion of her works' (MacCarthy [1946]1994: 66). Even in 2017, Cavendish's metaphysics was dismissed as 'admittedly more poetic than analytic' (Skrbina 2017: 207). The same reluctant dismissal is not made there of Johannes Kepler, who argues that earth's ensoulment is evinced by geysers, which are the nocturnal *jouissance* of the earth upon the ministrations of the moon.

The most affecting expression of this sentiment, loving and vehement, comes from Virginia Woolf. In *A Room of One's Own*, Woolf presents Cavendish as a paragon of squandered feminine intellect:

> What could bind, tame or civilise for human use that wild, generous, untutored intelligence? It poured itself out, higgedly-piggedly, in torrents of rhyme and prose, poetry and philosophy which stands congealed in quartos and folios that nobody ever reads. She should have had a microscope put in her hand. She should have been taught to look at the stars and reason scientifically. Her wits were turned with solitude and freedom. No one checked her. No one taught her…What a vision of loneliness and riot the thought of Margaret Cavendish brings to mind! as if some giant cucumber had spread itself over all the roses and carnations in the garden and choked them to death.
>
> (Woolf [1929] 2015: 46)

Isn't this wish that an unparalleled genius had been better 'checked', 'disciplined', and 'tamed' a strange one? It is an especially sad irony

---

1   Members of the British intelligentsia, mostly.

that in a book lamenting wasted feminine potential, Woolf cannot appreciate its realization because it doesn't have the accepted marks of serious inquiry.

Cavendish herself often pointed out that the ways that we check, civilize, and tame the mind can impede our natural capacity for an authentic cognitive relationship with nature. And philosophers are starting to appreciate anew that to really love wisdom means to pursue it wherever it lives: in poetry, oral traditions, sermons, autobiographical narratives, political action. The thing is, Cavendish's greatness is not so difficult to recognize. Her treatises look a lot like other philosophical treatises from her time, and she gives us a deep, original, comprehensive, and coherent vision of reality in the mold of familiar heroes like Hobbes, Spinoza, and Leibniz. To appreciate that, one just has to heed to her plea: 'if you'll give an impartial judgment of my philosophy, read it all, or else spare your censures' (OEP 13). Recently, philosophers have finally begun to do that, and so shall we. But first, an introduction to this 'erratic and lovable personality' with the 'freakishness of an elf' and a 'sympathy with fairies and animals so true and tender' (Woolf 2022)—who also happened to be one hell of a philosopher.

Section 1.1 Early life

Margaret Lucas was born in 1623 to an aristocratic family in Colchester, Essex, the youngest of eight children. After putting the family in the bad graces of the crown by killing a rival in a duel, Cavendish's father died when Margaret was two, and the household was managed for most of her life by her mother and her older brother, John. In her short autobiography, *A True Relation of My Birth and Breeding*, Cavendish describes a childhood filled with warmth, harmony, and civility. Her brothers 'practiced justice, spoke truth, were constantly loyal, and truly valiant'; her sisters were her cherubic confidantes. The children each had their own servant and were spared any want so that they would not develop unbecoming 'sharking qualities' (Cavendish 'True Relation').

It is not part of Margaret's recounting that the Lucases were totally despised by the people of Colchester. It seems that the family was as committed to exploiting the townspeople as they were to pampering their children, including cutting off the town's water supply in a conflict over property lines (Whitaker 2002: 6). So it is perhaps not too surprising that as the parliamentary crisis intensified and the neighbors caught wind that John was amassing troops for the king, the Lucas's estate was stormed and ransacked and the family was thrown into jail. It is not certain where Margaret was at the time, but the events of the civil war—which would see her exile, the confiscation of her husband's estate, and the death of two of her brothers—hardened her sense that class hierarchy was necessary to keep things orderly and pleasant in a chaotic world.

After three days in the local jail, their estate uninhabitable, and London increasingly inhospitable to royalists, the Lucases followed the king and queen to Oxford. There, 19-year-old Margaret asked to join the court of Queen Henrietta Maria. Margaret had almost no experience of the world outside her home. She was debilitatingly shy and perhaps a bit over-attached to her family. In an early letter, Margaret apologizes to her favorite sister for repeatedly waking her in the middle of the night to make sure she wasn't dead (Whitaker 2002: 27)—an episode that speaks to a mixture of tenderness, anxiety, and morbidity that seems to have remained a feature of Cavendish's personality for the rest of her life. Not just Margaret's mother but her entire family thought that court was a bad idea given how little experience she had of the world, but they relented.

It was a bad idea. Margaret's awkward, dreamy introversion was taken for 'simplicity' or aloof superiority, and her resentment of the meanness, hypocrisy, and superficiality of the court is evident from its depiction in her later plays. But her family insisted that she honor her commitment, and when the queen was forced to flee England for Paris, barely holding onto her life, Margaret followed. She was miserable in Paris, too, until William Cavendish—amiable Cavalier, expert horse breeder, enthusiastic poet—came to town. A widower 30 years her senior, William seemed to Margaret to embody all of the highest virtues: she describes him as worldly, curious, honorable, romantic, attentive, earnest. After some embarrassing love poetry, and with the reluctant capitulation of the queen, the two were married.

Section 1.2 Exile and early writings

The marriage was a lucky one for philosophy. A decent man, if a bit of a womanizer, William admired Margaret's intellect and supported her ambition, forgiving, as she put it, that she 'somewhat Err'd from good Huswifry, to write natures Philosophy' ('True Relation'). William had much more life experience than Margaret did and shared Margaret's interest in philosophy, literature, and writing. Their conversations stimulated Margaret and gave her confidence, and together the two would come to be counted among England's most lovable weirdos.

The couple was never able to conceive, which was probably also lucky for philosophy. Margaret expressed disappointment that she did not provide William—who already had a son and several daughters— with another heir, because it is 'the part of every Good Wife to desire Children to Keep alive the Memory of their Husbands Name and Family by Posterity' (SL 93). But she also observed that 'no good' is brought to a woman herself by having children, as she 'Hazards her Life by Bringing them into the World, and hath the greatest share of trouble in Bringing them up' (SL Letter 93), while gaining neither comfort nor happiness nor posterity by them. Cavendish saw her works as her progeny instead, their 'paper bodies…Destinated to Live, and I hope, I in them, when my Body is Dead, and Turned to Dust' (SL 143).

The Cavendishes spent the first 16 years of their marriage in exile as the civil war dragged on. For four years in Paris, they lived on credit and sometimes, Cavendish alleges, on the edge of starvation. One wonders whether things were *quite* that bad (she never did have to sell her jewels), but it does seem to have been a stressful time for them. In 1648, they followed Charles II to Antwerp, where they lived in the rented house of the artist Peter Paul Rubens, and entertained celebrity guests including, on one occasion, the dethroned regent himself.

For us, however, the more interesting guests were intellectual luminaries both expatriate and continental. Before their exile, William and his brother Charles, a mathematician and scholar who lived with Margaret and William, had made their family estate at Welbeck the center of a patronage circle known as the Welbeck or Cavendish Circle. Thomas Hobbes was especially close with the brothers, whose orbit also included Kenelm Digby and Walter Charleton. In Paris and Antwerp, their meetings were attended by René Descartes, Christiaan Huygens, Marin Mersenne, and Pierre Gassendi. Margaret was not at the center of their conversations but listened in on them, reporting, for example, that William impressed Hobbes with his answer to a question put to the men gathered, whether human beings could ever fly by flapping their wings like birds. ('No', because human shoulder joints were not like the wing joints of birds.) The Cavendish's Paris abode was even the location of Hobbes's widely publicized debate with John Bramhall over the compatibility of free will and necessity.

Margaret and Charles went to London in November 1651, staying for 15 months while attempting to recover some of the Newcastle estate. The parliamentary government allowed a wife to petition for support out of her husband's confiscated wealth, since women were not considered political actors. But the tribunal denied Margaret's request on the grounds that she had married William after he was exiled, and so knowingly married a traitor. Charles had more success (perhaps because he couldn't choose his brother?), and he was able to recover Welbeck Abbey and some other assets.

It was during this time that Cavendish published her first work, *Poems and Fancies*. She had gained a degree of notoriety already, thanks to her petition to Parliament but also to her increasingly spectacular persona. Cavendish never grew out of her painful social anxiety, and would blush, tremble, and stutter when faced with strangers or large groups of people. She appears to have compensated for this by adopting a highly affected manner, filling awkward moments with words, exclamations, and gestures. Sniped Mary Evelyn, a friend (allegedly) of the Cavendishes:

> I was surprised to find so much extravagancy and vanity in any person not confined within four walls. Her habit peculiar, fantastical....Her mien surpasses the imagination of poets, or the descriptions of a romance heroine's greatness: her gracious bows, seasonable nods, courteous stretching out of her hands, twinkling of her eyes, and various gestures of approbation, show what may be expected from her discourse, which is as airy, empty, whimsical and rambling as her books…I hope, as she is an original, she may never have a copy.
>
> (as quoted in Evelyn 1906:731)

Others, including Mary's husband John, were 'much pleased with the extraordinary fanciful habit, garb, and discourse of the Duchess' (Evelyn 1906: 293). Cavendish's love of fabulous clothing was also noted by Dorothy Osborne, who begged her husband to 'for God's sake' get ahold of *Poems and Fancies*, for 'they say tis ten times more Extravagant than her dresse' (Osborne 1912: Letter 18). Once she read it, Osborne concluded that 'there are many soberer People in Bedlam'. Others concluded that William must have written it, because it was too good to have been written by a woman.

It was very unusual for women to publish under their own names in England at that time, and those who did usually wrote on religious and social topics. In contrast, the *Poems and Fancies* develop an atomistic world picture, offering charming corpuscularian explanations of phenomena like the behavior of liquids, the etiology of disease, the attractive power of the sun and the earth, and of fire:

> The reason why fire burns, and burning smarts,
> Is that it hath so many little parts—
> Which parts are atoms sharp, and wound more fierce
> If they so far into our skins do pierce—
> And like an angry porcupine, doth shoot
> His fiery quills, if nothing quench them out.
> (P&F Of Burning, Why it Causes Pain)

If Cavendish ever held a version of atomism in earnest, she came to reject it very quickly: in *Philosophical Fancies*, which was published in the same year as *Poems and Fancies*, she already defends a continuum theory of matter. But the *Poems* evince Cavendish's deep and abiding interest in corpuscularian explanations, which explain natural phenomena in terms of the interactions of particles. Cavendish continues to give such explanations, sometimes calling such particles 'atoms', even as she denies that they are indivisible and distinct from one another in the sense that atoms were purported to be (e.g. PL 4 9). Everything, including life and death, mental phenomena like wit, understanding, and the passions, and social phenomena like war, can be explained by the relationships among bits of matter and changes in those relationships. This likely reflects the influence of the Cavendish Circle, a central goal of which was the development of atomist theories.

Corpuscularianism was strongly associated in the early modern period with Epicurus. Epicureanism had been revived by the 15th-century publication of Latin translations of both Lucretius's Epicurean *De rerum natura* and Diogenes Laertius's *Lives of the Philosophers*, which contained accounts and selections of Epicurus's writings. Cavendish would likely have had access to a published English translation of the latter and may have had access to a draft of Lucy Hutchinson's important translation of the former. She would likely have been acquainted as well with her friend Walter Charleton's *Physiologia Epicuro-Gassendiana*, which presented a version of Epicureanism scrubbed of its associations with libertinism, atheism, amoralism, and materialism.

Cavendish embraced a variety of broadly Epicurean tenets, including that the world is eternal and infinite, that self-caused motion is the source of all change, that infinite worlds populate the cosmos, that human beings are not special among animals, that the human soul is material, and that God is not concerned with human affairs. Cavendish was not nearly as concerned as Charleton was to explain away allegedly impious consequences of these views. Instead, she insists that nothing she writes as a natural philosopher has theological implications. Natural philosophy and theology are entirely distinct realms of inquiry—a methodological principle which is itself Epicurean.[2]

Cavendish's *Philosophical Fancies* was published once she was back in Antwerp, and she was incredibly prolific during the remainder of her time there, publishing or composing the *World's Olio*, *Nature's Pictures*, *Plays*, and *Orations*. These display her dazzling versatility as a writer, but most interesting was the publication, in 1655, of the 'darling of my affections' (Whitaker 2002: 249), the first edition of the *Philosophical and Physical Opinions*. Building on the *Fancies*, this was a first sketch of what would become her mature philosophical system.

Section 1.3 The Philosophical Letters

Upon the restoration of the crown in 1660, the Cavendishes returned to England. They settled at Welbeck Abbey, where Cavendish had the time and the freedom to study and to write.

As a girl, Cavendish had been given almost no formal education in philosophy, natural science, mathematics, or logic, little instruction

---

2   Cavendish doesn't accept every tenet of Epicureanism. Of note is that Cavendish denies, contra Epicurus, that there are atoms and empty space, and that there is chance, as we will see (OEP 263).

in writing, and none in languages other than English. She made her lack of cultivation an important part of the philosophical persona that she projected, emphasizing the originality and lack of 'artifice' in her work. She even claimed that it was 'against nature for a woman to spell right' (WO 93). But Cavendish had begun to feel that her ability to communicate was impeded by her unfamiliarity with philosophical background and jargon, judging that the first edition of her Opinions, while 'not defective for want of Sense and Reason', was 'defective for want of Terms of Art' (PL Preface). So she began to read a lot of philosophy. Eight years would pass before she published the second edition of her Opinions and her Philosophical Letters.

The Philosophical Letters, which 'confute' some of Cavendish's important philosophical contemporaries, provide a glimpse into Cavendish's ongoing philosophical development. Addressed to an anonymous and likely imaginary partisan of her targets whom Cavendish calls, simply, 'Madam', the Letters are divided into four sections: one on Hobbes and Descartes, one each on Henry More and Jan Baptist Van Helmont, and one on various other philosophers including Charleton, Harvey, Galileo, and Constantijn Huygens. The letters demonstrate that the foundations of Cavendish's views were very much in place before her encounters with the work of these philosophers but illuminate how she refined and clarified them in light of her self-education.

Van Helmont, whom Cavendish discusses at the greatest length, was an influential Belgian physician and chemical philosopher whose work would have exposed Cavendish to Aristotelianism, Paracelsian chemical philosophy and alchemy, and Galenic medicine. Cavendish accuses him of unintelligibility, both in his expressions, which she calls 'obscure, mystical and intricate', and in the substance of his views, which 'are built upon...strange grounds and principles' (PL 3 11). Cavendish criticizes Van Helmont's reliance on Aristotelian metaphysics and on what she considers immaterial principles like his so-called Archeus, as well as his tolerance of the pretensions of alchemists. But the positive influence of Van Helmont is apparent in Cavendish's account of tripartite active matter, and she engages his views on particular natural processes like breeding and grafting, the tides, digestion, disease, and magnetism.

Hobbes and Cavendish are bound together by a deep commitment to a then-extremely unpopular view: materialism. Like Cavendish,

Hobbes is mostly unconcerned to deflect the impious implications of his Epicurean-flavored atomism. Cavendish agrees with Hobbes more often than any other target of the *Letters*, and when she is critical of him, it is often on the grounds that his materialism does not go far enough or is inconsistently maintained.

In the same section, Cavendish also addresses Descartes, whom she criticizes for his dualism, his account of animal life, and his theory of motion and its propagation. Their shared section is plausibly an acknowledgement of their shared association with the mechanical philosophy, sometimes called 'mechanism'. Corpuscularianism and mechanism were two overlapping categories of natural philosophical approaches, which themselves in turn contain a lot of diversity and so are difficult to characterize concisely. We can, however, make a few generalizations. Corpuscularianism, as we have seen, was the earlier and broader project, explicitly associated with ancient atomic theories, and focused on the explication of phenomena in terms of the particles that make things up and their arrangements. In his *Origin of Forms and Qualities*, Robert Boyle lays out the central tenets of what he calls corpuscularianism, but they indicate the emergence of what would be called the mechanical philosophy, of which Boyle was one of the most important proponents. That can be seen from Boyle's emphasis on the quantitative features of particles, especially their shape and size, as well as on the role of local motion and impact. Boyle frames this work as a rejection of Aristotelian natural philosophy and specifically of its explanations in terms of forms, which rejection, as we shall see, we find even more radically pursued by Cavendish than any other mechanical philosopher.

As we have seen, Cavendish never loses her interest in broadly corpuscularian explanations, which is to say explanations of observed phenomena in terms of the interactions of their parts. However, despite a temptation in early work by geometrical explanations akin to those of the mechanists, she ultimately rejects the mechanist emphasis on spatial qualities and structures, as well as the fundamentality of local motion. Cavendish also harshly criticizes the reliance of natural philosophers on applied mathematics, while the mathematization of natural philosophy was a central motivation of many mechanists, perhaps most notably Descartes and his mentor Isaac Beeckman, who described their project as 'physico-mathematics'.

Moreover, as is also most explicit in Descartes, the mechanistic emphasis upon the geometrical properties of bodies was in part licensed by the believe that the sole essence, or at least part of the essence, of matter is extension in space. Descartes identified these basic properties as modes of extension (Descartes 1985: 229); Boyle called them 'mechanical affectations' because 'to them men willingly refer the various operations of mechanical engines' (Boyle 1666: 1).

As that comment illustrates, another distinctive feature of some articulations of mechanism is their reliance on an analogy between natural systems and machines. While part of the motivation behind this analogy is that machines can be explained in terms of the interactions of their parts, it also invites a comparison between God and a human artificer. This is something that Cavendish passionately rejects, arguing that to 'similize our reason', will, and other faculties to God's is nothing but 'presumption' and 'blasphemy' (OEP 198) and diagnosing as rank impiety the idea that 'nature, or the God of nature, did produce the world after a mechanical way' (OEP 74).

Finally, Cavendish roundly rejects the central mechanistic tenet that matter is inert, along with its commitment to causal explanations in terms of impact and transfer of motion. More generally, Cavendish shares with the mechanical philosophers her rejection of the Aristotelian explanatory framework in favor of structural explanations, holding that given the homogeneity of matter, the only explanations of the great diversity of natural phenomena will arise from the structure and activity of matter. She also shares with them the notion that structures that are accessible at the creaturely level can be found at a more fundamental level. But those structures are compositional ones and not spatial ones, and changes in them are divisions and compositions rather than local motion and trajectories.

'The mechanical philosophy' is an extreme oversimplification, given the differences among positions that go under that name, but it is a useful one. In this book, when we discuss mechanical philosophers, we will focus on Descartes, Robert Boyle, and Hobbes. Descartes and Boyle were two of the most visible and influential exponents of this school; they both were contemporaries of Cavendish, and she obviously read both. They also represent an important dichotomy among mechanical philosophers: according to plenists like Descartes (and Cavendish), matter is infinitely divisible, and a vacuum is impossible, while according to atomists like Boyle, there is empty space and (at least naturally) indivisible particles of matter. Hobbes's physical and psychological theories diverge from Descartes and Boyle in several important respects, but he is especially important because unlike Descartes and Boyle, Hobbes holds that matter is the only substance. For Hobbes, as for Cavendish, a theory of matter and motion is not just a theory of the physical world but a theory of everything.

The final principal target of the *Letters* is Henry More, one of the most prominent English philosophers of this period. Impressed at first by the promise of Cartesian natural philosophy, More eventually distanced himself from it, principally on the grounds that inert matter cannot generate life and motion. On this point, Cavendish agrees with More. But while Cavendish concludes that matter itself is active, More, agreeing with the mechanists that matter is essentially passive, concludes that there is an immaterial active principle in nature, which he calls spirit. Morean spirit has a fair bit in common with Cavendishian animate matter. For one thing, it is extended. But Cavendish clearly interprets Morean spirit as an immaterial natural substance and attacks More on that ground. A central reason why Cavendish denies that Morean spirit is immaterial is that his spirit is indivisible, but divisibility is essential to matter.

More is interesting also because of his association with Anne Conway. Conway was a powerful and fascinating philosopher, who was very close to More and whose metaphysics is instructively compared with Cavendish's. More tells Conway in one letter that he has been 'inform'd that that Marchionesse of Newcastle has in a large book confuted Mr. Hobbs, Des Cartes, and myself, and (which will make your Ladiship at least smile at the conceit of it) Van Helmont also to boot' (Conway 1930: 234).[3] A year later, More complains to Conway that Cavendish

is affrayd some man should quitt his breeches and putt on a petticoat to answer her in that disguize, which your Ladiship need not. She expresses this jealousie in her book, but I beleave she may be secure from any one giving her the trouble of a reply.

Alas. What a philosophical gold mine such a reply would have been.

---

3 The parenthetical comment likely refers to Conway's close philosophical friendship with Van Helmont's son, the Cabbalist Francisco Mercurius Van Helmont.

Cavendish sent her *Letters* to Van Helmont and Hobbes, too—not to Descartes, who had died in 1650—but Van Helmont did not reply, and Hobbes did not reply substantively. In contrast, three men engaged Cavendish somewhat more seriously: Joseph Glanvill, Walter Charleton, and Constantijn Huygens. These were friends of Cavendish, and Charleton had been her physician for a time. Charleton was at least passingly familiar with her work, telling her that 'your natural philosophy may be, for ought I know, excellent: but give me leave, Madam, to confess, I have not yet been so happy as to discover much therein that's Apodictical, or wherein I think myself much obliged to acquiesce' (*Letters and Poems* 1676: 111). (Charleton is himself a fascinating philosopher, but I doubt anyone would describe anything in his system as 'Apodictical' either.) Huygens wrote that the 'delightful atoms' of Cavendish's *Poems and Fancies* 'kept him up at night'; he also sought her opinion of the cause of the curious behavior of Prince Rupert's drops or 'exploding glasses'. And Glanvill and Cavendish debated the existence of witches, with Cavendish arguing, against Glanvill, that their existence is improbable, much as she argues elsewhere against the existence of demons, genies, and other 'hobgoblins'.

Section 1.4 A system develops

The first edition of the *Observations upon Experimental Philosophy* was published in 1666 and the first edition of the *Grounds of Natural Philosophy* in 1668. Cavendish presented the *Grounds* as a revision of the *Fancies* and of both editions of the *Opinions*, all of which aimed to articulate the foundations of her natural philosophical system. It is challenging to make sense of the many differences between these works. Sometimes, it is clear that Cavendish's view on some topic has changed between editions; for example, the concept of spirit in the *Opinions* is gone from the *Grounds*, replaced in some of its functions by animate matter. But what should we make of the relative absence of sympathy and love as metaphysical principles in later versions? Has Cavendish decided there is no such force, perhaps replacing it by sense and reason, or something else? Or is it just going under another name now, like 'consent' or 'agreement'? If the latter, is the name change philosophically significant?

The *Grounds* that ultimately results is a systematic and speculative treatise that begins with Cavendish's most general principles: that only matter exists, that it is self-moving, and that everything has knowledge and perception. The second part concerns creatures and their particular perceptions and knowledges, including a materialist account of the activities of the human mind. The third and fourth parts concern natural productions, including animal generation, and the fifth through ninth parts return to man and his activities, including the activities of his mind. The last four sections concern all manner of natural phenomena including magnetism, the motions of the planets, the cause of darkness and light, the variety of creatures far from our own world, the elements from which nature is composed, death, and the effects on the health of various kinds of purgatives and cordials.

The *Grounds* is followed by a five-part appendix, which treats questions that are more speculative than the rest of the work, as Cavendish acknowledges. The first two parts discuss God, sin, and resurrection—topics that Cavendish tells us elsewhere are not legitimate targets of natural philosophy. One way to read the appendices is as examples of divinity, or speculation upon the supernatural, and not as natural philosophy. At the same time, however, Cavendish for the most part makes claims about nature and matter, providing naturalistic explanations of what religion would explain in supernatural terms. Sin, for example, arises from the varieties of irregular motions, and Cavendish attempts a materialist account of resurrection. Either way, it is clear that Cavendish has entered a more speculative and uncertain mode. Parts three and four, accordingly, concern the nature of creatures in worlds beyond our own. This is a legitimate target of natural philosophy, since those worlds are material parts of nature, but not having perceptual access to those worlds, we cannot in fact know what they are like. Finally, Cavendish announces that the parts of her mind do not wish to dissolve their pleasant disputational society, so they conduct a long and curious debate about whether and how animals can be brought back to life.

The *Grounds* lays out a systematic and speculative metaphysical system along the lines of Spinoza's *Ethics* or Leibniz's *Monadology*, beginning with her most basic metaphysical commitments and applying them to questions about persons, the mind, and our relationship to other creatures. It does not, unlike those works, provide us with a rationalist epistemology or method to underwrite its claims—an observation that we will discuss at more length in Chapter 7. The work that contains Cavendish's detailed philosophy of mind, perception, and knowledge is the *Observations upon Experimental Philosophy*.

Section 1.5 Some observations upon experimental philosophy

On 30 May 1667, Cavendish was the first woman to attend a meeting of the recently formed Royal Society. Samuel Pepys reported on her visit in his typically catty style, commenting on her clothes and her attractiveness and reporting that she was full of 'empty admiration' as she watched Roberts Hooke and Boyle perform experiments (Pepys: https://www.pepysdiary.com/diary/1667/05/30/). We may speculate that it was Cavendish's shyness and not any emptiness that prevented her from saying more, because in her *Observations upon Experimental Philosophy*, published a year before that visit, she paints a nuanced and much more ambivalent picture of the experimental exploits of philosophers including Hooke and Boyle. There Cavendish argues that experimental philosophy could be useful and instructive, but as it was actually being practiced—that is to say, without the guidance of reason—it was not only useless but led to error, its practitioners nothing but 'boys that play with watery bubbles' (OEP 52).

The *Observations* is, in part, a critical work like the *Letters*, focused on experimental philosophers like Hooke, Power, Boyle, and Bacon instead of systematic philosophers like Van Helmont and More. It also includes three sections entitled 'Observations upon the Opinions of Some Ancient Philosophers', which critically discuss the work of Plato, Aristotle, Epicurus, Democritus, Thales, and others. Cavendish holds that there is as much truth in ancient opinions as in modern ones (PPO2 To the Reader),

> although it is probable, that some of the Opinions of Antient Philosophers in Antient times are Erroneous, yet not all, neither are all Modern Opinions Truths, but truly I believe, there are more Errors in the One, than Truth in the Other, but that is not saying very much.

At the same time, Cavendish departs in many respects from her sources, and she details some of those departures here. As these sections evidence, an important source of information for Cavendish about the history of philosophy was Thomas Stanley's History of Philosophy in Eight Parts. Knowing this helps elsewhere to identify Cavendish's debt to Stoicism, as Stanley discusses Stoicism at length in that work, particularly as it was articulated by Chryssipus.

Like the Letters, however, the Observations is far from merely critical. It contains Cavendish's most sustained original treatments of perception, cognition, epistemology, and methodology, and while it is less focused on presenting Cavendish's system than is the Grounds, two parts of the Observations are especially valuable for understanding Cavendish's metaphysical system.

The first is the Argumental Discourse, a careful defense of one of the most fundamental parts of Cavendish's metaphysics: the triumvirate of matter. It is a rhetorically delightful dialogue between Cavendish's 'former' and 'latter' thoughts, inspired by the fact that when she was done writing her Opinions,

> The Parts of my Mind grew sad, to think of the dissolving of their Society: for, the Parts of my Mind are so friendly, that although they do often Dispute and Argue for Recreation and Delight-sake; yet, they were never so irregular, as to divide into Parties, like Factious Fellows, or Unnatural Brethren: which was the reason that they were sad, to think their kind Society should dissolve, and that their Parts should be dispersed and united to other Societies, which might not be so friendly as they were.
>
> (GNP 5 1)

So Cavendish's former and latter thoughts dispute—they really dispute, with Cavendish's latter thoughts asking her former thoughts the hardest questions they can come up with about her philosophical system (but still nicely). Reading it causes one to wonder why philosophers so rarely admit to being of two minds.

The second part of the Observations that is especially important for understanding Cavendish's metaphysics is a terse numbered list of the principles of her natural philosophy, which Cavendish asks us in the preface to read alongside the Letters and the Grounds if we want a complete picture of her philosophy (OEP 13). Cavendish doesn't argue for these principles, as she does in the Grounds, but they distill her thinking in a way that, I think, points to her ultimate priorities. The system that emerges from the Grounds and the Observations is quite consistent. However, when there are inconsistencies and differences in emphasis between the two, I tend to side with the Observations. While the Grounds was published two years after the Observations, the Grounds is presented as a revision of the previous Opinions, whereas the Observations is produced from scratch. In my opinion, the Grounds shows its older bones, and the Observations feels like a more definitive expression of her system. Whether that is right or not, to the extent that this system changes between works, this book emphasizes its expression in the Observations.

As an appendix to the Observations, Cavendish published The Blazing World, an allegorical tale that she presents as an articulation of her philosophy that might be more palatable to ladies. It tells the story of a beautiful princess who is kidnapped and finds herself adrift alone after the gods send a great storm to punish her captors. She drifts into a new world, populated by all manner of animal-men, each of which represents some social or intellectual demographic: the Bear-men are the experimental philosophers, the Bird-men are astronomers, the Parrot-men are orators, and the Fox-men are politicians. The beautiful princess is made the empress of the Blazing World and uses her new power to interrogate the motley population on all manner of natural philosophical questions; these questions and their answers reflect the contents of the Observations.

Section 1.6 Conclusion

Cavendish died on 15 December 1673 at Welbeck Abbey, outlived by William, who commissioned some elegies and poems in her honor. In one of them, the poet Knightly Chetwood wrote:

> Philosophy herself shall hold the Pall,
> (She's the chief Mourner at this Funeral)
> (Letters and Poems 1676:168)

During her life, Cavendish often reflected on fame and its relationship with posterity. She had celebrity, but she wanted to be appreciated for her philosophy—and she was, a little bit. The colleges at Oxford and Cambridge welcomed copies of her works and replied with letters of flattery addressed to 'Margareta Novo-Castrensis'. And Bathsua Makin wrote in her 1673 pamphlet, 'An Essay to Revive the Antient Education of Women': 'The present Dutchess of New-Castle, by her own Genius, rather than any timely Instruction, over-tops many grave Gown-men.'

But for the most part, Cavendish was regarded as a mere 'pretender to philosophy' (Evelyn 1906: 294), a sentiment echoed by frenemies like Woolf, as well as by more recent literary theorists and philosophers. In his 2009 biography of Hobbes, A.P. Martinich opines that Cavendish was 'a philosopher, although not a very good one' (Martinich 2009: 319)—so confidently as to have no need of evidence. In response to Martinich, Cavendish might lament that it 'is impossible to Expect my Book should be Understood of every one that Reads it', for that requires significant 'Strength of Brain' (SL 144); moreover, 'it is harder' for some to understand her works 'because they are New Opinions' (SL 144). The *Observations* expresses some tentative hope that such new opinions might one day be appreciated:

> I [do] not persuade myself, that my philosophy being new, and but lately brought forth, will at first sight prove master of understanding, nay, it may be, not in this age; but if God favour her, she may attain to it in after-times: And if she be slighted now and buried in silence, she may perhaps rise more gloriously hereafter; for her ground being sense and reason, she may meet with an age where she will be more regarded, than she is in this.
> (OEP 12)

It has taken 300 years, but thanks especially to some wonderful philosophers like Eileen O'Neill, Karen Detlefsen, Sarah Hutton, Marcy Lascano, Jacqueline Broad, David Cunning, Deborah Boyle, and Susan James, that age has arrived.

Further reading

Battigelli, Anna. 2021. *Margaret Cavendish and the Exiles of the Mind*. University Press of Kentucky.

Boyle, Deborah. 2018. Chapter 1. *The Well-Ordered Universe: The Philosophy of Margaret Cavendish*. New York, NY: Oxford University Press.

Broad, Jacqueline. 2007. 'Margaret Cavendish and Joseph Glanvill: Science, Religion, and Witchcraft.' *Studies in History and Philosophy of Science Part A* 38(3): 493–505.

Clucas, Stephen. 1994. 'The Atomism of the Cavendish Circle: A Reappraisal.' *The Seventeenth Century* 9(2): 247–273.

Rees, Emma L. E. 2003. *Margaret Cavendish: Gender, Genre, Exile.* Manchester, UK; New York: Manchester University Press.

Sarasohn, Lisa T. 2010. *The Natural Philosophy of Margaret Cavendish: Reason and Fancy during the Scientific Revolution.* Baltimore: Johns Hopkins University Press.

Whitaker, Katie. 2002. *Mad Madge.* New York: Basic Books.

Two
Nature

The sun crowns Nature's head with beams so fair;
The stars do hang as jewels in her hair.
Her garment's made of pure bright watchet sky,
Which round her waist the zodiac doth tie.
The polar circles are bracelets for each wrist;
The planets round about her neck do twist.
The gold and silver mines, shoes for her feet,
And for her garters are soft flowers sweet.
Her stockings are of grass that's fresh and green;
The rainbow is like colored ribbons seen.
The powder for her hair is milk-white snow,
And when she comes, her locks the winds do blow.
Light, a thin veil, doth hang upon her face,
Through which her creatures see in every place.
(P&F Nature's Dress)

'Nature' is perhaps the central concept of Cavendish's philosophy. She uses it to refer to what we might call the universe, the cosmos, or the world. Some will add to that list another synonym: everything. Others will not, holding that there is something other than this world, whether it is something supernatural like an afterlife or God, some possible worlds or a multiverse, or something besides the natural world, like a spirit realm, a sphere of moral facts, or a Platonic heaven stocked full of abstract ideas. Almost all of Cavendish's contemporaries in England and Europe were committed to monotheism and so they denied that nature is all there is.

DOI: 10.4324/9781003107255-3

Does Cavendish think that nature is all there is? This is a surprisingly hard question to answer. On the one hand, Cavendish tells us that there is an immaterial God outside of nature on whom nature depends, and she sometimes writes that we have immaterial souls that live beyond our earthly bodies. On the other hand, much of what Cavendish tells us about nature strongly implies or even entails that it comprehends everything that there is. And while Cavendish tells us that there are or might be 'Immaterials' outside of nature, like God and immortal souls, she also tells us that there are no immaterial *substances*, even outside of nature, and that we can have no ideas of immaterials, including God.

Some of this tension can be resolved by attending to a distinction that Cavendish makes between natural philosophy, which is the source of our knowledge of nature, and theology, or divinity, which is the study of the supernatural. But as we shall see, despite some church-appeasing rhetoric, Cavendish does not in fact count the latter as knowledge at all. Instead, she holds that the boundaries of nature are the boundaries of what we can possibly know.

More than that, as I will argue in this chapter, nature, for Cavendish, is all that there is, as far as it could possibly concern us. The meaning of this will hopefully become clearer by the end of the chapter. But the idea is that nature comprises everything that we can possibly be related to, including anything that we can interact with, perceive with our senses, think about, or know about. In Cavendish's view, these relationships are all grounded by the fact that we are parts of nature, as are all of the things that we can be in relationships with.

The flip side of this is that what is not a part of nature with us, we cannot possibly be related to. So our possible experience and knowledge of things are limited to natural things. 'No part of nature', Cavendish writes, 'can conceive beyond itself, that is, beyond what is natural' (OEP 17). To talk about what is beyond nature is to talk nonsense. It will take not just this chapter but the book to understand this, as we see why parthood and composition are so important for Cavendish, and how she conceives of the relationship between the natural, the material, and the rational. But it is important to start with a broad view of how Cavendish conceives of the natural and the non-natural, and how that relates to her natural philosophical project. Because it takes a broad view, this chapter contains a number of promissory notes, that I intend to honor in future chapters.

Section 2.1 Nature as we find it

Cavendish does not think that we can deduce what there is from reason alone; instead, we must look around us to discover what world we have ended up in. When we do that, she thinks, four facts are evident. Cavendish does not provide arguments for these metaphysical starting points, and only later in the book will we grapple with whether Cavendish's epistemology provides a framework for their justification. They are, however, extremely minimal, so much so that almost all philosophers (particularly in Cavendish's tradition, tracing back to the Greeks) have taken them for granted.

First, there is something rather than nothing.

Second, and only slightly more controversial, there is change. Cavendish shares Aristotle's conviction, against Parmenides, that natural philosophers 'must take for granted that the things that exist by nature are, either all or some of them, in motion which is indeed made plain by induction' (Aristotle, *Physics* 1 2). The things in nature are not fixed, but alter, and they alter in different ways and at different rates.

Third, there are many things. Nature is full of both quantitative and qualitative variety—indeed, infinite variety. There are numerically distinct things: 'what is one Part is not another Part, no more than one Man is another Man' (PPO2 Preface). And things differ from each other in their natures and characters:

> An Oak is not like a Tulip or Rose, for Trees are not like Flowers, nor Flowers like Roots, nor Roots like Fruit, nor all Flowers alike, nor all Roots alike, nor all Fruits alike, nor all Trees, and the rest; and so for Minerals, Gold is not like Lead, nor a Diamond like a Pibble-stone; so there may be Infinite several Kinds of Creatures, as several Sorts that we can never imagine, nor guess at.
>
> (PPO2 4 10)

Fourth, nature is what Cavendish calls 'orderly'. While there is an infinite variety of things, this variety is a 'harmonious variety' (OEP 34), not a random grab-bag of unconnected beings and events. Cavendish understands harmony as a type of coherence, and she thinks that things cohere because nature is in some sense one. Cavendish sometimes articulates the third and fourth point together, writing that nature displays a 'poise and balance' between variety and unity.

So Cavendish's basic commitments about nature are: something exists, what exists is both many and coherent, and there is change. Cavendish takes these facts as her target of explanation in articulating the principles of her natural philosophy.

Section 2.2 Nature is matter

Given that nature as we find it has these features, Cavendish thinks, it must be made of self-moving matter. Chapter 3 ('Matter') will shed further light on why matter is uniquely qualified to explain these facts about nature, but one very important reason is that matter can explain why nature is 'poised and balanced' between variety and unity. That is because, as we shall see, the structure of matter is parthood and composition. All variety is variety of parts, and there is unity because those parts are composable with one another, making nature 'one only infinite body' (OEP 190).

Moreover, Cavendish holds that there is only matter in nature: 'Nature contain[s] nothing within her but what is substantially, really, and corporeally existent' (PL 3 2). Even stronger than that, Cavendish holds that the natural and the material are 'one and the same' (OEP 137; see also 253) and that the phrase 'Immaterial Natural substance' is 'non-sense' (PL 3 11). Chapter 3 will offer a deeper analysis of the meaning of this claim and of Cavendish's reasons for holding it. Here, we need only appreciate that Cavendish identifies matter as the 'principle' of natural being and that she assimilates matter with what exists in nature.

Section 2.3 Nature is infinite

Three of the most important facts about nature, according to Cavendish, are that it is infinite, eternal, and self-moving. All three of these were strongly associated by Cavendish's contemporaries with atheistic naturalism of an Epicurean persuasion. The next three sections, which treat each of these features, will hopefully make clear why this is so and why these positions seem to push Cavendish towards the view that there is nothing besides nature. We begin with nature's infinity.

Nature, according to Cavendish, is infinite in many respects. The very first chapter of the first edition of the *Opinions* establishes that nature contains infinite figures and so

> if infinite figures, infinite sizes; if infinite sizes, infinite degrees of bignesse, and infinite degrees of smalnesse, infinite thicknesse, infinite thinness, infinite lightnesse, infinite weightinesse; if infinite degrees of motion, infinite degrees of strengths; if infinite degrees of strengths, infinite degrees of power, and infinite degrees of knowledge, and infinite degrees of sense.

In the second edition, infinite matter is infinite in 'Quantity, Bulk, Space, Place, Continuance…Parts and Whole…Positives, Negatives, and Potentials' (PPO2 xxviii). And in the *Letters*, Cavendish explains that there are 'several kindes of Infinites', including infinity in number, magnitude, degree of quality, and degree of motion, 'and so Infinite Creations, Infinite Compositions, Dissolutions, Contractions, Dilations, Digestions, Expulsions; also Infinite degrees of Strength, Knowledg, Power, &c' (PL 1 2). While the polemical role of the infinite is somewhat tamed in the later *Grounds* and the *Observations*, its philosophical role is not, though the respects in which nature is infinite are more pared down. In those works, Cavendish focuses on the claims that nature has infinite parts; infinite creatures and varieties of creatures; infinite effects, motions, and actions; and infinite varieties of effects, motions, and actions. This is an important part of Cavendish's gradual move toward the parsimonious ontology that will be developed in this book.

Cavendish defines the infinite in general as 'that which has no terms, bounds or limits' (OEP 130), which she relates to the claim that 'the infinite cannot be reckoned, nor numbered' (BW 45). In the case of particular finite creatures, parts, or effects, to be infinite means to be uncountably many or innumerable, that is, 'Infinite and Numberless' (GNP 1 9). Cavendish also claims, however, that nature, and matter, are infinite, period, and that nature is 'one infinite body' and 'one infinite whole' (OEP 31). This kind of infinity cannot, of course, be understood as uncountably many. So how should it be understood?

In the *Letters*, Cavendish writes that nature is infinite in 'quantity or bulk, that is such a big and great Corporeal substance, which exceeds all bounds and limits of measure, and may be called Infinite in Magnitude' (PL 1 2).This use of 'quantity' evokes the scholastic and early modern usage of the term to describe continuous extension in three spatial dimensions. But there are reasons to question whether what Cavendish means by infinite quantity is infinite extension in space. In the Argumental Discourse, Cavendish argues that it is 'certain that nature consist[s] of infinite parts; which if so, she must needs also be of an infinite bulk or quantity' (OEP 31). But the argument that she provides has nothing to do with spatial considerations:

> for wheresoever is an infinite number of parts or figures, there must also be an infinite whole, since a whole and its parts differ not really, but only in the manner of our conception: for, when we conceive the parts of nature, as composed in one body, and inseparable from it, the composition of them is called a whole; but, when we conceive their different figures, actions and changes, and that they are divisible from each other, or amongst themselves, we call them parts.
>
> (OEP 31)

This argument that the whole of nature is infinite depends not on an argument from the nature of extension or spatial parts, but upon a conceptual claim about the relationship between part and whole. Wherever there is an infinite number of parts there is an infinite whole not because, say, an aggregate of an infinite number of extended things yields an infinite extended thing, but because a whole and its parts differ only in the manner of our conception. This suggests that Cavendish takes 'infinite whole' and 'infinite bulk' to be interdefined with 'something with infinite parts'. Cavendish also argues that matter must be infinite because it is the cause of its parts, and 'it is not probable that a finite can have infinite effects' (OEP 31)—another argument that does not depend upon spatial infinity.

The next chapter will argue further that it is not essential to Cavendishian matter to be extended in spatial dimensions. So I do not think that we should understand nature's infinite body to be infinite spreading-out in spatial dimensions. Rather, we should understand nature's infinite body simply as an infinite whole. Cavendish stresses that while nature has infinite parts, they are joined in a 'body of continued infiniteness' (OEP 127). For nature to be continuous is for all the parts of nature to be joined with other parts of nature, *ad infinitum*, which need not involve spatial continuity. That nature is infinite parts and an infinite whole is an important aspect of what Cavendish calls nature's 'poise and balance':

> as there are Infinite Divisions, so there are infinite Compositions, so that the Infinite Compositions do Equalize or make an Unity with Infinite Divisions, for one Infinite doth Counterpoise an other Infinite, which makes Order and Method in Infinite Nature.
> (PPO2 3 20)

Infinite nature is infinite parts, infinitely composed.

Section 2.4 There is 'nothing exterior' to nature

As we will continue to see, Cavendish holds that to be composed with other parts is to be dependent upon them, in the sense that no parts of nature can exist 'by themselves, precised or separated from all the other parts' (OEP 126), and can 'only join and disjoin to and from parts, but not to and from the body of nature' (OEP 48). Among other reasons for this, Cavendish argues that there would be no place for such hypothetical disconnected parts to go. She identifies space and body (OEP 128), and thus holds that void space is impossible. So there is no empty space beyond infinite matter.

More than that, however, Cavendish often expresses that there is nothing beyond infinite nature. Sometimes she makes the weaker claim that there is no matter beyond infinite nature, as when she argues that nature's infinite body '[is] called Only matter, to Exclude all other Matter whatsoever' (PPO2 xxxiii). In both editions of the *Opinions*, Cavendish frequently describes matter as 'infinite and only matter'. Similarly, in the *Observations*, Cavendish characterizes nature as 'but one body' with 'no sharer or co-partner…And thus Nature may be called…"individual", as not having single parts subsisting without her, but all united in one body' (OEP 47–48). Other times, however, Cavendish does not restrict this claim to matter; for example, she tells us that nature's infinity entails that it 'cannot have anything without, or beyond itself' and that it 'is all within itself' (OEP 131, 126).

This association between nature infiniteness and its 'onlyness' is an important one. When Cavendish tells us that there is 'nothing exterior with respect to infinite' (OEP 130), we should not understand this as a claim about three-dimensional space—or, at the least, not only that. What she means is that nature takes up all the ontological space that there is. The problem with simply accepting this as Cavendish's view is that she also sometimes claims that there are or might be things outside of nature that are not material. Most significantly, she holds that God exists and is a supernatural and immaterial being. We will return to this tension in Section 2.9, which argues that nature is all that there is, as far as that could possibly concern us. Infinite and only nature has no bounds but does represent the bounds of our experience.

Section 2.5 Nature is self-moving

Cavendish holds that there is change in nature and that change must have a cause. She concludes from this that nature must be self-moving and that 'were there no self-motion, there could be no action' (OEP 167). We will further explore Cavendish's arguments that nature is self-moving in Chapter 5, but her view is at least partly motivated by the notion that there is nothing outside of nature to move it—at least, nothing that can interact with it. As she argues in the *Grounds*:

> As for a First Motion, I cannot conceive how it can be, or what that First Motion should be: for, an Immaterial cannot have a Material Motion; or, so strong a Motion, as to set all the Material Parts in Nature, or this World, a-moving; but (in my opinion) every particular part moves by its own Motion.
>
> (GNP 2)

A first motion outside of nature would have to be something non-natural and hence immaterial, since nature contains all the matter that there is. But Cavendish holds that immaterial things cannot affect material things. Cavendish does not think that God is material, so it follows that not even God can set nature into motion.

Cavendish does not hold that only some matter is self-moving, but that every part of matter, and every creature, is self-moving. From this she concludes that matter's self-motion is 'the only cause and principle of natural effects' (OEP 18). One part of matter, or one creature, cannot move another, though one part can 'influence' or 'occasion' another part to act. We will see the arguments for these claims in Chapter 5 and 9.

In holding that all of nature is self-moving, Cavendish radicalizes Aristotle's influential definition of the natural as what has 'a principle or cause of change and of remaining the same' that belongs to it 'in virtue of itself' (*Physics* 2 1). He called this internal principle of change a '*phusis*' ['*natura*', in Latin], which derives from the word for a plant's growth. Aristotle used the word '*kinêsis*' ['*motio*', in Latin] to refer to all changes, not just to local motion, or change of place. For now, we should understand Cavendish's use of 'motion' in that light: it is change, and self-motion is self-caused change.

For Aristotle, however, the cosmos itself is not self-moving, and only some of the things within it are self-moving. The motion of the cosmos and the motion of living creatures both require causes; a supernatural prime mover, in the case of the cosmos, and souls, in the case of individual creatures. Cavendish rejects these explanations of the self-motion of nature and the things in it. Instead, nature itself is truly natural, in the sense that both infinite nature and its parts contain their own principle of motion.

It is a manifest and significant feature of natural change, according to Cavendish, that things change gradually and at different rates. It is a result of matter's variably gradual actions that things are characterized by time. Just as space depends upon matter and cannot be abstracted from it, time depends upon change and cannot be abstracted from it:

> [T]here can be no such thing as Time in Nature, but what Man calls Time, is onely the variation of natural motions; wherefore Time, and the alteration of motion, is one and the same thing under two different names.
>
> (PL 3 17; see also GNP 16)

So as there is no space outside of nature, neither is there time, and while there are space and time in nature, nature itself is not in time any more than it is in space. Criticising Van Helmont's delightful characterization of time as 'Certain Fluxes of Formerlinesses and Laternesses', Cavendish writes:

> But when I say, Time is the variation of motion, I do not mean the motion of the Sun or Moon, which makes Days, Months, Years, but the general motions or actions of Nature, which are the ground of Time (PL 3 17).

'I would rather believe Solomon', she continues,

> who says, that there is a time to be merry, and a time to be sad; a time to mourn, and a time to rejoyce, and so forth: making so many divisions of Time as there are natural actions; whenas your *Author* makes natural actions strangers to Nature, dividing them from their substances. (PL 3 17)

What is fundamental are matter and its merry and mourning actions. Seconds and days are mere abstractions.

Section 2.6 Nature is eternal

Cavendish argues that it follows from the fact that nature is infinite that it is eternal (and vice versa; PPO2 xxxi; OEP 32; PPO1). While she defines the eternal as what is 'Infinite in Time or Duration' (PL 8), this cannot mean what is unbounded in time, since we know that nature is not in time. As Georgescu points out, a better definition can be found elsewhere in the *Letters*: 'Eternity consists herein, that it has neither beginning nor end' (PL 1 3; see Georgescu n.d. 5). Nature's motions have no beginning or end (OEP 220).

Cavendish does not provide the details of the inference from nature's infinity to its eternity, but it suggests the influence of Epicurus, who argues in the Letter to Herodotus that the eternity of the world follows from the principle that 'nothing comes into being out of what is non-existent'. While the spirit of this principle goes back at least to Parmenides, at Cavendish's time the canonical formulation came from Lucretius's Epicurean poem *De rerum natura*: '*ex nihilo nihil fit*'—'from nothing, nothing comes'. In his *Physiologia Epicuro-Gassendo-Charletoniana*,

Charleton describes the *ex nihilo* principle as Epicurus's 'first branch of ever-flourishing truth' (Charleton 1654: 85).

As we have seen, Cavendish often writes or implies that there is nothing outside of nature that could have created it. However, she does not make this argument explicitly, because she does not (at least explicitly) hold that there is no God. Instead, she makes a different argument, one that echoes Epicurus's second argument for the eternity of the universe. It proceeds not from the claim that nothing can come from nothing, but from a second branch of ever-flourishing truth: that something can only be changed or destroyed by something:

> the sum total of things was always such as it is now, and such it will ever remain. For there is nothing into which it can change. For outside the sum of things there is nothing which could enter into it and bring about the change.
>
> (Diogenes Laertius 1925: 569)

This argument, like the first, has an impious corollary: assuming that God is not already a part of the sum total of things, it implies that God lacks the power to destroy it all. But this implication is more easily blocked than the first. Cavendish simply allows that it is impossible for nature to be annihilated *except* by God, who 'by His omnipotency…may reduce the world into nothing' (OEP 262–263).

In the *Philosophical Letters*, Cavendish anticipates that despite this caveat, her interlocutor will be 'offended at my Opinion, that Nature is Eternal' (PL 13). In fact, as Cavendish recognizes, charges of atheism will be invited not only by her claim that nature is eternal, but also by her other two Epicurean claims: that it is infinite and self-moving. As she writes 'To The Reader' of the *Observations*,

> There remains yet one obstruction more to be removed. Perhaps the wise among my readers cannot, and the superstitious will not, allow nature to be infinite or eternal. If so, I am not unwilling, that both sorts should waive that opinion, and enjoy their own: nor is it necessary for me to be rigorous in asserting it.
>
> (OEP 21)

Cavendish goes on in that paragraph to dismiss a number of reasons for associating nature's infinity, eternity, and self-motion with atheism.

Returning to nature's eternity, the offended party might worry that even if God could destroy nature if he felt like it, the argument still entails that nature does not depend upon God for its existence. She may also worry that to attribute eternity to nature is to attribute to it an attribute that should be reserved for God. Cavendish denies that these impious implications follow. To the latter, Cavendish replies by adopting a traditional distinction between two different senses of eternity. Nature is eternal in the sense that it is everlasting, or without beginning or end. God is eternal in a different sense, reserved for him: time, and change, do not apply to God at all (PPO2 7). To the former, she replies by denying that eternity is incompatible with divine dependence.

Well, sort of.

While God does not create nature in time, nature does depend upon God as an 'eternal servant upon an eternal master' (OEP 17; GNP 1 4). 'Eternity', Cavendish writes, 'doth not take off the dependance upon God, for God may nevertheless be above Matter'. However, she continues: 'You may ask me how that can be? I say, As well as any thing else that God can do beyond our understanding' (PL 2 22). Elsewhere, she writes that the compatibility of nature's eternity with its dependence on God 'cannot be comprehended by natural reason' (OEP 262; see also PL 14), cannot be treated by 'natural Arguments and Proofs' (OEP 16), and is 'against the rules of logic' (OEP 217).

This all seems to be an admission that at least within a certain domain—the domain of natural reason, natural proof, and 'understanding'—nature's eternity is incompatible with its divine dependence. We can go some way towards squaring this with Cavendish's claim that nature depends upon God by considering Cavendish's account of the scope of natural philosophy.

Section 2.7 Natural philosophy and theology

Cavendish defines natural philosophy as 'rational inquisition into the causes of natural effects' (OEP 158). As this suggests, it encompasses all kinds of inquiry into nature: it is 'the only study that teaches men to know…the several composed parts of nature' (OEP 244) and it is the 'guide…to other sciences, and all sorts of arts' (OEP 217).

Some kinds of inquirers were distinguished at Cavendish's time from natural philosophers, including chemists, physicians, historians, architects, and Cavendish herself sometimes distinguishes 'experimental philosophers' from natural philosophers (OEP 247). But Cavendish would describe them all as doing natural philosophy to the extent that they are seeking the causes of natural effects, writing that 'all Arts and Sciences are produced in one kind or other from Natural Philosophy' (PPO2 Epistle to My Reader). Natural philosophy, then, is the way that we come to knowledge of nature.

Cavendish contrasts natural philosophy with divinity, or theology, which she defines as the study of the supernatural. Supernatural topics include God, of course, and the life of the soul after this one (PPO2 Epistle to My Reader), but also the grounds of morality and the possibility of free will (PL 225). According to Cavendish, these, being supernatural, are emphatically not the proper subjects of natural philosophy.[1]

Cavendish's claim that the subject of natural philosophy is nature might sound obvious, even tautological. In fact, it was a controversial minority opinion. Most of Cavendish's English contemporaries endorsed so-called natural religion or natural theology on the grounds that God is a legitimate subject of natural philosophy. He is, after all, the ultimate cause of all natural effects. Boyle, for example, took 'nature, scripture, and conscience' to be all three the proper subjects of study for 'both our Divines & our Philosophers' (Boyle [1649] 2000: 147). Fifteen years after Cavendish's death, Newton would present his *Philosophiæ Naturalis Principia Mathematica*, one of the greatest works of mathematical physics ever produced, as evidence for the existence of God, writing that 'to discourse of [God] from the appearances of things, does certainly belong to Natural Philosophy' (Newton 1729: 392).

---

1 A caveat is necessary here. The appendices to the *Grounds of Natural Philosophy* appear to be Cavendish's best attempts to address apparently supernatural questions on the assumption that they are in fact natural questions. So, for example, Cavendish speculates there that heaven and hell are in fact parts of material nature. These appendices, as evidenced by the fact that they are set apart from the main text, are obviously and self-consciously speculative. But they make clear that questions like these may in fact be questions about nature, and if they are, then they are not in principle unaddressable by natural philosophy.

Cavendish, in contrast, mercilessly mocks philosophers 'who mince philosophy and divinity, faith and reason, together', thereby finding themselves in 'such a gallimaufry of Philosophy and Divinity, as neither can be distinguished from the other' (OEP 239). It is, 'an injury to the holy Profession of Divinity to draw her to the Proofs in Natural Philosophy' (PL 1 1), for 'God and his heavenly mansions are to be admired and wondered at with astonishment, and not disputed on' (P&F). Contrariwise, 'as Pure natural Philosophers do not meddle with Divinity, or things Supernatural, so Divines ought not to entrench upon Natural Philosophy' (OEP 239), and should instead 'let those whom Nature hath indued with such a proportion of Reason, as is able to search into the hidden causes of natural effects, contemplate freely, without any restraint or confinement' (PL 3 30; see also PL 4 10). This is quite canny. Many of Cavendish's English contemporaries took special satisfaction in condemning the views of other philosophers on the grounds that they entailed atheism. By maintaining that no inference can be valid between the two realms, Cavendish blocks such assaults, entreating her readers that 'since it is natural Philosophy, and not Theologie, I treat on, pray account me not an Atheist, but beleeve as I do in God Almighty' (PPO1 An Epistle to My Readers).

Cavendish tries to pitch this strict division between theology and philosophy as a good thing for the church, claiming that there is 'but one fundamental truth in each' of natural philosophy and divinity (OEP 10) so that neither can threaten the other. But her position is more subversive than she lets on. Cavendish does not, in fact, think that theology counts as knowledge. While 'Philosophy is Built all upon Human Sense, Reason, and Observation'

> Theology is only Built upon an Implicit Faith, which is an Undoubted Belief of that, which the Nature of the Creature cannot possibly Comprehend or Conceive, whilst it is in this World, and in the State of Ignorance; Wherefore Poor Ignorant Man must rest upon Faith, which is Beyond Human Sense and Reason, until such time as he hath a Glorifi'd Body and a Purifi'd Soul.
>
> (PPO2 xii)

Philosophy and theology are not, after all, different kinds of knowledge concerned with different kinds of truth. Rather, philosophy is knowledge of nature, and theology is a speculative stopgap for our worldly ignorance of what lies beyond.

On what grounds, exactly, does Cavendish hold that 'what is Supernatural cannot be naturally known by any natural Creature' (PL 2 29)? Some of Cavendish's arguments for this are specific to human perceptual faculties, which includes both sensitive and rational perception. For example, as we will see in Chapter 6, we perceive and understand things outside of us by patterning them, which requires that both the perceiver and the object are material and have parts. Immaterial beings like God are 'void of parts' and so they 'can in no ways be subject to perception' (OEP 38; see also PL 2 3). But we can say something more informative for our current purposes here, about why we are condemned to ignorance of the supernatural. It is not just that supernatural things are not made of the same stuff as we are, but that they are not part of nature with us. As we will see throughout the book, to know something else, for Cavendish, is to join with it, and if we cannot join with something we cannot know it. In fact, any causal, rational, perceptual, or cognitive connection with anything requires that we be joined with it. It is because we are parts of nature that we can join with other parts of nature and comprehend them. We cannot comprehend immaterials because immaterials are not comprehended in nature.

Section 2.8 God

Despite her frequent and clear insistence that neither we nor any other 'natural figure' can perceive or comprehend God (OEP 17, 38), Cavendish writes that we do have some kind of knowledge of God, which is moreover 'innate, and inherent in nature and all her parts' (OEP 17). This knowledge, however, is not of God's essence or of any of God's attributes, for we cannot conceive 'what God is in himself' (OEP 17) and 'God's infinite attributes are not conceivable' (PL 2 3). Occasionally, Cavendish seems to claim knowledge of one or another of God's attributes, including that God is supernatural, indivisible, atemporal, unchanging, and spiritual. But we should not take these to be positive attributes of God. Rather, they are expressions of a negative theology. This is obvious enough in the case of 'supernatural', which we may interpret to mean, simply, not natural. But divisibility, temporality, change, and materiality are all essential and exclusive to nature. So Cavendish's attribution of indivisibility, atemporality, and permanence to God may be interpreted as different ways of emphasizing that God is not natural. This is also true of 'spiritual'. As material beings, we cannot conceive spirits or the essence of spirit (e.g. OEP 88-89). So this too can only be another way or saying that God is not natural. (It is worth noting that Cavendish does not usually characterise God's attributes as perfections in contrast to nature's, only as differences.)

The knowledge of God that we can have as natural philosophers is only that God exists (OEP 17, 38, 40) and that nature depends upon God as its 'author' (OEP 89). How, though, can we know this? In light of Cavendish's denial that we can perceive anything that is not natural, we might interpret her claim that we have 'innate self-knowledge' (OEP 16) of God to mean that our knowledge of God's existence has some special, a priori source. I do not think this is right, though the full argument for will require understanding Cavendish's epistemology. The source of our knowledge of God is the same as the source of all of our other knowledge: our experience of nature. Nature manifests the effects of a great power, 'which power all the parts of Nature are sensible of' (OEP 89). But we do not know what that power is, 'like as the perception of sight seeth the ebbing and flowing of the sea, or the motion of the sun, yet knows not their cause; and, the perception of hearing, hears thunder, yet knows not how it is made' (OEP 89). Our knowledge that God exists is simply the knowledge that nature must depend upon something outside of it. But it is not knowledge of what that something is, nor of the nature of that dependence.[2]

---

2 In reading Cavendish as arguing that we can know nothing about God or how God created nature, I am in agreement with Cunning (2016) and Lascano (2023:19). Boyle and Detlefsen, in contrast, argue that we can know something about God and about how God created Nature, and that God plays a role in our explanations of natural things and happenings.

Section 2.9 The power of God and the power of nature

But how, exactly, do we know that nature must depend on something outside of it? Cavendish does not tell us directly, but the passage is illuminating: 'I do not say, that nature has her self-moving power of herself, or by chance, but that it comes from God the Author of Nature' (OEP 220). This trilemma provides the basis for an argument by elimination for God's existence. In this context, to occur 'by chance' is to occur without a cause (GNP 16) or reason (OEP 82). Cavendish, as we will see, holds that nothing happens by chance (OEP 264). Everything requires 'a sufficient Cause to produce such effects…which Effects could not be produced if any of those Causes were wanting' (GNP 16). Thus, the trilemma reduces to a dilemma: either nature has its existence and fundamental character of itself, or due to an external cause.

Given that Cavendish holds that nature is eternal, and eternally self-moving, we might expect her to hold that nature exists and has her self-moving power 'of herself'. Moreover, she tells us that nature's power is 'infinite', which sounds pretty powerful. But Cavendish does not hold that nature is self-caused in this sense.

To understand why, we begin with a distinction Cavendish draws between what she calls infinite natural power and infinite divine power. Nature has omnipotence of a sort, because nature's power, or the power of self-moving matter, provides a complete explanation for everything that happens within her body. Everything in nature is caused by natural matter's self-motion (OEP 37, 220).

This does not, however, mean that nature can do anything at all. Nature does what she does because it is in her…well, nature. Nature 'cannot work beyond herself, or beyond her own nature; and yet hath so much liberty, that in her particulars she works as she pleaseth' (OEP 109). True omnipotence, in contrast, would be the ability to anything at all, and in particular the ability to create *ex nihilo*. 'God' is the name for what has true omnipotence, or infinite divine power, which consists in the ability to do anything 'by an absolute will and command' (OEP 212).

Building on these two kinds of power, we can understand a bit more about the sphere of the natural. We are able to understand nature in its most general and fundamental principles, and thereby to explain everything that happens within nature. But we are not able to understand, by considering nature herself, why she has the nature she does. Our ability to understand everything that happens in nature is complete. Our ability to understand why nature is the way it is, however, is not only incomplete but utterly nonexistent. True omnipotence is not constrained by our understanding, but it also cannot be touched by our understanding.

In this sense, the sphere of nature is the sphere of our understanding. And Cavendish's argument that God exists is not an argument to a positive claim about a certain kind of being, but a point about the limits of our knowledge. This is also why it is 'beyond our understanding' how any kind of dependence upon God is compatible with nature's eternity. From our perspective, nature is everything that there is and has no bounds. But it points beyond itself for an explanation.

Cavendish takes nature's infiniteness, onlyness, and eternity to mean that there is 'nothing exterior' to nature. And to some extent, these license us to make universal claims within the scope of natural philosophy. Given that we cannot reach beyond nature, there is always an asterisk next to such claims: 'in nature, that is'. But when speaking in the voice of a natural philosopher, we are allowed to drop the asterisk. Cavendish's claims that nature is infinite, self-moving, and eternal do not depend on arguments from a point of view that would transcend nature itself. Rather, they consist in an epistemic bracketing of what is outside of nature.

This epistemic bracketing is something more than an expression of ignorance. It is not merely that we happen to lack knowledge of what is outside nature. Cavendish has a metaphysical story about why we cannot conceive anything outside of these boundaries: because we can only conceive of what is part of nature with us.[3] It concerns

---

3 Scholars disagree about the epistemic versus metaphysical interpretation of Descartes' view. Some of what Descartes says in his correspondence with More seems to bring him closer to Cavendish's positions, e.g. 'True, our mind is not the measure of reality or of truth; but certainly it should be the measure of what we assert or deny. What is more rash or absurd than to want to make judgments about matters which we admit our mind cannot perceive. I am surprised that you seem to wish to do this when you say "is infinite only in respect to us, it will be, in reality, finite"' (Descartes (to More) 1991: 364).

what is possible for us to know because it concerns what is possible for us to be related to in any way—what we can conceive, perceive, interact with, and know. Nature is the realm about which we can speak meaningfully. It is what there is, as far as it concerns us.[4]

Section 2.10 Natural modality

Most of the time, when Cavendish tells us that something is possible or impossible, she is speaking relative to nature's power. In this sense, something is possible or impossible, as Cavendish puts it, given 'nature considered, not what she might have been, but as she is, and as much as we are able to perceive by her actions' (OEP 158). By this, Cavendish means not 'given that certain creatures or parts exist', but given the most basic facts about nature outlined in this chapter: that nature is made of matter, which contains both unity and multiplicity, and that matter is self-moving. It is in this sense of impossibility that Cavendish holds that a vacuum (GNP 4) and inanimate matter (OEP 16, 158) are impossible. We may call this kind of Cavendishian modality 'natural modality'. Something is naturally possible or impossible when it is possible or impossible given the most general features of nature.

To say that something is naturally possible is not to say that it is actual, because there are many ways that nature could have been that are consistent with these general features. Nor is natural modality merely epistemic modality despite Cavendish's description of it as

---

4 It is interesting to compare Cavendish here with Kant, who would come later. Cavendishian nature is analogous to the Kantian phenomenal realm in that it is in one important sense causally and explanatorily self-contained, and our relationship to that realm both grounds the legitimacy of our claims about it and establishes a limit to those claims. But for both, our knowledge of nature, or the phenomenal realm, points beyond our cognitive capacities. Cavendishian nature is not constituted by the mind in the way that it is for Kant, however; rather, the mind is constituted by nature. It depends on the fact that our minds—which are just our bodies—are parts of nature, which is structured in a certain way. It is a kind of transcendental argument, but for metaphysical conditions of possibility and not cognitive and perceptual conditions of possibility.

what is possible 'as we are able to perceive by [Nature's] actions'.[5] It is true that naturally impossible worlds are worlds that are impossible, given some things that we know. But we know those things because they are true of nature.

Cavendishian natural necessity is usefully compared to what contemporary philosophers refer to as 'nomic necessity', which is necessity relative to the laws of nature. As Boris Kment describes nomic necessity, natural necessity 'form[s] a sphere around actuality'—a sphere defined by these universal features of nature (Kment 2014: 189). Cavendishian natural necessity is analogous to nomic necessity only if we recognize how very deep and fundamental the basic features of Cavendishian nature are. We cannot understand how a world without these features could be characterized by time, could change as we encounter it, could hold a variety of things, or could maintain order or coherence. So it is not like nomic necessity if one thinks, for example, that we can easily imagine a world in which some physical laws or constants were different. Another interesting comparison is with Bigelow, Ellis, and Lierse's 1992 'The World as One of a Kind', which argues that the actual world is a member of natural kind and that 'we can imagine worlds which would be of the same natural kind as ours; but we can also imagine worlds which would not' (Bigelow et al. 1992: 371). (Cavendish does not think that we can imagine anything about worlds that are not natures, but she definitely thinks that we can imagine that there are such worlds.)[6]

Cavendish has a useful and beautiful device for thinking about what is naturally possible. Inspired by Epicurus's claim that there are 'infinite worlds both like and unlike this world of ours' (Letter to Herodotus), Cavendish holds that if 'Nature be infinite, there must also be infinite worlds' (OEP 264). A world, as Cavendish uses that term, is just a region of nature. It is a complex part of nature, made of a blend of all three kinds of matter (GNP 255), and diversified

---

5 As, for example, Shaheen (2022) interprets these kinds of modal claims.
6 Other comparisons of interest include Deutsch's 'real possibility' (1990), Fine's 'Varieties of Necessity' (2002), and Sider's 'Crash Course on Natural Necessity' (2018).

into a variety of creatures. Because worlds are parts of nature, they are causally integrated with one another, and so travel between worlds is possible, like the voyage of the Empress to the Blazing World (GNP 255–256).

However, these different worlds have vastly different varieties of creatures, which form somewhat self-contained realms. Other worlds 'may be so different from the Frame, Form, Species, and Properties of this World, and the Creatures of this World, as not to be any ways like this World, or the Creatures in this World' (GNP 234). Our world is the world of the solar system and the Milky Way, of hydrogen and carbon and bees and lupines and golden retrievers and parliaments. In other worlds, these may be replaced by entirely different 'kinds and sorts' of creatures. The differences between creatures may be drastic and deep: there may be worlds without lupines and carbon but also without gravity, light, heat and cold, or dry and wet.

Our world is not necessarily the best world nor the happiest nor the most regular of all the worlds. The fact that there are human beings in it doesn't give it any particular dignity—in fact, the presence of human beings in a world is pretty bad news for our world, at least:

> I wish Men were as Harmless as most Beasts are, then surely the World would be more Quiet and Happy than it is, for then there would not be such Pride, Vanity, Ambition, Covetousness, Faction, Treachery, and Treason, as is now.
>
> (SL To His Excellency the Lord Marquess of Newcastle)

When Cavendish has a theologically inclined audience in mind, she describes our world as the one whose creation is described in Genesis, but she does not really take that story literally. God only created our world in the sense that self-moving matter depends upon him; everything else depends on the motions of self-moving matter.

Cavendish clearly understands these worlds as tools for probing natural possibility. This happens most obviously in the Appendix to the *Grounds*. The First Part establishes that immaterial substances are naturally impossible. The Second through Fourth Parts go on to ask, about a variety of kinds of worlds, whether they are possible. The arguments that Cavendish gives proceed, for the most part, from considerations that constrain natural being.

Cavendish definitely thinks that some naturally possible worlds exist, finds it 'probable' that many of them exist, and sometimes speculates that infinite worlds exist (WO The Infinities of Matter). Although she does not claim that they all exist, I wonder whether she is tempted by that view. Descartes claimed that in infinite matter given infinite time, all possibilities are eventually realized. Leibniz plausibly saw this as Descartes' attempt to ground modal claims in the natural world. Perhaps Cavendish is trying to do something similar? In one short section of the Grounds, Cavendish entertains the question that 'some may ask, *Why there are such sorts of Creatures, as we perceive there are, and not other sorts?*' She answers that ''tis probable, we do not perceive all the several kinds and sorts of Creatures in Nature: In truth, it is impossible (if Nature be Infinite) for a Finite to perceive the Infinite varieties of Nature' (GNP 25–26). This does not demonstrate that Cavendish thinks that all possible sorts of creatures exist. But it is telling that Cavendish thinks that appealing to the infinity of creatures counts as some kind of response to the question why some sorts of creatures and not others actually exist.

If all naturally possible worlds exist, it opens the door to holding that nature, as we find it, is the only possible nature. In other words, it opens the door to necessitarianism, in the realm of the natural. Sometimes Cavendish expresses necessitarian sentiments, as when she writes that 'all motions are so ordered by nature's wisdom, as not any thing in nature can be otherwise, unless by a Supernatural Command and Power of God' (PL 4 17). We will return to this question later in the book.

Section 2.11 Metaphysical modality?

Many philosophers in both Cavendish's time and our own who accept something akin to nomic or natural modality also recognize a further kind of modality, that is nowadays called 'metaphysical modality'. If what is naturally possible is determined by what natures are possible, what is metaphysically possible is determined by what realities more generally are possible. Contemporary philosophers describe these as possible worlds (using that term differently than Cavendish does). For many philosophers, the metaphysically possible worlds outstrip the nomically or naturally possible ones, and a reality or state of affairs might be possible that does not, say, conform to the laws of nature.

Many early modern philosophers identified what is metaphysically possible with what is within God's power. Given Cavendish's distinction between infinite natural power and infinite divine or absolute power, she may seem to countenance a similar distinction. While nature can do whatever she wants consistent with being a material, self-moving body, God can do whatever he wants, period. Cavendish occasionally seems to deploy this stronger sense of possibility. Most significantly, she sometimes claims that a world of inanimate matter, though naturally impossible, is possible in this sense, writing that God could have created 'a dull, indigested and unformed heap and chaos' (OEP 207). This is not a possible nature, but, it would seem, it is a possible creation.

It is clear that there is a sense, for Cavendish, in which other worlds that are not natures are possible. That is because, as we have seen, natural necessity is not absolute. There is always that implied asterisk: as far as it concerns us. Herein lies an acknowledgement that many realities are possible that are not ours. However, as we have also seen, and will continue to see, Cavendish holds that all our possible experience and knowledge is constrained by nature. What is completely beyond nature is completely beyond our ken. So to say that a world is metaphysically but not naturally possible can only be an acknowledgement of our ignorance about any possible world that is not a possible nature.

So, similar to Cavendish's claims about God and about supernatural entities, these sorts of possibility claims must be understood purely negatively. When Cavendish writes that animate and inanimate matter are 'so closely intermixt' that they 'cannot be separated from each other, but by the power of God' (OEP 33), she means: they cannot be naturally separated from each other, which is to say, separated from one another, as far as we know. As for what God can do: who can say. I do not think that we should read this, then, as a positive claim that animate and inanimate matter can be separated.

Cavendish does not think that she has positive knowledge that a world of inanimate matter is possible. This stands in stark contrast with many early modern as well as contemporary accounts of metaphysical possibility, according to which we can positively determine what is metaphysically possible and impossible by considering what is conceivable or inconceivable. For Cavendish, what is outside of nature is inconceivable for us, but that does not mean that we can declare it impossible. Nor can we declare it possible. It is not right to imagine naturally possible worlds, for Cavendish, as a subset of all the possible worlds. It is especially not right to attempt to identify these by making claims about what God can and cannot do, which impiously proposes to 'limit God's action' (PL 4 10). Cavendish even admits that what is 'against the rules of logic' is nonetheless 'not above the power of God' (OEP 217). So even logical necessity is not a guide to metaphysical necessity.

Cavendish's deployment of natural modality reflects the fact that natural philosophy, which includes most of what we would call metaphysics, is relativized to nature. So as natural philosophers, natural necessity is all the necessity we should be concerned with. This is an interesting perspective for contemporary debates over the relationship between conceivability and possibility. It is an attempt to recognize the cognitive access that we do have to unrealized possibilities, while still recognizing that our minds cannot transcend the world we are in fact parts of. Conceivability is a guide to natural possibility, but not to metaphysical possibility.[7]

Section 2.12 Conclusion

Nature, for Cavendish, is what there is, what we can be in any way related to, what we have cognitive access to, and what we can

---

7 Cavendish does sometimes appeal to inconceivability to argue impossibility in a third way, an example of which we will see early in the next chapter, when we see that Cavendish rejects the possibility of an immaterial substance. That is because an immaterial substance is straightforwardly incoherent or contradictory based on how she understands those terms. In an unpublished manuscript, O'Leary argues that it is only in such cases where Cavendish argues from inconceivability to impossibility.

meaningfully talk about. Cavendish allows that there may be something outside of nature, and even that there must be, because nature, as far as we can tell, is not self-caused. But we cannot know anything about what is outside of nature, including anything about God.

In our experience of it, nature has some obvious general features. It exists, there is change, and it contains variety as well as unity. From that we can conclude that it is made of matter, and we will explore what that means in the next chapter. What there is might have been a different way, but we cannot say what other ways it might have been, other than negatively. That nature is this way, and we are a part of it, is what allows us to be related to the rest of it, including cognitively. Natural philosophy is the inquiry into what nature is like, and the fruits of natural philosophy are all that we can know about what there is.

Further reading

Detlefsen, Karen. 2009. 'Margaret Cavendish on the Relation between God and World.' *Philosophy Compass* 4(3): 421–438.

LoLordo, Antonia. 2011. 'Epicureanism and Early Modern Naturalism.' *British Journal for the History of Philosophy* 19(4): 647–664.

Three
Matter

And if that matter with which the world's made
Be infinite, then more worlds may be said.
Then infinites of worlds there may be found,
If infinite of matter has no bound.
(P&F The Infinites of Matter)

What is matter? I asked some friends this question, and most of them replied: 'stuff'. Some of them just said 'stuff'; others said 'stuff you can see and touch', 'the stuff that makes up the earth and other planets', or 'I don't know…hard stuff?'

What are they reaching for with that word 'stuff'? I think it is something like 'whatever there is' or 'what exists'. And that is what Cavendish means by it, too. Matter is what there is—in nature, at least, which is all that possibly concerns us.

Cavendish tells us that 'the principle of nature is matter' (OEP 253, see also 251). A principle, for Cavendish, is an ontological foundation; it is that 'out of which all other creatures are made or produced' (OEP 205). Usually, Cavendish tells us that there is one principle: self-moving matter (e.g. OEP 205), and she is loathe to treat matter and motion as separate principles, as we will see. But as her claim that the principle of nature is matter suggests, she sometimes treats matter as the principle of the being of things in nature and self-motion as the principle of change and variety:

> For first, all effects of nature are material; which proves, they have but one principle, which is the only infinite matter. Next, they are all self-moving; which proves, that this material principle

DOI: 10.4324/9781003107255-4

has self-motion; for without self-motion, there would be no variety or change of figures, it being the nature of self-motion to be perpetually acting.

(OEP 239)

So while we must eventually tackle what it means that Cavendish denies any distinction between matter and (self-)motion, we begin by focusing on the principle of natural being, which is matter. We will consider motion in the next chapter, and at the end of that chapter, we will have in place Cavendish's principles.

This chapter develops Cavendish's conception of matter and the meaning of her materialism and, in the process, argues for two central interpretive points.

The first is that Cavendish's materialism should not primarily be understood as a commitment to the claim that a certain kind of substance exists. Matter is not a kind of substance for Cavendish, and it is specifically not extended substance, as it notably is for Descartes and many of their contemporaries. Rather, matter is substance, period: which is to say, matter is what there is, as far as that possibly concerns us. One important consequence of this is that while Cavendish in no way admits the existence of spiritual or thinking substances, we distort the significance of her materialism when we approach it primarily as an intervention in debates over dualism, or the view that both material and spiritual or mental substances exist.

The second is that while matter is not a kind of substance, we can still say something substantive about it, which is that it has compositional structure. So Cavendish's materialism is also, centrally, a commitment to the claim that all fundamental metaphysical structure is compositional structure. As such, it is a rejection of a number of alternative kinds of metaphysical structures, including atomism, Aristotelian hylomorphism, and the fundamental spatial structure of the mechanical philosophy. As we shall see, Cavendish's preference for compositional structure results from the fact that she is deeply motivated by ontological parsimony and holds that compositional structure can best account for nature's variety and coherence without multiplying principles, kinds of entities, quasi-entities and dependent entities, distinctions without differences, and other metaphysical 'hobgoblins'. In its context, her account of matter is strikingly original, but it is inspired by the spirit of her Democritean and Stoic forebears, and it echoes and purifies some of the guiding commitments of the mechanical philosophers.

Section 3.1 Matter is what there is

Given how abstract is the question of what is or what has being, it is helpful to situate Cavendish a bit in the history of that debate, which in European philosophy has often been conducted in response to Aristotle. Aristotle posed the question of what has being 'in the primary sense', naming whatever that turned out to be '*ousia*', which became '*substantia*' in the Latin tradition. Specifying exactly what that 'primary sense' is can be tricky—so, too, explaining what a non-primary sense of existence could even be—and doing that was a central goal of metaphysicians in the Aristotelian tradition. But we can understand 'substance' to mean: what exists, for real, or what *is*, most basically or most fundamentally.

In his quest to discover what has such being, Aristotle took as one of his primary targets an influential answer that he attributes to Democritus along with Heraclitus, Anaxagoras, and Thales, according to which

> the principles which were of the nature of matter were the only principles of all things. That of which all things that are consist, the first from which they come to be, the last into which they are resolved (the substance remaining, but changing in its modifications).
>
> (*Metaphysics* 1 3)

In holding that matter is the principle of all being, these *physikoi* held that the existence and nature of something is explained once we posit *what it is made of*, in the sense in which statues are made of bronze, mountains are made of granite, and birds are made of organs.

Aristotle argued, against this view, that matter alone is 'inadequate to generate the nature of things' (*Metaphysics* 1 3). A statue is not just bronze but bronze in the shape of a fallen hero, and a bird is not just a pile of organs, but organs arranged bird-wise. Such entities require that a form (*eidos* or *morphê*) be added to their matter (*húlē*). *Húlē* liter-ally means 'timber,' but Aristotle used it to refer to whatever some-thing is made out of: timber for a house, bronze for a statue, and blood and sinew for an animal. 'Hylomorphism' is thus the name for the view that only form and matter, united, are sufficient to make a thing with being in the primary sense and can thus earn the label of 'substance'.

In this Aristotelian tradition, forms did two crucial bits of meta-physical work. First, forms were necessary to account for the fact that there is both qualitative and quantitative variety in nature. While it might seem from the examples of matter given, like organs and bronze, that matter has a nature of its own, we can always ask what makes the organs of the bird organ-like and what makes the bronze of the statue bronze-like. The Aristotelian answer will always be a form, so matter without form would be, as described in Burgersdijk's Scho-lastic textbook, 'free of and open to all forms, and so is called pure potentiality' (Pasnau 2013:35). Second, forms give substances the powers that they have. Aristotle conceived of matter as purely passive, and so it requires combination with an active principle in order to act.

To the extent that the question 'what is substance' means 'what has primary being', Cavendish answers with the Democriteans. What has primary being is matter, although Cavendishian matter is not formless or passive, like so-called 'prime matter'. Cavendish often uses the words 'matter' and 'substance' interchangeably (e.g. PPO2 Epistle to the Readers, 4 34; OEP 20, 140). Other times, she uses 'substance' to refer to a specific kind of stuff, like milk, leather, or fire (PPO2 4 27, 5 44; OEP 65). Still other times, she treats 'substance' and 'being' or 'substance' and 'thing' as interchangeable (PPO2 3 16, 3 19; PPO1 31). By identifying matter and substance, Cavendish is trying to convey that matter is what exists in the primary sense; there 'can be no Being without a Body, nor no Body without a Being' (PPO2 30). As we shall see, Cavendishian matter shares some other features in common with Aristotelian substance, including that it has a particular kind of unity and that it persists through changes.

But by Cavendish's time, the term 'substance' had accumulated other senses and implications, becoming a technical term not only for Aristotelians but also for innovators like Descartes. We should be wary of reading those senses and implications into Cavendish's use of the word.[1] When Cavendish uses the word 'substance', she is translating her own ontological framework into terms that are more familiar to her readers, but it is not a term native to her ontology. And as we shall soon see, Cavendish is extremely critical of hylomorphism as well as of the Cartesian conception of substance. So we must take care with the observation that matter is substance, for Cavendish.

That there is only matter in nature is the very first point established in the *Grounds*. There, Cavendish gestures at an argument that if there were anything in nature that was not matter, we could not know about it. This may not seem like much of an argument. After all, Cavendish admits that there is a lot about nature that we cannot know, but that doesn't make it false. But as we discover in the *Observations*, it is not simply that we couldn't know about immaterials in nature, but that it is 'impossible for the mind to conceive a natural immaterial substance' (OEP 86). And the fact that a natural immaterial is inconceivable means that it is not merely unknown but naturally impossible (see also OEP 75, 89, 193).

Given how often Cavendish relativizes her materialist claims to nature, we may ask whether she holds that immaterial substances are possible outside of nature. The answer is that she does not. In the *Grounds*, Cavendish discusses substance in detail in two places: the first chapter of the first part, Of Matter, and the first chapter of the first Appendix. The former establishes that there are no immaterial substances in nature, and the latter asks, 'Whether there can be a Substance, that is not a Body' (GNP Appendix 1 1). Cavendish answers that 'What a Substance, that is not Body, can be, (as I writ in the First Chapter of the Book) I cannot imagine' (GNP Appendix 1 1). She does not relativize the claim to nature there. And she continues on explicitly to ask whether 'There may be a Substance, that is not a Natural Substance; but, some sort of Substance that is far more pure than the purest Natural Substance.' Her answer is that 'Were it never so pure, it would be in the List or Circle of Body: and certainly, the purest Substance, must have the Properties of Body' (GNP Appendix 1 1).

---

1 For a contrasting reading, that argues that Cavendish deploys not one but two technical senses of 'substance' with roots in both traditions, see Shaheen (2022).

So Cavendish holds that immaterial substances are impossible, even outside of nature.

That said, Cavendish does allow that what she calls 'immaterials' are possible outside of nature. This is especially important because it allows her to leave open that God and immaterial souls exist. But we can interpret her claim that immaterials are possible just as we interpreted the claims that God and divine souls exist. To allow that an immaterial is possible is to allow that many things may be possible beyond the bounds of nature, which are also the bounds of our possible experience, conception, and knowledge. Cavendish's claim that immaterial substances are nonetheless impossible is a signal that she does not intend to make a positive claim about what can and cannot exist outside of nature. So, too, is her claim that 'an immaterial is no object, because it is not a body' (OEP 89), which is part of a discussion of God and so applies to him. Cavendish never characterizes God as an object or a substance in any context that suggests that she accepts that characterization. To claim that would be to definitely claim that an immaterial being is possible rather than to point to our ignorance of the world beyond nature.[2]

Like Cavendish, Hobbes held that 'being and body are one and the same.'[3] This was no doubt an influence on Cavendish, and it is useful to compare her view with Hobbes's. One argument that Hobbes gives that an incorporeal being is impossible is that it is inconceivable because it is not imaginable, and it is not imaginable because it is not extended. Cavendish's argument that immaterial being is inconceivable does not, in contrast, depend upon matter's spatial extension. She does argue that immaterials cannot be perceived because they do not have a 'form' or 'figure' (e.g. OEP 88), but 'figure' here again means 'compositional structure', and things without compositional

---

2 Cavendish has been accused of inconsistency on this point (see e.g. Duncan (2012)), but she is in fact quite careful on it.

3 According to Duncan (2022), Hobbes, especially in his early work, has a view that is much closer to the one I ascribe here to Cavendish. While he thinks that we cannot have an (imagistic) idea of anything immaterial, this does not license us to conclude that nothing immaterial exists.

structures cannot be patterned by matter.[4] So the argument depends upon matter's divisibility, not its extension. Cavendish's position is not based, as Hobbes's is, on an introspective description of a mental state but rather on her metaphysics of perception. We will see the details of that in Chapter 6, and we will also see there that the deepest reason why immaterials are inconceivable by us is that they are not a part or possible part of nature with us.[5]

Section 3.2 Matter cannot be created or destroyed

While matter is 'subject to infinite and eternal changes' (OEP 18), it 'admit[s] of…no new creation nor annihilation' (OEP 36). We already know that Cavendish does not think that nature as a whole can be created or destroyed. But she also holds that all of nature's parts are eternal, because the destruction of any part would entail the destruction of the whole, which is impossible (OEP 261, 137, 237, 255, 261). So every bit of matter is also indestructible (except, of course, by God).

At Cavendish's time, both Burgersdijk's Scholastic textbook and Charleton's *Gassendo-Epicurean* treatise declared it to be a 'unanimous consensus' and a matter of 'universal agreement' that there is something that remains the same through all changes (see Pasnau 2013). With them, Cavendish holds that while matter is 'subject to infinite and eternal changes' of figure (OEP 18), 'the ground of the figure, which is natural matter, never changes' (PL 4 10). The permanence of matter is one of the few points on which Cavendish is proud to don the mantle of philosophical tradition, calling it an opinion 'Older than Eternity' (PPO1 The Text to my Natural Sermon). 'Older than Eternity' may be a bit of a stretch, but Cavendish is right that it is old. More specifically, what is old is the idea that there is something incoherent about genuine being that is not permanent, a position especially associated with Parmenides. Being itself cannot contain the seeds of non-being, so unless something else comes along to destroy a genuine thing, it stays being.

---

4   Cavendish does describe an idea here as a 'picture'; the meaning of that and similar claims will be assessed in Chapter 6.
5   For a defense of the view that Cavendish does think of conceptions as imagistic, see Cunning (2016, Chapter 1).

The depth of Cavendish's commitment to the claim that only matter exists, alongside her claim that matter is permanent, can make it hard to see how she can maintain that anything in nature is impermanent and thus how there can be change. As we'll see in Chapter 5, this tension is eased by her denial of the Aristotelian view that change must be analysed in terms of a thing coming into or going out of existence. And Cavendish does not, of course, agree that matter is inert; rather, matter causes all the changes in itself.

Section 3.3 Against hobgoblins

Just as Cavendish does not hold that matter is inert, she does not hold that it cannot differentiate itself. While self-motion is part of the cause of that differentiation, motion does not constitute natural variety, and we will see in the rest of this chapter, and in Chapter 5, how Cavendish does account for the distinctions and differences between birds and statues. Before we see how she does that, however, we will see how she definitely does *not* do it: she does not do it by adding any further entities to her metaphysical principles. As this section will argue, she forbids not only Aristotelian forms but also a huge variety of ontological posits by other philosophers meant to do the work of differentiating matter.

Aristotelians distinguished between substantial and accidental forms: substantial forms are responsible for the fact that things are what they essentially are, while accidental forms, like colours and fevers, are responsible for the features they can gain or lose. We will talk some more about substantial forms in the next chapter, when we discuss Cavendish's account of creatures. Here, we consider Cavendish's unsparing attack on accidental forms, or accidents, because it vividly illustrates a central aspect of her materialism.

The late Scholastic consensus was that where substances had being in the primary sense, accidents had what was called 'diminished' being. Colours and fevers were supposed to be entities, but entities that exist in some lesser sense than the full or primary sense in which substances exist. Cavendish confesses that she does not really know what people mean by the word 'accident' (OEP 271), and her attacks on accidents flatten centuries of the subtlest metaphysical debate. But her target is clear enough to give us a sense of the implications of this critique for her own metaphysics.

She characterizes the Scholastic conception of an accident as 'something between body and no body' (OEP 271, see also 275) and a 'mean between something and nothing' (OEP 231). Her argument against such beings is simple: they are, by definition, not matter, and so they do not exist.

The precise nature of such diminished beings was very much a matter of debate, and Cavendish directly rejects several ways of rendering it more comprehensible. Drawing on Aristotle's identification of 'what is primary' with 'that upon which other things depend' (*Metaphysics* 1003b11), an accident was characterized as something that essentially depends upon another thing for its existence, as the warmth of a cozy cat depends upon the cat, while the cat can exist independently. To this, Cavendish replies that nothing can exist whose 'being is to subsist in another body' (OEP 36). It was, further, considered an important mark of the dependence of an accident on a substance that it is inseparable from that substance. Cavendish also rejects this approach to distinguishing between primary and diminished being, holding that nothing exists which 'cannot subsist of, and by itself...as a substance' (OEP 36).

That diminished beings do not exist may seem like an obvious corollary of Cavendish's materialism. But in fact, most versions of materialism do not go so far, and most conceptions of the material are not so austere. Cavendish's materialism is not just the claim that everything that exists is material, but that everything that exists is matter, which is to say, material *substance*: 'something or nothing, body or no body, substance or no substance' (PL 2 24). Of course, 'material substance' is pleonastic, for Cavendish, so her materialism is the view that only substance exists. In other words, Cavendish's materialism is the view that there is only one sense of being, primary being, and nothing with dependent or secondary being.

In rejecting accidents, Cavendish is very much of one voice with the mechanical philosophers, who took such Aristotelian mysteries as among their primary targets. Cavendish's anti-Aristotelian contemporaries characterized accidents and other forms as 'occult qualities', vacuous posits that offer no true explanation of natural phenomena. Boyle, for example, promised to provide explanations of 'almost all sorts of qualities, most of which have been by the schools either left unexplained, or generally referred, to I know not what substantial forms' (Boyle 1666:1). As the poet Thomas

Shadwell eulogized Cavendish 'She never did to the poor Refuge fly/ Of Occult Quality or Sympathy' (*Letters and Poems* 166).

As we shall see, Cavendish and the mechanical philosophers inherit from Democritus the view that qualitative diversity depends upon arrangements of matter rather than on forms, and that activity, which is just motion, need not be caused by forms. But Cavendish's rejection of occult entities is much more sweeping than any of her contemporaries, and it captures some of the mechanists' own posits in its scope. For example, Descartes characterizes shape, size, and local motion as modes of matter, which he defines as essentially dependent entities. Cavendish rejects essentially dependent entities, as we have seen, and she explicitly includes 'manner and modes of Substances' (PL 2 23) in her long lists of ontologically suspect 'hobgoblins'. Cavendish gives us many such lists, which include 'Non-beings, and Neutral-beings, Corporeals and Incorporeals, Substances and Accidents' (PL 2 23), 'intentionals, accidentals, incorporeal beings, formal ratio, formal unity, and hundreds the like' (PL 4 18). There is no reason to think that Cavendish would not include Boyle's 'mechanical affections' among those hundreds.

Even Hobbes, who (arguably) characterizes accidents as nothing but ways of conceiving of bodies, comes in for criticism, fairly or unfairly. Cavendish targets Hobbes' claim that

> An accident's being said to be in a body is not to be taken as if something were contained in that body—as if, for example, redness were in blood the way that blood is in a bloody cloth, that is, as a part in the whole; for if so then accident would be a body, too.
>
> (Hobbes 1656 8 3)

Cavendish demurs:

> I answer…that redness is as well in blood, as blood is in a bloody cloth, or any other colour in any thing else; for there is no colour without a body, but every colour hath as well a body as any thing else, and if Colour be a separable accident, I would fain know, how it can be separated from a subject, being bodiless, for that which is no body is nothing…
>
> (PL 1 16)

Cavendish's response to Hobbes demonstrates how committed she is to the claim that if something exists, it is material substance.

It also raises a further important question about Cavendish's own view. Does she hold that qualities like colour are bits of matter, distinct and separable from their bearers, and joined to them as a part is joined to other parts? This interpretation is further suggested by Cavendish's comments that reflect Stoic arguments that qualities are matter as well as arguments made by medieval defenders of real accidents, most notably John Duns Scotus, according to whom accidents have the full-fledged being of substances (though not matter, since he did not identify substance and matter). Thomas Stanley reports that the Stoics hold that

> Qualitatives have a subsistence, and are separate from their subjects. For qualities (as all other accidents) are bodies, seeing that according to Zeno [of Citium], nothing can be effected by that which is incorporeal, nor can that which is incorporeal effect any thing; whatsoever effecteth is a body. Effective quality therefore is a body.
>
> (Stanley 1656:388)

Compare this to Cavendish's rejection of Van Helmont's accident-based etiology of disease:

> A disease is a real and corporeal being, and...not an abstracted quality...for no immaterial quality will do any hurt, if it be no substance...wherefore apoplexy, leprosie, dropsie, and madness, are corporeal beings, as well as the rest of diseases, and not abstracted qualities, and I am sure, persons that are affected with those diseases will tell the same.
>
> (PL 3 27)

Like the Stoics, Scotus argued that accidents have full being because they have causal efficacy, as well as on the basis that they are 'principles of cognizing substance' and are the 'per se objects of the senses.' This is reminiscent of an argument that Cavendish makes in the *Letters* that colours, scents, and so on are matter:

> [A]s for colours, scents, light, sound, heat, cold, and the like, those that believe them not to be substances or material things, surely

their brain...moves very irregularly...for what objects soever, that are
subject to our senses, cannot in any sense be denied to be corporeal.
(PL 1 2, see also GNP 12)

This realist interpretation of Cavendishian accidents is an interesting
one, and it is more congenial to Cavendish's metaphysics than are
accidents with diminished being. It is a reading that is reminiscent of
L.A. Paul's recent articulation of a 'one-category' ontology, inspired
by Peter Van Inwagen, which takes properties and property-bearers
to have the same kind of being, and takes them to be related to
one another by composition just like substances (Paul 2017; Van
Inwagen 2011). I do not, however, think that it represents Cavendish's
ultimate view of accidents. The letter responding to Hobbes begins
with Cavendish 'willingly consent[ing]' to Hobbes's claim that 'an
Accident...is nothing else, but the manner of our Conception of
body, or that Faculty of any body, by which it works in us a conception of it self' (PL 1 16). She goes on to affirm that 'what they call
Accidents, are in my opinion nothing else but Corporeal Motions.'
The argument against Hobbes's account of accidents may be read as
a *reductio*: if red is a separable accident, then it is in blood as blood
is in a bloody cloth. But it is not a separable accident, as the rest of
the passage implies, with Cavendish going on to argue that 'natural
colour cannot be taken away from any creature, without the parts
of its substance or body' and that the removal of artificial colour is
the separation of two bodies. This suggests that natural colour is not
matter distinct from its bearer but rather identical to its bearer, or,
as twenty-first century metaphysicians like to say, nothing over and
above its bearer. And while artificial colour is distinct from the coloured thing, it is not a distinct material accident. Rather, in the case
of artificial colour, the colour is identical with another body, like
paint, and its removal is like stripping paint from a house.

As we shall continue to see, Cavendish takes the apparent qualities
and features of matter to be akin either to arrangements of matter
or actions of matter rather than separate bits of matter themselves.
'All that they name qualities of bodies', Cavendish writes, 'are not
distinct substances' (PL 1 43). Colour, warmth, smell, shape, and the
like are the 'actions' or 'effects' of matter (PL 1 16; GNP 13 6).

Cavendish relates the proliferation of weird entities like accidents
and 'hundreds the like' to two other inflationary metaphysical

instincts: the proliferation of distinctions and the proliferation of relations. To take one example of this, Descartes holds that, there are three kinds of distinction: a modal distinction, a conceptual distinction, and a distinction of reason. A mode, Descartes argues, is not distinct from a substance in the same sense that another substance is. Meanwhile, Cavendish writes that 'men are apt to make more distinctions then Nature doth' (PL 3 23) when in fact nature is 'as plain as an un-plowed, ditched, or hedged champion' (PL 4 18). This allergy to distinctions is an important aspect of Cavendish's metaphysical intuition. It is reflected in her frequent claims that something or other is 'all one thing with matter.' Accidents, qualities, and the like 'are but one and the same with body, without any separation or abstraction' (OEP 253; see also OEP 108, 193, 270). So too are seemingly more fundamental features of matter, including place (OEP 48), motion (OEP 73,137), colour (OEP 45), and magnitude (OEP 81,128). We will investigate these claims further in their place.

Different kinds of entities and their different kinds of distinction also invite a proliferation of kinds of relationships. In the case of many of these entities, their dependence upon a substance was characterized as 'inherence'. This is a special kind of relationship that is different from the relationship that two substances have to one another, which for Cavendish means it is distinct from the relationship that two parts of matter have to one another. While the relationship between two parts is not hierarchical, the relationship between a mode, property, accident, or other inherent entity is.

Cavendish's rejection of diminished beings, and with it of different kinds of distinctions and relations, is more central to her materialism than her rejection of immaterial substances. Consider, for example, Cavendish's criticism of Van Helmont's appeal to accidents in explaining natural phenomena. She rejects accidents alongside other immaterial things like 'Van Helmont's Lights, Gases, Blaze and Ideas; and Dr More's Immaterial Substances or Daemons' (PL 1 16). But she continues: 'Dr More hath the better, that his Immaterial Substances, are beings, which subsist of themselves, whereas accidents do not, but their existence is in other bodies'.[6] At least More thinks ghosts

---

6 For a more detailed account of Cavendish's critique of accidents and other diminished beings, see Peterman (2024).

are beings. Van Helmont's claim that accidents exist, on the other hand, is tantamount to claiming that a nonexistent thing exists.

Section 3.4 Matter is not extended substance

In place of forms and accidents, the mechanical philosophers attributed the qualitative and quantitative diversity in nature to the geometrical features of bodies like size and shape (sometimes alongside texture, solidity, or impenetrability, especially for atomistic mechanists), as well as to the (spatial) arrangements and local motions of such particles. Despite Cavendish's assessment, the mechanists thought that these modes or mechanical affections were ontologically and explanatorily different from occult qualities for a number of different reasons. One of those reasons is that the matter of the mechanists is not prime matter, with no nature or character, but a particular kind of substance, namely, substance extended in length, breadth, and depth. Descartes identified spatial extension as the entire essence of matter (Descartes 1984: 224), while for Boyle extension was part of its essence, making matter 'a Substance extended, divisible and impenetrable' (Boyle 1666: 97).

This conception of matter was not a new one. A number of Aristotelians dealt with the paradoxes generated by the concept of prime matter by identifying extension as the essence of matter, or part of it. More precisely, it was of the essence of matter to have *partem extra partem*, or parts next to parts. This made divisibility essential to matter but, specifically, divisibility into parts with spatial dimensions and arrayed in space.

Because Cavendish adopts some of the rhetoric of the mechanical philosophers, she may seem to join them in identifying extension as at least part of the essence of matter. She describes the natures of things as their 'figures', for example, which makes them sound like geometrical shapes, and she holds that all change is 'motion', which echoes the mechanists' claim that all motion is change of spatial place. However, we will see in the next two chapters that Cavendishian figure is not geometrical figure and Cavendishian motion is not change of spatial place.

It is only with these arguments, along with the development of Cavendish's positive conception of matter, that the argument against a spatial interpretation of matter will be complete. Here, however, we can offer a few general considerations against assuming that Cavendish's conception of matter is that of the mechanists.

First, Cavendish never tells us that it is of the essence of matter to be extended in space, and she almost never relies on spatial concepts to describe nature or matter at the fundamental level. This alone is an important reason to hesitate before assimilating her conception of matter to that of the mechanists. While sometimes Cavendish speculates about particular creaturely motions in terms of circles and squares, these are not fundamental descriptions of matter, and it is moreover far from clear, especially in later work, that she has literal geometrical circles in mind. For example, the *Observations* explains a number of phenomena in terms of 'circle-lines,' but writes that there might be a variety of circle-lines that make water, for 'some circle-lines may be gross, some fine, some sharp, some broad, some pointed, etc. all which may cause a different weight of water' (OEP 108). Occasionally other shapes come up, like triangles and square, but she seems to associate these with exterior figures, which, as we shall see in Chapter 6, reflect how bodies are perceived and not the 'truth of the interior nature of bodies, or natural creatures' (OEP 93).[7] Rather, precise geometrical figures are human constructions that are not found in nature.

Second, in stark contrast to the relative absence of spatial concepts, Cavendish incessantly describes nature, at all levels including the fundamental, in terms of parthood and composition. And she explicitly analyses a number of spatial concepts in terms of compositional ones. Most significantly, as we have seen and will see in more detail, a 'figure' is a thing's compositional structure. And as Chapter 4 argues in detail, Cavendishian motion is not change of place, or motion though space, but, rather, the 'chief and general action of matter' is 'dividing and composing'.

Third, as we saw in the last section, Cavendish does not seem to think that reliance upon spatial structure has allowed the mechanical philosophers to divest themselves of peripatetic hobgoblins to

---

7 Cavendish does describe matter as extending in the context of discussions of contraction and dilation; we shall consider that in Chapter 5.

the extent that they liked to think. While Cavendish does not explicitly argue that there is no possible way to develop an extension-based metaphysics that succeeds in doing that, it does seem that she doubts that the mechanists can explain the relationship between matter and its affections or modifications, or between matter and local motion, without proliferating entities and distinctions. For example, Cavendish holds that both Boyle and Descartes get the relationship between matter and motion wrong. For Descartes, motion is a mode that can be lost and gained by a body, on Cavendish's interpretation (PL 1 30), and she describes Boyle as making matter and motion into two separate principles. We will see, in Chapter 5, why she thinks her own view of matter and motion fares better, and, in the rest of this chapter, why she thinks that she does a better job of eliminating forms and qualities.

Section 3.5 Matter is not a kind of substance

Finally, and most importantly, Cavendish does not hold that matter is extended substance because she does not hold that matter is a *kind* of substance at all. An initial way of understanding this claim is in terms of Cavendish's rejection of qualities and similar entities. Not only does Descartes characterize a body's size and shape as dependent modes, but he takes those modes to follow from the fact that matter is a substance whose primary attribute is extension. Descartes, of course, also holds that there are other substances, minds or souls, whose primary attribute is thought. So at the most fundamental level, Descartes replicates the kind of metaphysical structure that Cavendish rejects: after all, she might ask, what is a 'primary attribute', and what is its relationship with the substance underlying it? For Cavendish, matter is substance, or what has primary being—at least, as far as it could possibly concern us. The identity of substance and matter is naturally necessary, and does not require that natural being have one attribute or another.

But the fact that matter is not a kind of substance goes deeper even than Cavendish's rejection of qualities and other hobgoblins. For Cavendish, matter is the principle of natural being and the ground and cause of all creatures. There is an infinite variety of creatures with infinite kinds and natures, as we shall see in the next section. Those kinds and natures are a result of their being complex compositions of matter. Matter itself has no particular nature, at least, not in the way that we attribute to creatures. To try to characterize the nature of matter, or describe it as a kind of thing, is to project the creaturely forms of our acquaintance onto matter itself. As Cavendish vividly makes this point: 'Infinite matter is not like a piece of clay, out of which no figure can be made [unless it is] clayey; for natural matter has no such narrow bounds, and is not forced to make all creatures alike' (OEP 222).

Clayeyness is a property of creatures, which are finite parts of matter, not matter itself. To describe matter as extended substance, or as substance of any kind, is like describing it as clayey. Just as no part of matter is bound to some creaturely feature, 'no particular parts are bound to certain particular actions, no more than Nature her self, which is self-moving Matter' (OEP 138–139).

In light of this, we should hesitate to understand Cavendish's materialism primarily as a rejection of dualism, the position that there are mental substances as well as material substances. Cavendish does, of course, reject dualism, as a matter of natural necessity. But if we overemphasize this framing, it is too easy to think of her materialism as a vote for one kind of substance over another. And that is indeed how most versions of materialism, both early modern and contemporary, are construed: as the claim that only one certain kind of substance exists. For example, a widely read philosophical dictionary from 1733 describes materialism as the claim that 'all the occurrences and operations of natural bodies are derived from the bare properties of matter, as from its dimension, shape, weight, confrontation and mixing' (as cited in Wolfe 2017: 965). Not only does this version of materialism postulate that only a certain kind of substance in nature, but the kind is characterized in terms of its properties—which, of course, Cavendish denies exist. Materialism's present-day cousin, physicalism, is also more often than not characterized in terms of the kinds of properties there are. The recent entry on physicalism from the *Stanford Encyclopedia of Philosophy* surveys a vast variety of positions known as physicalism, almost all of them articulated in terms of the relationship between physical and non-physical properties (Stoljar 2001). Cavendish's materialism should not be understood in this way.

In lacking any kind, Cavendishian matter may start to sound like Aristotelian prime matter. But in fact she holds that '*materia prima* are two Latine words that mean nothing' (PPO1 An Epistle). For matter to be 'capable of, and subject to all forms,' it cannot be 'void of all quality, form and species' (OEP 253). There is variety and change in nature, and there must be something in natural matter that accounts for that. But Cavendish rejects the Aristotelian idea that this means that there are entities or quasi-entities like forms in addition to matter. Form and matter cannot be distinguished from one another:

> Form and matter are but one thing; for it is impossible to sep-arate matter from form, or form from matter; but what is not divisible, is not compoundable; and what cannot be separated, cannot be joined.
>
> (OEP 252)

No further entity but matter is required to explain nature, including the infinite forms that creatures can take and the infinite changes that they undergo.

Section 3.6 Matter is one

Matter is the principle of natural being, and its permanence is what grounds matter's permanence is essentially connected to nature's eternity. Matter is also, it turns out, what ground's nature's ability to strike a 'poise and balance' between variety and coherence, which is ultimately the source of nature's order. This section will introduce the sense in which matter is one, and the next section will introduce the sense in which matter is many.

Cavendish often insists that nature is one; there is 'but one matter, and the motion of that matter is the action by which it produces several actions and effects...the various effects alter not the nature of unity of the onely matter' (PL 4 18; see also, e.g. OEP 236). But in what sense or senses is matter one. The answer, it turns out, is com-plex and changes over Cavendish's career.

In both editions of the *Opinions*, Cavendish holds that the only, or at least the most important, sense in which matter is unified is unity of kind, which we will call its homogeneity. She writes that 'Nature tends to Unity' because it is 'but of a kinde of Matter' (PPO 1 15; see also PPO2 vii 1 and 1 1; PL 4 18) and that this 'One kind of Matter, is the union, conformity and order of and in Infinite Matter' (PPO2 1). In the preface to the second edition of her *Opinions*, Cavendish dilates upon this sense of unity, writing that 'Like and the Same are not all one thing': just as two men are not the same man but are alike in being men, two bits of matter are alike in being matter but are none-theless distinct individuals. This distinction between 'like' and 'same' resembles a distinction we nowadays draw between 'qualitative' and 'numerical' identity: two men are qualitatively alike in being men but numerically distinct. Similarly, while two bits of matter might be numerically distinct bits, they are alike in being both of them matter.

Cavendish emphasizes matter's unity of kind less often in later work, although she does write in one place in the *Observations* that 'infinite matter in itself, and its own essence, is simple and "homo-geneous," as the learned call it, or of the same kind and nature, and consequently is at peace with itself' (OEP 199).

We may wonder, at this point, in what sense matter is homo-geneous, that is, what is the 'same kind and nature' that all matter shares. As Section 3.8 argues, matter should not be understood as having a 'kind' at all, which is part of why, while Cavendish still recognizes matter's homogeneity in later work, a second kind of unity comes to dominate. As we have seen, it is not only that the parts of nature are alike but that they are united with one another into compositions:

> No part can subsist singly, or by itself, precised from the rest; but they are all parts of one infinite body; for though such parts may be separated from such parts, and joined to other parts, and by this means may undergo infinite changes, by infinite compositions and divisions; yet no part can be separated from the body of nature.
>
> (OEP 137)

Matter has what we may call compositional unity, because all the parts are composed with other parts of nature. Moreover, Cavendish describes nature itself here as 'one united material Body' (GNP 1 3) and as one whole (OEP 31, 47, 121).

This latter point seems to represent a significant change from the *Opinions*. The first edition declares that 'In infinite no union can combine' (PPO1 1 9) and the second that while 'there is a union in the nature of Infinite matter, yet there cannot be a Union in the Infiniteness' (PPO2 1 14). The very first sentence of the second edition establishes that there is no such thing as 'the Whole Matter... for there is no such thing as All in Infinite' (PPO2 1 1).[8] What exactly is going on with this change?

It is not as if the compositional sense of unity is completely absent from the Opinions. Cavendish already emphasizes there that the parts of nature are all joined with and depend upon the other parts of nature, and in the preface she describes nature as a 'whole' from which 'the parts cannot be divided' (PPO2 xxvii). What she is concerned to reject is anything that implies that nature is 'circum-scribable', which she further relates to something's being 'perfect', 'exact', and 'absolute'. She takes all of these to imply some kind of limitation, and the infinite has no limits (PPO1 1 4). Alongside her denial that nature is one perfect unity in the relevant sense, Cavendish denies that nature has 'an Exact form or figure, by reason it is Infinite' (PPO2 1 7); that it has an 'Absolute Power' (PPO1 1 18; PPO2 1 14); and that it has an 'Absolute Knowledge' (PPO1 1 7)—in fact, she writes that the infinite 'cannot possibly Know [even] itself' (PPO2 1 13).

Part of what is going on here reflects Cavendish's insistence that the infinite is not subject to measure or number, which includes not being countable as one. And in arguing that nature has no 'exact form or figure', Cavendish clearly means, in part, that nature has no geometrical figure, which would limit it by a particular shape and size. For example, Cavendish writes in the Letters:

> it is a contradiction to say an Infinite Cube or Triangle, for a Cube and a Triangle is a perfect circumscribed figure, having its certain compass and circumference, be it never so great or little; wherefore to say an Infinite Cube, would be as much as to say a Finite Infinite.
>
> (PL 156–157)

---

8 Though in the preface, she refers to nature as a 'whole' from which the parts cannot be divided (PPO2 xxvii).

But I do not think that Cavendish's point here is limited to the inapplicability of number and measure to the infinite. The fact that nature has no form is related to the fact that we 'cannot positively know what infinite is' (OEP 130). The infinite outstrips, not only our mathematical concepts, but all of our concepts.

Cavendish explicitly tells us in the *Grounds* that she has changed her mind on the question of whether nature can have a figure:

> I questioned, Whether Nature could have an Exact Figure, (but, mistake me not; for I do not mean the Figure of Matter, but a composed Figure of Parts) because Nature was composed of Infinite Variety of Figurative Parts: But considering, that those Infinite Varieties of Infinite Figurative Parts, were united into one Body; I did conclude, that She must needs have an Exact Figure, though she be Infinite.
>
> (GNP 1 12; see also OEP 138)

She further concludes, in contrast with her claims in the PPO, that 'Infinite Parts must of necessity be Self-knowing' and have 'an Infinite Knowledge and Perception' (GNP 1 8), and that infinite nature has 'both an United Knowledg, and an United Power' (GNP 1 12). But Cavendish still insists that nature is not 'absolute' in the sense of having a 'limited and circumscribed figure' (OEP 32):

> [I]nfinite is what has no terms, bounds or limits, and therefore it cannot be circumscribed; and if it cannot be circumscribed as a finite body, it cannot have an exterior magnitude and figure, as a finite body; and consequently, no measure. Nevertheless, it is no contradiction to say, it has an infinite magnitude and figure: for, although infinite nature cannot have anything without, or beyond itself, yet it may have magnitude and figure within itself, because it is a body: and by this the magnitude and figure of infinite nature is distinguished from the magnitude and figure of its finite parts; for these have each their exterior and circumscribed figure, which nature has not.
>
> (OEP 130–131)

These changes reflect a deep and important change in Cavendish's conception of matter. Note that she continues to deny that infinite nature has 'the Figure of Matter', by which she means a fixed size and geometrical shape, or any other kind of boundary. But it does have a figure in the sense that will become primary in Cavendish's system: it has a 'composed Figure of Parts', which means that it has a compositional structure. Unlike a geometrical shape, this does not imply any kind of boundary, but rather concerns the overall structure of infinite matter, which is infinite parts composed in an 'infinite whole' (OEP 31). Just like finite bodies, infinite matter has a body, and 'whatsoever hath a body, has a figure' (PL 2 9)—at least in this sense.[9]

Section 3.7 Matter is many

In the *Opinions*, despite the claim that infinite matter is not one whole, Cavendish sometimes treats infinite matter as what grounds unity, and its parts as derivative from or less fundamental than infinite matter. For example, she describes the parts as 'inherent' in infinite matter (PPO2 xxviii), which is reminiscent of certain readings of Cartesian extended substance and foreshadows Spinoza's claim that creatures are modes of the one infinite substance. However, as Cavendish's conception of matter evolves, she no longer holds that matter's unity is prior to its variety. In the next chapter, I will argue that Cavendish does not ultimately conclude that motion constitutes the parts of matter, but that it causes the divisions in matter (as well as the compositions), so that the parts exist independently of any motions. Here, we consider some independent evidence that Cavendish takes the fact that matter has parts to be equally fundamental to the fact that it is unified.

For one, this is reflected in Cavendish's intervention in a debate among medieval and early modern philosophers concerning whether the parts of matter are actual parts, or merely potential parts until they are actually divided from other parts. Despite, as we shall soon see, her agreement with Digby as to the centrality of parthood and composition to the nature of matter, Cavendish targets his claim that matter is 'but one whole that may indeed be cut into so many severall partes'

---

9   As we will see in Section 8.3, Cavendish's claim that nature has a figure does not mean that nature has some bounds. More specifically, it does not mean that nature is one composite or one creature. Much of Cavendish's system needs developing before we see exactly why and how to conceive of infinite nature's figure.

but that the parts are 'not really there, till by division they are parcelled out: and then, the whole (out of which they are made) caseth to be any longer' (Digby 1644: 10). Against Digby, Cavendish argues:

> I do not understand those that say, that a whole Figure may be Divided into many several Parts, but yet those Parts are not really there as in the whole Figure, untill by Division they are parceled out, and then the whole Figure, out of which they were made, ceases to be any longer a Whole, for then every several Part becomes a Whole, so that the Parts are not yet in it, that may be made of it, and that the Parts in the Whole be a bare Capacity...
> (PPO2 3 20)

The potential parts theorists think that for a part to become actual, it must be 'parceled out', or separated from the whole. As an important later proponent of actual parts, Samuel Clarke, puts it, to be actual parts, bits of matter must be 'actually unconnected' from other matter, and to be 'truly distinct Beings', which 'exist separately and have no dependance one upon another' (Clarke 1731: 100). We have already seen, and will continue to see, that Cavendish completely rejects this view. If one bit of matter were 'parceled out' in Clarke's sense, it would be no longer a part at all. Division, as Clarke understands it, is what entirely severs the connection between parts. To claim that this is required to *create* parts, according to Cavendish, is absurd. To be parts, two bits of matter must be connected by being joined, even as they remain two parts, so Clarke's sort of division precisely destroys parts:

> single parts...are such as can subsist by themselves; neither can they properly be called parts, but are rather finite wholes: for it is a mere contradiction to say single parts, they having no reference to each other, and consequently, not to the body of nature.
> (OEP 31)

Just as it is essential for Cavendish that matter is unified, Cavendish holds that matter, and only matter, essentially has parts:

> Matter cannot be without parts. (GNP 1 1, see also OEP 137, 162)
>
> Nothing has parts, but what is corporeal, or has a body. (OEP 36)

[W]heresoever is body, there are also parts; so that divisibility is an essential propriety or attribute of matter or body.[10] (OEP 263)

The depth of Cavendish's commitment to both the necessity and the sufficiency claims is evident from many of her arguments. She argues both from the materiality of things to their divisibility, as well as from the divisibility of things to their materiality. Perhaps the most striking examples of the second are arguments that appeal to the manifest divisibility of the mind to establish that it is material (e.g. GNP 6 2)—arguments that we will revisit in Chapters 6 and 7.

While for many philosophers, to hold that matter has actual rather than potential parts means that its parts are quite independent of one another; this is not true for Cavendish. Matter's variety does not negate its unity, nor vice versa. To have actual parts is to be both actually divided and actually united:

> the Parts are in the Whole, although divided, and the Whole in the Parts, when divided…Parts and Motions live or lie in the Substances, whether Divided or not Divided…as there are Infinite Divisions, so there are infinite Compositions, so that the Infinite Compositions do Equalize or make an Unity with Infinite Divisions.
>
> (PPO2 3 20)

As we will see in the course of this chapter, Cavendish's refusal to pick a side is at the heart of her metaphysics.

Section 3.8 Matter is continuous

Cavendish's commitment to the unity of matter is a crucial motivation for her rejection of atomism and her embrace of a continuum theory of matter that was likely influenced by the Stoics as well as by Descartes's own continuum theory of matter.

---

10 Note that while Cavendish characterizes matter as divisible rather than divided here, her gloss on that shows that she means that matter has actual parts.

According to the atomists, Cavendish thinks, matter both fails to be homogeneous and fails to have compositional unity. It fails to be homogeneous because it has a fundamentally disjunctive essence. Atoms are matter, and things composed of atoms are matter, and Cavendish does not see any deeper connection to unite these two classes of matter. An atomist like Boyle might disagree, arguing that both atoms and compositions of atoms are extended in space, and so it is their shared nature as extended things that unites them. But as we shall see, Cavendish does not hold that extension in space is the essence of matter. And as Boyle himself recognized, the claim that atoms are both extended and indivisible yields a bit of a paradox if, like many philosophers have, one holds that spatial extension entails divisibility of some kind. In holding that some matter is divisible and some indivisible, Cavendish thinks, the atomistic conception of matter is not one in kind. In contrast, she holds that 'Matter, or Body, cannot be so divided, but that it will remain Matter, which is divisible' (GNP 1 5; see also OEP 263).

Atomism also fails to make matter one composed body. At least on Cavendish's interpretation of atomism, atoms are too independent of one another to be able genuinely to combine into one body. An atom would be what Cavendish calls a 'single part', which is, as we saw in Section 2.4, a (hypothetical) bit of matter that can be separated from and has 'no reference' to the other parts of nature (OEP 126). The single parthood of atoms follows from their alleged spatial separation, but as Cavendish argues, 'Nature cannot divide or compose from her self' and so 'there cannot possibly be any Vacuum' (GNP 1 1). This rejection of spatial discontinuity is a consequence of her deeper and more general rejection of ontological discontinuity. A world of atoms would not be one world at all, but rather 'every part...would make some kind of a finite world...having no relation to one another' (OEP 262). To constitute nature as we know it, matter must be something with infinite parts that 'cannot be taken from the Infinite Body' (PF Of Infinite Matter).

Instead of atomism, Cavendish holds that all the bits of matter in nature are 'parts of one continued body' (OEP 126) and that nature 'is a body of a continued infiniteness, without any holes or vacuities' (OEP 127). Parts of matter can divide and compose from other parts, 'yet they cannot quit all parts' (OEP 127). Cavendish's view that matter is continuous was almost certainly inspired either directly or indirectly by the matter theory of the Stoics, who, like Cavendish, identified matter as 'that of which every thing is made' and that which 'hath two names, Substance, and Matter' (Stanley 1656: 102). Like Cavendish, the Stoics also held that matter is continuous, so that there is no vacuum, and that matter is divisible ad infinitum (Stanley 101). Besides this, there are a number of further similarities between Stoic matter theory and Cavendish's, perhaps most notably the view that natural matter is a complete mixture of an active and a passive principle—a doctrine that somewhat imperils Cavendish's claim that matter is homogeneous, a peril that we will tackle in Chapter 4.

In holding that substance is matter and that matter is continuous, Cavendish is not just resisting atomism but also Aristotelianism. For Aristotle, a substance is always *a* thing with *a* form, like a human being or a bunny or a plant. While Cavendish, as we shall see, does think that human beings and bunnies and plants exist, what fundamentally exists—what substance is—is not things but stuff. Stuff is unambiguously a mass noun, like 'ectoplasm', not a count noun, like 'ghosts'. Metaphysicians nowadays have adopted 'stuff' as a quasi-technical term—it refers to what there is, or what has being, without committing us to an ontology of objects. This word wasn't around for Cavendish to adopt. But she did have the word 'matter', and that's what she meant by it: stuff.

As Cavendish's arguments against atomism highlight, a continuum theory of matter relates the two kinds of material unity. We said in Section 3.3 that matter does not have a kind, and we did not say any more about what it means for matter to be homogeneous. But as the rest of this chapter will argue, we can say something more about matter, which is that it both has parts and is composite—in other words, that it has what we will call compositional structure. In this way, matter's very homogeneity guarantees both its complexity—because it means that all matter has parts—as well as its compositional unity.

This elegant feature of Cavendish's view would not be one if Cavendish held that the primary sense in which matter is homogeneous, continuous, and divisible was spatial. As the centuries-long debate over actual and potential parts makes clear, the relationship between divisibility, spatial extension, and matter is not at all obvious. It is not clear whether an infinite substance, continuously spread out in three dimensions, is or is not divided into actual or even potential parts. It is clear, however, that an infinite substance that is essentially divided and composed is.

Section 3.9 Matter is being, compositionally structured

At this point, I think we have enough evidence to preliminarily conclude that matter is, simply, being, whose essence is 'to be divisible, and capable to be united and compounded' (GNP 238). Further evidence for this will come from seeing, in the rest of this book, how central Cavendish makes compositional structure to her natural philosophy.

We have seen throughout this chapter that Cavendish, on the one hand, has an extremely parsimonious view of matter and infinite nature, according to which it is simply matter, without any forms, modes, or other metaphysical structures. In this sense, Cavendish shares an 'impulse towards monism'[11] with Parmenides. On the other hand, she also deeply struck, like Heraclitus, by the fact that nature is filled with infinite variety and constant change. Cavendish squares these instincts by seeking a minimal metaphysical posit to account for the fact of unity in diversity (along with positing that matter acts to cause changes in itself). This leads her to hold that nature is dividable and composable; it has diversity because it has parts, and it has coherence or unity because the parts of nature are composed together. The very first principle of Cavendish's natural philosophy, according to her brief synopsis in the *Observations* is: 'There is but one matter, and infinite parts' (OEP 191). This book explores the implications of this fundamental structure.

Some readers might be tempted to interpret Cavendish's claim that all distinctions are parthood distinctions very capaciously. We speak of many kinds of things as having parts, from minds to poems to cocktails. Also, some philosophers have described form

---

11 I borrow this phrase from Dea et al. (2018) who use it to characterize early modern rationalists. As we will see, Cavendish has rationalist as well as empiricist intuitions. For a contemporary realization of this impulse, and a consideration of its history both ancient and early modern, see Della Rocca (2020).

and matter as 'metaphysical parts' of a substance. If Cavendish has such a capacious understanding of parthood, then her claim that all distinctions are parthood distinctions is much less radical. It can, for example, accommodate substance-property or substance-mode structure, as long as we imagine that substance and property are parts and joined by composition.[12]

I do not think this is Cavendish's view. Rather, she has a very specific reading of material parthood that rejects the kinds of entites and structures that generalized metaphysical parts would represent. This is evident, for example, in her reply to Hobbes about the relationship between blood and a bloody cloth. One reason that Cavendish gives for rejecting accidents and the like is precisely that they are supposed to be distinct from matter in a way that is not as two parts are distinct, and related to matter in a way that is not the way that two bits of matter are related to one another.[13] As we have already seen, Cavendish rejects the coherence of this view. All that exists is matter, and all matter is distinct from other matter by being distinct parts, so the only distinctions are distinctions between parts. 'There is no variety,' she writes, 'but of parts' (OEP 18).

Cavendish does distinguish between what she calls 'effective parts,' which are the parts of nature that interest us here, and the 'constitutive' or 'essential' parts of nature. The latter refer to inanimate and animate matter, which are mixed together to create the self-moving matter of nature. We can ignore these kinds of parts, for now. Chapter 5 will discuss them and ultimately argue that they should not be called 'parts' at all. The effective parts of nature are those parts of matter, and of creatures, that are changed by division and composition.

What is unusual about Cavendish's position is not that she holds that matter is necessarily (and even sufficiently) divisible. It is that she holds that divisibility *alone* is essential to matter, independently of any other considerations about its nature. Most strikingly,

---

12 For a view like this, see again Paul (2017). On Paul's view, properties are joined to their bearers by composition.

13 This reflects not just Hobbes's view, but also Descartes', who holds that 'a body is a substance, and a mode cannot be a part of a substance' (Descartes 1984: 292).

Cavendish does not hold that matter is divisible because it is essentially extended in three dimensions, making its divisibility parasitic on its spatial character. Rather, the essence of matter is simply and fundamentally to be divisible being.

While Cavendish's position is unusual, it is not completely unique. As Laura Georgescu's work has demonstrated, one philosopher comes close to Cavendish's view here: her friend and physician Kenelm Digby. According to Digby, quantity is the 'primary affection of bodies,' and 'quantity is nothing else, but the extension of a thing' (Pasnau 2013; see also Georgescu 2022). Quantity, in turn, is dependent upon divisibility, as is matter's extension in space, so divisibility, for Digby, is the most fundamental feature of bodies.[14] But while Digby and Cavendish agree that divisibility is essential to bodies, Digby derives spatial extension from divisibility, while Cavendish does not seem concerned with spatial extension at all. As we shall see, she offers reductions of spatial concepts like place, space, motion, size, and shape to compositional concepts, sometimes chalking up their spatial significance as misunderstandings of concepts that can be completely articulated in terms of parts and wholes.

It is possible to see Cavendish's view of matter as an elegant and logical purification of certain corpuscularian and mechanistic inclinations. As we have seen, Cavendish and the mechanical philosophers share a desire to replace Scholastic metaphysics with one that, inspired by predecessors like Democritus, explains the variety of natural phenomena in terms of structures. As Descartes swaggered:

> compare my assumptions with the assumptions of others: that is, compare all their real qualities, their substantial forms, their elements, and almost infinitely many other such things, with my single assumption that all bodies are composed of parts. (Descartes (to Morin) 1991: 200)

---

14 Compare to the view of the Coimbrans: 'Matter of itself, apart from quantity, has substantial parts from which it is intrinsically composed. It does not have them extended and arranged in order, however, one outside another, without the aid of quantity. It is the role of quantity to take those parts, which would otherwise be mixed up and entangled, and spread them out and unfold them' (cited in Pasnau 2013:96).

Marleen Rosemond argues that divisibility is more central to the early modern conception of the material than is extension (Rozemond 2014). If that is right, then Cavendish can be said to have the purest version of this conception of the material. But both Descartes and Boyle also make the modes of extension or mechanical affections, especially the geometrical properties of shape and size, at least as fundamental as parthood structure, and sometimes more fundamental. Descartes, for example, writes that physical phenomena can be 'explained without the need to suppose for their effect any other thing in their matter besides the motion, size, shape, and arrangement of its parts' (Descartes 1985: 89). These two kinds of structure do not always fit easily together. Cavendish, in contrast, puts all her money on parthood structure.

What makes Cavendish think that parthood and composition is the best candidate for metaphysical structure? And why does she tie it so closely to the concept of matter and to her materialism?

Plenty of materialists have seen materialism as compatible with a variety of structures: geometrical structure, for example, or substance-property or substance-mode structure. We have already seen reasons why Cavendish rejects some of these other options. They are inconsistent with her materialism, according to which there is only one kind of being, the being of stuff. Because there is an infinite multiplicity of creatures, this stuff must have some structure, but one that least runs afoul of parsimony. Cavendish thinks that this is parthood and composition.

The first reason that parthood and composition fit this bill is that it minimizes the kind of stuff that there is. Not only are parts the same stuff as each other, but parts and composites are the same stuff as each other. To borrow some terminology from more recent discussions of the metaphysics of stuff, Cavendishian matter is cumulative and dissective: when you put together matter you get matter, and when you divide matter up, you get matter (Burge 1977: 106). Atomist matter does not have these features, as we have seen, which is why Cavendish has a continuum theory of matter.

The second good feature of compositional structure is that it eliminates relationships of hierarchical dependence. This may not be immediately apparent, because most philosophers have thought that there must be some kind of hierarchical dependence relationship between part and whole. The majority of philosophers in the Aristotelian tradition thought that wholes depend on their parts, but some argued that parts depend upon their wholes, at least for some kinds of wholes. Cavendish does not hold that parts are more fundamental than their composites or that composites are more fundamental than their parts. (I use 'composite' and 'whole' interchangeably for Cavendish.)

This captures one intuition about parthood: that compositions are nothing more than their parts. As David Lewis writes, 'if you are already committed to some things, you incur no further commitment when you affirm the existence of their fusion. The new commitment is redundant, given the old one' (1991, 81–82). To borrow an example used by Lewis and Donald Baxter, if a grocery clerk rang up a six-pack of soda to charge us for each bottle and then again for the six-pack, we would rightly object. According to Cavendish, however, this does not mean that composites are just the parts, taken together. 'When I speak of the parts of Nature,' Cavendish writes, 'I do not understand, that those parts are like grains of corn or sand in one heap, all of one figure or magnitude, and separable from each other' (OEP xxvii). The same two bits of matter may be parts of some particular composition, or not.

For Cavendish, composition is identity, namely, the identity of some parts with one thing: 'a whole and its parts,' she writes, 'yet are one and the same thing, several ways' (OEP 193), and 'a whole is nothing but a composition of parts, and parts are nothing but a division of the whole' (OEP 32, see also 164).

At the same time, no bit of matter may fail to be part of anything at all, and all bits of matter are together at least co-parts of the whole of nature. This is clear from Cavendish's rejection of single parts. The fact that whole does not depend upon parts nor do parts depend upon whole does not mean that there is no dependence at all in Cavendish's system: the parts of nature depend upon one another.

Given that parthood and composition is the fundamental structure of matter, there is nothing in virtue of which parts form a whole. The fact that some parts do or do not form a whole is brute; to borrow a phrase from Ned Markosian, composition is brutal.[15]

---

15 Markosian defends a version of brutal composition in Markosian 1998 but later repudiates it.

This way, Cavendish accounts for relational facts without appealing to metaphysical relations in anything like the sense that many philosophers have conceived of them throughout history. For one thing, many philosophers both past and present have thought of relations as property-like. Some medieval philosophers described relations as properties with a foot in two substances; today, relations are often modeled as 'two-place predicates,' which logical structure some metaphysicians take to be reflected in reality. Cavendish rejects all such entities. As we will see in more detail in Chapter 6, on perception, parts are related to one another only insofar as they are composed together.

This is reflected in another argument that Cavendish makes against atomism, which is that it can never account for order. Cavendish holds that 'where Unity is not, Order cannot be' (GNP 1 4), and she argues accordingly that order is impossible in an atomistic world. It is impossible, if atomism were true, that nature would 'be able to rule those wandering and straggling atoms, because they are not parts of her body, but each a single body by itself, having no dependence upon each other' (OEP 129). It is not *prima facie* obvious why a world of atoms could not come to be ordered despite their not being part of one body, but Cavendish's denial that they can makes clear that she takes composition to be necessary for relations.

'Structure' is not a word that Cavendish uses very often, though she does write of the wisdom in the 'fabric and structure of [nature's] works' (OEP 60) and occasionally describes the figures of creatures as their structures (e.g. OEP 62, 70). All the uses are from the *Observations*, where, I think, this account of nature is most dominant. In one place there, Cavendish asks 'whether the parts of a composed figure do continue in such a composition until the whole figure be dissolved?' her answer is that while 'some parts of a figure do disjoin from one another, and join with others; yet the structure of the creature may nevertheless continue' (OEP 130). The implied answer to the question is that the creature will survive as long as its structure does, even as parts divide and compose from it. We will consider this claim more fully in Chapter 5, when we consider the survival conditions for a creature. The point is that, even though it is clear in many places that the nature and actions of a creature are a result of the arrangement of its parts, here is one spot where Cavendish explicitly identifies that with a creature's structure.

'Structure' can mean a lot of things, and I don't mean to put too much weight on the term. It is simply a helpful frame, I think, as we try to get a grip on Cavendish's motivations. As we have seen in this chapter, we certainly do not want to suggest too much of a distinction between the structural features of matter and its nonstructural features, lest we begin to echo the form/matter distinction of hylomorphism. The appeal of identifying compositional facts as the fundamental metaphysical facts is that a case can be made that it avoids abstracting structure from matter. What it means to be a composition is to be two parts of matter, joined as one.

Section 3.10 Conclusion

Readers familiar with Cavendish may have some objections at this point to the claim that we have exhaustively characterized matter as being with compositional structure. What about self-motion? Sense and reason? Self-knowledge? While Cavendish does not seem to think that all of these are essential to matter, they are certainly true of matter in our world and seem to be real features of it that specify it beyond just being divisible substance.

Cavendish does indeed tell us that both motion and self-knowledge are ubiquitous in matter, and she even speaks of both at times as if they are essential to matter. Chapter 4 will address the question of matter's self-motion and its relationship with matter. For now, we should not be tempted to think about it as some property that matter has, but rather something that matter does. What is important is that Cavendish does not reify matter's power to move itself, turning it into a property or accident of matter. Chapter 7 will address matter's self-knowledge. It will turn out that self-knowledge is contained in the definition of matter as divisible stuff.

I have argued in this chapter that we should not think of Cavendish's materialism as a commitment to the existence of substance of a certain kind. It is simply being. That said, we can say more about it: we can say that it is dividable and composable. Should divisibility be considered as a feature, mode, property, quality, accident, or whatever, of matter? No. Matter must have structure because there is quantitative and qualitative variety, and Cavendish identifies the structure that is necessary as divisibility. For Cavendish, compositional structure is the way that being must be structured in order to explain the manifest fact that nature contains variety and is nonetheless coherent. What fundamentally motivates Cavendish's materialism, then, is an extreme application of Ockham's Razor at the fundamental metaphysical level, combined with an acknowledgment that natural variety is undeniable. With perhaps the most austere ontology on offer in the early modern period, Cavendish attempts to explain nature's infinite effects; in the rest of this book, we shall see how she does it.[16]

Further reading

Cunning, David. 2006. 'Cavendish on the Intelligibility of the Prospect of Thinking Matter.' *History of Philosophy Quarterly* 23(2): 117–136.

Boyle, Deborah. (2018). Chapter 3. In *The Well-Ordered Universe: The Philosophy of Margaret Cavendish*. New York, NY: Oxford University Press.

Duncan, Stewart. 2012. 'Debating Materialism: Cavendish, Hobbes, and More.' *History of Philosophy Quarterly* 29(4): 391–409.

Rozemond, Marleen, and Alison Simmons. 2023. 'It's All Alive! Cavendish and Conway against Dualism.' in *The Routledge Handbook of Women and Early Modern European Philosophy*, edited by K. Detlefsen and L. Shapiro. New York: Routledge.

Shaheen, Jonathan L. 2019. 'Part of Nature and Division in Margaret Cavendish's Materialism.' *Synthese (Dordrecht)* 196: 3551–3575.

---

16 Some might think that Spinoza gives Cavendish a run for her money in terms of austerity. Maybe. I do think that Spinoza, like Cavendish, self-consciously wants to minimize the ontological structure he appeals to. I understand Spinoza's metaphysics to be an investment in precisely the kind of ontological structure that Cavendish denies—hierarchical structure of dependence or inherence—and a denial of precisely the kind of ontological structure that Cavendish invests in—structures of parthood and composition.

Four
Motion

> I perceive man has a great spleen against self-moving corporeal
> nature, although himself is part of her, and the reason is his ambi-
> tion; for he would fain be supreme, and above all other creatures,
> as more towards a divine nature: he would be a God, if arguments
> could make him such.
> (OEP 209)

It is manifest, according to Cavendish, that there is change in nature.
In fact, change is constant, and there are an infinite variety of
changes. While Cavendish acknowledges that experience informs us
of this infinite and indeed irreducible variety of creaturely changes,
it turns out that she holds, based on empirical as well as *a priori* considerations, that there is one fundamental kind of change, which she
calls 'motion' or 'corporeal (figurative) motions'. While Cavendish
shares with the mechanical philosophers this goal of identifying
one intelligible kind of change underlying all of nature's blooming
and buzzing, Cavendishian change is not local motion, or change of
place. Rather, it is dividing and composing, which we will call 'compositional motion'.

Because nature contains only matter, and because there is nothing
outside nature that can interact with it, Cavendish holds that all
the changes in nature are made by matter itself. In this chapter, we
will take a look at Cavendish's reasons for holding that matter is
self-moving, and we will conclude that the deepest reason is that
she denies the coherence of one thing's acting on another. Just as
the fundamental facts of nature are compositional facts, fundamental

DOI: 10.4324/9781003107255-5

natural change is composing and dividing, making 'the chief actions of nature are composition and division' (OEP 132).

Self-motion is the cause of all the variety in nature, but Cavendish does not think that the mere fact that matter moves itself can explain that variety. Since matter is homogeneous and homogeneously self-moving, there must be some explanation of why it acts het-erogeneously. Cavendish concludes that this requires that nature is constituted by an active and a passive principle, leading her to hold that natural matter is a perfect commixture of animate and inani-mate matter. This is the subject of one of Cavendish's deepest meta-physical struggles, which plays out dramatically in the Argumental Discourse, a section of the *Observations* primarily devoted to analysing and explaining the relationship between matter and change.

Section 4.1 Compositional motion

We have not yet discussed what, exactly, Cavendish means by 'creatures', and we will do that at length in the next chapter. For now, what is important is that Cavendish calls all the things that we encounter in nature 'creatures', which she further identifies with the parts and effects of infinite natural matter. These are the everyday objects of our acquaintance, including animals, vegetables, minerals, and even, as the next chapter will argue, artifacts. Cavendish thinks that even things that are apparently motionless are in fact teeming with motions that we cannot perceive (e.g. OEP 131).

Cavendish is fascinated by the infinite variety of creaturely changes, which include processes like the bruising of flesh, the melting of water, an animal's digestion of its meal, and the unwreathing of a sprig inside the grain of a wild oat. While Cavendish describes these all as 'motions', we should not take that to mean change of place, as we commonly use the term today. For now, we should understand all these 'motions' simply as changes, just as Aristotle used the word. Cavendish holds that the varieties of such creaturely motions are infinite, and they cannot be reduced to one determinate kind or a finite number of kinds. 'Nature doth not work in all creatures alike', Cavendish writes, nor does nature have 'one primary or principal sort of motions, by which she produces all creatures'. It is 'a very wild and extravagant conceit', Cavendish tells us, to measure the infinite actions of nature according to the rule of one particular sort of motions' (OEP 72).

Though Cavendish holds that 'not any particular corporeal figurative motion can be said the prime or fundamental', she continues: 'unless it be self-motion, the architect and creator of all figures' (OEP 55). While the variety of creaturely motions is infinite and irreducible, that does not mean that there is nothing more that we can say to characterize motion (and self-motion, which is its cause). Cavendish frequently writes that all creaturely motions are ultimately nothing but 'corporeal motions':

> When I speak of motion, I desire to be understood, that I do not mean any other but corporeal motion; for there is no other motion in nature: So that generation, dissolution, alteration, augmentation, diminution, transformation; nay, all the actions of sense and reason, both interior, and exterior, and what motions soever in nature, are corporeal.
>
> (OEP 128, see also 69)

In telling us that all motion is *corporeal* motion, Cavendish is not simply telling us that all change is change in bodies (*corpora*). Rather, she is characterizing motion, generally and fundamentally, and telling us that creaturely changes arise from motion in that sense.

What, then, is corporeal motion? In the *Grounds*, Cavendish writes that 'all Corporeal Motion is Local; but only they are different Local Motions' (GNP 11 8). The accepted meaning of 'local motion' at that time was 'change of place', and in claiming that all corporeal motion is local, Cavendish evokes the mechanical philosophers, who held that all fundamental natural change is change of place. Despite her (very) occasional use of the phrase 'local motion', however, Cavendish does not hold that corporeal motion is change of place.

One reason for that is that it is impossible for a body to change its place, according to Cavendish. Following Hobbes, Cavendish identifies the place of a body with the space that it takes up. But the space that a body takes up, in turn, is identical with that body's magnitude. A body can no more lose its place than it can lose its magnitude, and while it can change its place in a sense, that just means that it can get bigger or smaller (OEP 125). True change of place, then, must be an intrinsic and not an extrinsic change, which is to say that it is a change in the object considered just in itself. As Cavendish puts it, if the place of a body changes, then the 'body must change also' (OEP 37). Because a body cannot lose its place, 'motion cannot be a relinquishing of one place and acquiring another, for there is no such thing as place different from body' (PL 1 17; PL 1 32).[1] Motion, Cavendish writes, is 'only improperly called change of place' (OEP 36; PL 4 31).

So what is motion, properly speaking? Cavendish's answer is that it is 'composition and division of parts' (OEP 136). A man's journey, for example, is 'nothing else but a division and composition of parts' (OEP 127), so that

> though it be a vulgar phrase, that a man changes his place when he removes, yet it is not a proper philosophical expression; for he removes only from such parts, to such parts: so that it is a change, or a division and composition of parts, and not of place.
> (OEP 37)

When someone takes a sea voyage, Cavendish writes, it is

> not place he changes, but only the adjoining parts, as leaving some, and joining others; and it is very improper, to attribute that to place which belongs to parts, and to make a change of place out of change of parts.
> (PL 1 32)

Our traveler does not quit some parts and join with others as a consequence of changing his place. His journey simply is a division from some parts and a joining to other parts.

Cavendish explicitly identifies compositions and divisions with natural change in general (OEP 238). She writes that compositions and divisions are the source of all changes of figures in nature, and of all nature's effects (OEP 30, 32, 236), giving composition and division a

---

1 Peterman (2019b) contains a fuller defense that Cavendishian motion is not local motion, along with more detail about Cavendish's account of place and magnitude and its relationship to that of Hobbes and Descartes.

generality that she gives no other kind of change. And perhaps most strikingly of all, Cavendish identifies composition and division of parts as 'the chief and general actions of nature' (OEP 192). Since the 'chief and general action' of nature can be none other than self-motion, self-motion must be the dividing and composing action of nature. This makes perfect sense, given the account of matter's structure laid out in the last chapter. Self-motion is the fundamental way that matter changes itself, so it stands to reason that self-motion is change in fundamental structure, which is compositional structure. Indeed, Cavendish writes, 'self-motion...is the cause of all the variety of natural figures, and of the various compositions and divisions of parts' (OEP 49). We may call fundamental Cavendishian motion, then, 'compositional motion'.

Section 4.2   Creaturely motions and compositional motion

How exactly does Cavendish explain all changes in terms of composition and division, including changes of place, mechanical affections, figure, posture, and all manner of qualitative changes? She offers some answers, which are no more or less speculative than the mechanists' attempts to reduce all creaturely changes to local motion. Despite the mechanists' claims that local motion is especially intelligible or observable, it is no more obvious from experience that all change can be reduced to change of place than it is that all change can be reduced to composition and division. We observe growth and decay, generation and death; we observe the Baconian-cum-Cavendishian processes of digestion, respiration, and so on; we observe changes in colors and textures and temperatures, melting and freezing, incineration and putrefaction. It is just as difficult to explain all these in terms of changes of place as it is to explain them in terms of composition and division.

We have already seen Cavendish's analysis of changes of place like creaturely journeys. That kind of motion involves the creature dividing from one composite and composing with a new one. Cavendish offers analyses of a number of other creaturely changes in terms of composition and division. For example, she tells us that growth and diminution are composition and division, writing that '*Increase* and *Decrease*' are only 'alteration[s] of corporeal figurative motions, as uniting parts with parts, and dissolving or separating parts from parts' (PL 4 33). (Note, too, how she identifies 'corporeal figurative motions' with uniting and separating parts.) Putrefaction is 'onely a dissolving and separating of parts' (OEP 119). Generation and destruction are compositions and divisions (GNP 2 1; OEP 55, 78), and death is 'only a change from the dissolution of some certain figure, to the composition of another' (OEP 225).

The creaturely motions that Cavendish analyses in terms of composition and division include motions that appear frequently on lists of what she describes as 'Ground or Principal Motions' (PPO2 1 18). The list changes from text to text but usually includes attraction, contraction, retention, digestion, dilation, and expulsion (e.g. PPO2 1 9). As Marcy Lascano explains, this list appears to be modeled on Francis Bacon's list of principal motions (2023), and Lascano argues that Cavendish holds these to be fundamental kinds of motions, which are not all reducible to division and composition.

Cavendish certainly holds that these complex motions are common to and important for the creatures that we observe in our corner of nature—which, as we know, represent only a small fraction of the variety of creatures and actions in other worlds. But it is not a list, exhaustive or otherwise, of fundamental kinds of change. One argument for this is that composition and division are not on this list. So if this were an exhaustive list of motions at whatever level of fundamentality it concerns, then composition and division are either more or less fundamental than these six. But it is very hard to believe that they are less fundamental, given the manifest importance Cavendish places on composition and division.

But also, Cavendish explicitly analyses the items on this list in terms of composition and division. Respiration, for example, is a 'dividing and uniting of parts' (OEP 54, 135). Sometimes it sounds like Cavendish might think that there are other ways of acting on parts; she characterizes retention, for example, as what 'fixeth Parts', expulsion as what 'disperseth Parts', and dilation as what 'inlargeth Parts' (PPO2 1 18). But in the *Observations*, after Cavendish characterizes respiration as 'a reception and emission of parts', she immediately clarifies that reception and emission are 'nothing else but a composition and division of parts' (OEP 14–15).

There are a handful of passages that seem directly to deny that all motion is composition. For example:

> All motions are not dividing or dissolving, but some are reten-
> tive, some composing, some attractive, some expulsive, some
> contractive, some dilative, and infinite other sorts of motions, as
> it is evident by the infinite variety which appears in the differing
> effects of nature.
>
> (OEP 238–239)

> [T]here are also retentive motions in nature which are neither
> dividing nor composing, but keeping or holding together.
>
> (OEP 55)

We can make sense of the first by distinguishing composition and division at the fundamental level from composition and division in complex creatures, which belongs alongside contraction and dilation, retention, attraction, and expulsion. If this sounds desperately *ad hoc*, consider that the mechanical philosophers are committed to a perfectly analogous position. Tree-level changes of place are among the many kinds of changes that we encounter in the world, and all these changes, they think, are explained by change of place at a more fundamental level. As for the second passage, we will consider retentive motions in Chapter 5 and show that they are not a distinct kind of activity from dividing and composing.

What about other kinds of changes? For example, how does Cavendish understand qualitative changes, like change of colour, warmth, smell, and sound, that do not seem obviously to involve division and composition? Cavendish holds that despite appearances, such changes do involve division and composition of the coloured or warm object, along with changes in how those objects are perceived by us. We will explore this in much more detail in Chapter 6, on perception.

Cavendish occasionally seems to recognize a special class of change that she calls change of 'posture', contrasting it with change of figure, as when she writes that a man can change his posture without changing his natural figure (OEP 93). But in this passage, Cavendish is arguing that creatures can change their exterior figures (or 'postures') without changing their internal figures. And as we will see in the next chapter, while it may be true that a man can change without changing his compositional structure, or certain parts of it, that does not mean that he can change without changing *any* compositional structures. A man and his parts are parts of lots of other compositions that may change without the man dissolving entirely.[2]

Section 4.3 Compositional motion and mechanical motion

Does Cavendish's identification of motion as composition and division run afoul of her imperative not to reduce natural motions to one kind? I do not think so. Composition and division are not kinds of motions, just as divisible stuff is not a kind of stuff. If that were the case, then matter would be confined to particular motions in the former case just as it would be clayey in the latter case. Rather, parthood structure is the fundamental structure of matter, and composition is, in nature, the way that that structure changes. Matter, in virtue of being matter, is dividable and composable; but 'dividable and composable matter' is not a kind of matter.

In denying that geometrical properties are fundamental and that change in spatial location is the fundamental kind of change, Cavendish is denying a central thesis of mechanism. But she shares with the mechanical philosophers a commitment to explaining change as structural change. From that perspective, Cavendish's analysis of motion can be seen as an internal critique of mechanism. What is more, as the last chapter argued, many mechanical philosophers are committed to compositional analyses and explanations of natural

---

2 This also addresses passages, that Lascano emphasizes, which seem to suggest that dilation and contraction involve no composition and division (e.g. OEP 124–125). Cavendish describes contraction and dilation there as 'effects' of parts and of self-motion, which should alert us that they are not fundamental kinds of change. In combination with the other evidence that self-motion is dividing and composing, this passage suggests that contraction and dilation are complex motions that can be ultimately resolved into division and composition. Cavendish's insistence that diminution is not a division of a thing from its *own* parts does not entail that diminution does not involve division *at all*.

phenomena, alongside analyses and explanations in terms of spatial structures. These two kinds of analysis do not always sit comfortably together, and this is a weakness of the mechanical philosophy that Cavendish's elegant system reveals. This is true of the dynamics of these structures as much as the structures themselves, and it is reflected in contradictions and unclarities in the mechanical account of motion.

For example, Descartes and Boyle both hold that all the variety in nature is due to local motion. Boyle argues that 'Matter being in its own nature but one, the diversity we see in Bodies must necessarily arise from somewhat else, then the Matter they consist of' (Boyle 1666: 3). Similarly, Descartes argues that because 'the matter existing in the entire universe is thus one and the same', 'all the properties which we clearly perceive in it are reducible to its divisibility and consequent mobility in respect of its parts'. It is not always clear, however, whether Descartes and Boyle think that motion is supposed to *ground* or merely *cause* the distinctions between bodies. To take Descartes: he claims that every part of matter is really distinct from the other parts (Descartes 1985: 213), and that matter's parts are necessary for there to be a variety of motions (Descartes 1985: 232). But he also tells us that motion is a mere mode of an extended substance and that a mode is not the kind of thing that can generate a real distinction. And he defines a part of matter, at least for the purposes of physics, in terms of relative motion, as 'every thing that is transferred at the same time, even if the thing in question can be made up of many parts which, in themselves, have other motions' (Descartes 1985: 233).

In either case, we are made to wonder: how, exactly, is local motion supposed to do the work of creating distinctions between parts? The relative local motion of two bodies seems to have nothing whatsoever to do with parthood, except maybe by presupposing it. For Cavendish, too, motion is required to generate the variety in nature, which is to say, its parts. However, there is no mystery as to how this works: it is because self-motion, the 'chief and general action of matter', simply *is* division and composition. It divides matter into parts because that is its job. In eliminating local motion, Cavendish cuts out the middleman.

Descartes and Boyle also struggle to explain what unites the parts of a creature into one. Sometimes they seem to want to give a reductive account of composition and division in terms of spatial structures and changes. How can local motion ground the unity of a material object? There seem to be two possible answers. One is that parts of matter are unified by certain kinds of kinematic relationships among their parts—or what Spinoza, articulating a broadly Cartesian story, called a 'ratio of motion and rest'. On this sort of account, a creature's unity is not a lack of division but rather a reunification of distinct parts. Another possible answer is that parts of matter are unified by rest—in other words, by the absence of motion. This, at least for some intents and purposes, was the story that Descartes told. Both answers have problems that were well known to critics of the mechanical philosophy. In contrast, Cavendish has no trouble explaining unity. It is the fundamental action of nature to compose, and the unity of a creature is a fundamental natural fact, one that is irreducible to any spatial or kinematic relationships among the parts.

Section 4.4 Variety depends on motion

For Cavendish, as for Descartes, it is sometimes ambiguous whether variety depends upon motion as its grounds or as its cause. That ambiguity is apparent even within one sentence:

> Diversity is only Change of Motion and Alteration of Figures; neither is there any such thing as several Kinds or Sorts of Creatures or Substances in Infinite matter, for several Kinds, Sorts and Particulars are but Changing or Forming of Matter into several Figures by Change of Motion.
>
> (PPO2 Preface)

The first part of this passage makes it sound like diversity simply *is* motion, while the latter part makes it sound like diversity is caused by motion, which results in a diversity of figures. In the *Grounds* and the *Observations*, however, the causal view emerges as the winner. Self-motion, which is the power to divide and compose, causes changes, or dividing and composings, in figures, which are compositional structures. This accompanies the shift from the *Opinions* view that the parts are inherent in infinite matter.

In later works, as we have already seen, Cavendish no longer characterizes parts as inherent in matter, and she holds that matter has actual parts and not potential parts. While self-motion can cause

matter to come to have parts, matter has parts independently of
motion. 'Were there no motion', Cavendish writes

> there would be no change of figures. It is true, matter in its
> own nature would be divisible, because wheresoever is body,
> there are parts: but, if it had no motion, it would not have such
> various changes of figures as it hath.
>
> (OEP 126)

We saw in the last chapter that Cavendish sometimes uses 'divisible'
to mean 'has parts'. In any case, she is explicit here that 'wheresoever there is body, there are parts' and that without motion, there
would not lack figure, only change of figure. Similarly, Q. 3 of the
Observations asks 'Whether the inanimate matter could have parts,
without self-motion'? Cavendish answers

> Yes: for, wheresoever is body or matter, there are also parts,
> because parts belong to body, and there can be no body without
> parts; but yet, were there no self-motion, there could be no
> various changes of parts or figures.
>
> (OEP 157–158)

· Self-motion causes changes of figures, or parthood structures, but
does not ground parthood distinctions.

Section 4.5 All motion is self-motion

Nature, or some part of it, is the only possible cause of the changes
in it, since nothing outside of nature can influence it or be otherwise
connected with it. Cavendish concludes from this not only that some
parts of nature must be self-moving in order to generate motion, but
that there is 'no part of the composed body of Nature which is not
self-moving' (OEP 28). Why couldn't some parts of matter, but not
all of them, be self-moving?

One argument that Cavendish gives is that 'no part of nature can
be inanimate; for, as the body is, so are its parts; and as the cause, so
its effect' (OEP 112). Note that Cavendish argues that we can infer
from the nature of a cause to its effects, and not from the nature of

effects to their causes. However, it does not seem that even this principle applies to finite bodies and effects, since creatures and their
parts and effects differ from each other in many ways. Cavendish is
presumably focused here on infinite natural matter as the relevant
body and cause, and she holds that whatever features infinite natural
matter itself has, every one of its effective parts, or effects, must also
have. Self-motion, being ubiquitous as a matter of natural necessity,
is 'cumulative and dissective' just as matter itself is:

> if Matter moveth it self, as certainly it doth, then the least part
> of Matter, were it so small as to seem Individable, will move it
> self; Tis true, it could not desist from motion, as being its nature
> to move, and no thing can change its Nature; for God himself,
> who hath more power then self-moving Matter, cannot change
> himself from being God.
>
> (PL 1 5)

Other than being divisible and composable, and (as we will see)
being self-knowing, self-motion is the only feature of the cause that
is subject to this kind of reasoning.

A second argument that Cavendish gives for the ubiquity of
self-motion is that 'it is not probable, that one part moving another,
should produce all things so orderly and wisely as they are in nature'
(OEP 73). We will consider her reasons for this premise further in
Chapter 9 ['Order'], but alongside the premise that if one part does
not move another, then all parts move themselves, it gets Cavendish to her conclusion. Elsewhere, however, Cavendish argues in the
other direction: that 'all the parts of nature, whensoever they move,
move by their own motions; which proves, that no particular creature of effect of composed nature, can act upon one another, but
that one can only occasion another to move thus or thus' (OEP 19).

Which is prior: the claim that one finite body cannot move
another, or the claim that everything is self-moving? In fact, they are
interrelated. The deepest motivation behind Cavendish's claim that all
motion is self-caused is how she thinks about action in general. To act,
for Cavendish, is to self-act, and she finds something incoherent in the
notion that one thing acts on another, especially if what is acted upon
is supposed to be inert or passive. One finite thing can 'occasion' or

'influence' the action of another, and as we shall see in Chapter 9, this kind of influence looks a lot like what many philosophers would call a cause, including in that it is a kind of counterfactual dependence. But this kind of influence is not, Cavendish thinks, what proponents of agent–patient interaction imagine that it is.

To see why, it helps to begin by considering Cavendish's arguments against a specific model of causal influence: the 'transfer' model of causation, according to which for one thing to act on another is for it to transfer a form, quality, or accident to another thing. Cavendish, of course, holds that anything that is transferred must be a substance, since only substances can exist independently (and, indeed, exist at all).

Most mechanical philosophers would deny that they accept such a model of causation. But Cavendish thinks that at least some are committed to it unawares. The most significant example of this is her critique of Descartes' claim that in collisions, one body transfers part of its quantity of motion to another. Cavendish interprets this as a kind of transfer theory and rejects it:

> motion being material and inseparable from matter, cannot be imparted without matter; and if not, then the body that receives motion would increase in bulk, and the other that loses motion would decrease…the contrary whereof is sufficiently known.
>
> (OEP 74–5; see also PL 1 30, 3 18)

If motion could be transferred, it would be matter, and we do not find that the eight ball becomes heavier in addition to speeding up when the cue ball hits it.[3] While Cavendish does sometimes seem to allow that transfer of motion is possible as long as matter is also transferred along with the motion, this is not a special kind of causation.[4]

---

3 Cavendish's argument is interesting in light of relativistic physics, one of the central discoveries of which is the equivalence of mass and energy. The inertial mass of a body, which is the more modern equivalent of quantity of matter, does in fact increase as its kinetic energy increases, which is a function of its speed.

4 Lascano (2021, 2023) argues that some interactions between bodies are transfers of substance and motion. I agree, inasmuch as a basic change is a part separating

Cavendish signals her agreement on this point with Hobbes, who writes that when a hand moves a pen to write, 'the motion doth not go out of the hand into the pen, and…the motion of the pen, is the pens own motion' (PL 1 16). While Cavendish does seem sometimes to allow that transfer of motion is possible, this does not mean that the motion of a self-moving part of matter can ever be separated from it. Rather, it means that some of the self-moving parts of one body detach from it and join another body, bringing their self-motion with them. Motion should not be understood as itself matter; motion should be understood as changes in matter, and self-motion as the actions of matter.

Cavendish's rejection of the transfer model of causation may seem like a niche philosophical concern, but it reflects a much more general critique of early modern accounts of so-called transeunt causation, or causation between two distinct things.[5] Consider a stop shot on an eight ball: the cue ball hits the resting eight ball, stops, and the eight ball starts moving. Now the eight ball is moving by itself. In what sense, Cavendish wonders, is the eight ball not *self*-moving? By whose motion is it moving if not its own? For Descartes, the answer is ultimately: God's motion, or the motion of another minded agent. But Cavendish does not think of self-motion that way. As it glides down the table, nothing is moving the eight ball but itself. Even if one does not explicitly accept that some entity, motion, is passed from one body to another, Cavendish thinks that to deny that the eight ball is self-moving is to implicitly posit that something—some power, or whatever 'motion' is—is injected by the cue ball into the eight ball:

> if a thing has no motion in it self, but is moved by another which has self-motion, then it must give that immovable body motion of its own, or else it could not move, having no motion at all; for it must move by the power of motion, which is certain; and then

from one body and joining another, and it would bring its self-motion with it. I do not think motion transfer is a special kind of causation or interaction.

5 Cavendish does not use this term, nor does she use the term 'immanent causation'. But immanent causation, in contrast, involves an actor acting on itself, and Cavendish describes nature's infinite natural power as 'the power to produce effects in her own self' (OEP 220).

it must move either by its own motion, or by a communicated or imparted motion; if by a communicated motion, then the self-moveable thing or body must transfer its own motion into the immoveable, and lose so much of its own motion as it gives away, which is impossible, as I have declared heretofore at large, unless it do also transfer its moving parts together with it, for motion cannot be transfered without substance. But experience and observation witnesseth the contrary.

(PL 3 18)

This is further illustrated in a subtle argument from the *Letters* that addresses more directly Descartes' claim that transeunt causation occurs by impact:

that Motion should proceed from another exterior Body, joyning with, or touching that body which it moves, is in my opinion not probable; for though Nature is all Corporeal, and her actions are Corporeal Motions, yet that doth not prove, that the Motion of particular Creatures or Parts is caused by the joining, touching or pressing of parts upon parts; for it is not the several parts that make motion, but motion makes them; and yet Motion is not the cause of Matter, but Matter is the cause of Motion.

(PL 1 5)

Matter's self-motion is the cause of everything that happens in it, which is to say, the joining and dividing of parts as well as any creaturely changes that depend on those, including the touching or pressing of parts on parts. To explain the motion of a part of matter by it being touched by another part is to get the order of explanation the wrong way around.

As all this demonstrates, Cavendish holds that all the parts of matter are self-moving because she denies the coherence of one thing's acting *on* another. As we will see in the coming chapters, this does not mean that one part of matter cannot act in response to another, or with another. Cavendish holds that parts 'influence' one another all the time, and she characterizes the influence of one part on another as an occasional cause. But to say that the cue ball is the occasion of the eight ball's motion is compatible with saying that the eight ball itself acts, moving itself.

This way of understanding Cavendish's claim dovetails with her Aristotelian-inflected understanding of the concept of nature. As we saw in Chapter 2, like Aristotle, Cavendish holds that for a thing to be natural is for it to have an internal principle of motion: 'all natural motion', she writes, 'is self-motion' (PL 3 18). But 'not any thing in Nature can move naturally without natural motion' (PL 3 18), and nothing moves that does not move naturally. So all of nature's actions are 'self-actions; that is, such actions whose principle of motion is within themselves, and doth not proceed from…an exterior agent' (OEP 19).

At the same time, it contrasts starkly with another aspect of the Aristotelian account of motion, one which is shared by some mechanical philosophers. According to Aristotle, it is essential to a change that it involves an agent and a patient. This is so fundamental to change that Aristotle argues that any self-motion in fact requires that the self being moved must be complex, so that self-motion can be analysed into agent and patient (Coope 2015: 36). The notion that all action requires an agent and a patient is accepted by Descartes and Hobbes, despite their rejection of the Aristotelian theory in many of its other aspects.

Cavendish's conception of action is radically opposed to this, at least at the level of effective parts, where 'there is no such difference as the learned make between patient and agent' (OEP 234). There is no need for a creature to act on anything in order to act. As Chamberlain (2024b) puts it, Cavendish denies that one body can 'reach into' another body to act in it. Cavendish's fundamental conception of action is self-action, and so all 'parts or creatures of Nature… move by their own motions', and 'no particular creature…can act upon another, but that one can only occasion another to move thus or thus' (OEP 27).

What motivates Cavendish to adopt this conception of action? We have already seen some reasons that she rejects the coherence of action-on. But it is also in keeping with her ontological parsimony. Cavendish holds that it is undeniable that there is natural change and seeks the minimal metaphysical posit to explain it. That minimal posit is simply that what there is, acts. No such thing as action-on is implied by this. It tells us that matter must be such as to initiate change, but it does not tell us that matter is such as to produce change in anything else.

Section 4.6 The triumvirate

In the Argumental Discourse, after reminding us that all of nature's actions are self-actions, Cavendish clarifies that in fact this is only true of the actions of the effective parts of the 'composed and mixed body of nature', or creatures, which 'whensoever they move, move by their own motions' (OEP 19). But that composed body of nature, and every part of it, is in fact 'a commixture of the…degrees of animate and inanimate matter', and 'the inanimate part of matter, considered as it is an ingredient of nature, is no ways moving, but always moved' (OEP 25–27). Cavendish often tells us, as she does here, that there are two principles, parts, ingredients, or 'degrees' that constitute self-moving matter: inanimate matter and animate matter. Other times, she posits three kinds or degrees of matter: inanimate matter, and two kinds of animate matter, one which she calls 'sensitive' and one which she calls 'rational'. Cavendish refers to these three constituents of nature as a 'triumvirate', because they are responsible, working together, for everything that happens in nature. While no effective part of nature can be moved by another effective part of nature, inanimate matter, 'having no motion of itself, is moved by the animate parts' (OEP 19).

Cavendish sometimes calls inanimate, sensitive, and rational matter the 'constitutive parts' or 'essential parts' of nature. But she carefully distinguishes the sense in which they are parts of nature from the sense in which the effective parts of nature are parts of nature. As their name suggests, the effective parts of nature, or creatures, are 'effects of the body of nature', while the constitutive parts 'constitute the body of nature' (OEP 28) and 'make it what it is' (OEP 27). The effects of nature depend upon the mixture of these constituents, but not as a composition depends upon its parts.

We should not think of the constitutive parts as parts of effective parts; for this reason, I will call the members of the triumvirate 'constituents' rather than 'constitutive parts'. Every effective part contains—in some sense, but not as parts—all three constituents: 'could matter be divided into an atom', Cavendish writes, 'that very atom would have a composition of these three degrees of matter' (OEP 168). In fact, the constituents are so thoroughly combined that it is still appropriate to say that matter is a perfectly homogeneous self-moving body. We will see how this works in more detail in the next section.

For now, we would like to know, along with Cavendish's questioning latter thoughts, what the sudden appearance of inanimate matter makes of our interpretation, in the last section, of Cavendish's reasons for holding that all motion is self-motion. In answering her latter thoughts, Cavendish likens the relationship between animate and inanimate matter to that between a horse and its rider and between a hand or animal and a stick that it carries. The metaphor is potentially confusing, because horses and riders and hands and sticks are all effective parts, and so in fact the stick, for example, 'cannot properly be said moved, but occasioned to such a motion, by the animal that carries it' (OEP 28). In contrast, Cavendish continues, 'the inanimate part cannot be said occasioned, but moved' (OEP 28).

But Cavendish is asking us to attend to how we tend to think—incorrectly!—a horse moves its rider, and to contrast that with how we think—again, incorrectly!—our cue ball moves the eight ball.[6] Unlike in the billiards case, where we imagine that motion is communicated from the cue ball into the eight ball, in the case of the horse and its rider, we imagine that

> the man was moved and carried along by the horse, without any communication or translation of motion from the horse into the man: Also a stick, say they, carried in a man's hand, goes along with the man, without receiving any motion from his hand.
>
> (OEP 27)

Inanimate matter is moved by animate matter more like that than like we imagine that the eight ball is moved by the cue ball.

So Cavendish's claim that inanimate matter is moved by animate matter does not affect her rejection of the transfer model of

---

6   This is a bit like when Descartes famously illustrates to Elizabeth how the soul is united to and moves the body by comparing it to how we incorrectly imagine the earth is drawn to the sun. Descartes argues that this is an incorrect description of what is going on in gravitation, but a more accurate description of what is going on in the soul-body union. Descartes thinks we believe that gravitation works this way because we project our own nature—as soul-body unions—onto bodies. I don't think that is going on here, but then again, we are made of animate and inanimate matter blended together, just as for Descartes we are unions of minds and bodies.

causation; in fact, it sheds even more light on why Cavendish rejects that model. If the motion of animate matter were communicated to inanimate matter, in what sense would inanimate matter still be inanimate? Here, we see the limits of the analogy with our billiard balls, since in fact, the eight ball is not inanimate but self-moving. How, then, does inanimate matter ever move? It is carried along by animate matter, as a rider on the back of a horse. It cannot move without being joined with animate matter as a rider is joined with its horse; this joining is not an interaction but a union.

This does not endanger the rule that every creature and every part of matter is self-moving; it just makes clear that it is restricted to effective parts and is directed at a certain widespread notion of transeunt causation. At the same time, it does force us to reevaluate the idea that Cavendish thinks that action is essentially action-on and that she cannot really make sense of one thing's acting on another. I still think this is true, but it requires a little more discussion. It requires asking, specifically, to what extent and in what respect animate matter counts as 'acting on' inanimate matter. And that requires seeing in more detail how Cavendish understands the metaphysics of the triumvirate.

Section 4.7 The problem of heterogeneity

Why does Cavendish decide that matter is a mixture of inanimate and animate matter? Why not simply say that all matter is self-moving?

As we saw in Section 4.3, Cavendish holds that self-motion is the cause of the variety in nature, because it divides and composes matter into parts and creatures. But this does not yet explain how those parts and creatures come to act differentially. If matter is homogeneously self-moving, why doesn't it all act the same way?

It is of course open to Cavendish to reply: 'it just does'. This would complement a reading of Cavendishian self-motion on which it is something like agency, so that bits of matter could have different wills to move in different ways. But this is not what self-motion is, and Cavendish is not satisfied by 'it just does', as the Argumental Discourse makes quite clear. Cavendish is after genuine explanations of natural phenomena, and natural phenomena are diverse while matter is homogeneous. All the variety in matter results from its effects, and self-motion is not an effect but the 'prime and only cause of natural effects' (OEP 116). As a principle, it cannot vary as matter's natural effects do.

Nor can Cavendish attribute the heterogeneity of matter's actions to some cause outside of nature. That is how Descartes and Boyle do it: for both, God imparts not just motion but 'various motions to the parts of matter' (Descartes 1985: 240); or, as Boyle puts it, natural diversity is the 'effect of variously determined motion' (Boyle 1666: 4). As we know, Cavendish does not think that God can be the source of variety, since God cannot act on matter at all.

So Cavendish concludes that matter cannot, after all, be perfectly homogeneous in every sense, and in particular it cannot be perfectly homogeneous in respect of the principle of natural effects: self-motion. Explaining this is the primary goal of the Argumental Discourse—'wherein', Cavendish announces, 'are contained the principles and grounds of natural philosophy, especially concerning the constitutive parts of nature, and their properties and actions' (OEP 13). This is an incredibly engaging and dense piece of philosophizing, and Cavendish admits that she stages it as a dialogue between the parts of her mind because the issues at stake

> caused a war in my mind: which in time grew to that height, that they were hardly able to compose the differences between themselves, but were in a manner necessitated to refer them to the arbitration of the impartial reader, desiring the assistance of his judgment to reconcile their controversies, and if possible, to reduce them to a settled peace and agreement.
>
> (OEP 23)

Cavendish begins by asking 'how it came, that matter was of several degrees, as animate and inanimate, sensitive and rational' (OEP 23). She answers that 'it could not be known how she came to be such, no more than a reason could be given how God came to be' (OEP 23). We simply do not know why what exists is this way rather than another way. We do, however, know that it does, because it is 'evidently perceived by [nature's] effects or actions' (OEP 24).

The primary fact about nature's 'effects and actions' that needs explaining, besides simply that there is variety, is that different changes take place at different speeds. It is as a result of this,

Cavendish thinks, that there is time. In a world of only inanimate matter, there would be no change at all, but in a world of only animate matter, all changes would happen 'in an instant' (OEP 26). In either such world, there would be no time because time depends on gradual change. The only way to explain this is to posit some matter that is self-moving and some matter that is not: 'The truth is', Cavendish writes, 'to balance the actions of nature, it cannot be otherwise, but there must be a passive degree of matter, opposite to the active; which passive part is what we call inanimate' (OEP 33).

Why can't we explain this by saying that there is some active matter that sometimes moves quickly and sometimes moves slowly, as natural matter does? Again, Cavendish seems to think that such heterogeneity of action requires explaining. I think this is important evidence that Cavendish does not mean to rely on fundamental agency in natural philosophical explanations, as many interpreters take her to; I will address this at greater length in Chapter 9. Cavendish demands that this heterogeneity be reflected in a heterogeneity in the principles themselves: it cannot be fundamental or unexplained.

She expresses this in the *Grounds*, where her 'major thoughts' insist that there cannot be degrees of strength of self-motion, because 'Self-motion could be but Self-motion' (GNP 1 15). Her minor thoughts object that 'the Self-motion of the Rational, [matter] might be stronger than the Self-motion of the Sensitive [matter]'. But her major thoughts reply decisively that 'there could be no degrees of the Power of Nature, or the Nature of Nature: for Matter, which was Nature, could be but Self-moving, or not Self-moving; or partly Self-moving, or not Self-moving'. They go on to explain that some parts of nature may be stronger than others in virtue of the number of parts, the 'manner and form of their composition', and the sorts of action they perform.

This confirms that Cavendish holds that the fundamental kind of action is to move or not move oneself, which is consistent with the interpretation of motion as fundamentally dividing and composing. Considered in abstraction from both the constitutive and effective structure of matter, we cannot make sense of variable motion. The difference between slow motion and quick motion cannot be left unanalysed, because just as all matter is equally self-moving, 'the slowest motion was as much motion as the quickest' (OEP 25).

Cavendish is expressing here that the difference between two speeds of motion cannot be a fundamental one. The only fundamental difference is between non-motion and motion. So motion at different speeds must result from a blending of these. Ultimately, this is the source of all variety; as Cavendish writes in the *Letters*, 'though Matter is but active and passive, yet there is great Variety, and so great difference in force and liberty, objects and perceptions, sense and reason, and the like' (PL 1 5).

One way that variable rate of change manifests itself in nature is that we find that some compositions are relatively stable. It stands to reason, then, that Cavendish holds 'were there no inanimate matter... there would be no solid figures' (OEP 157). That is not, I think, because inanimate matter has some special power to glue parts together or that inanimate matter is especially associated with composition and animate with division—after all, composition and division are both actions. Rather, it is because without inanimate matter, everything would be constantly in flux, and so 'there could not be such solid compositions of parts as there are' (OEP 157).

Section 4.8 What is 'sensitive and rational' about sensitive and rational matter?

I have argued that the Argumental Discourse is Cavendish's attempt to explain the diversity of natural motions through animate and inanimate matter. As Cavendish puts it in the *Letters*, 'though Matter is but active and passive, yet there is great Variety' (PL 1 5). What should we make, then, of Cavendish's claim that there are two different kinds, or 'degrees', of animate matter: sensitive and rational? Based on Cavendish's names for them, it would be easy to think that sensitive and rational matter each have some further feature, or capacity to act in some way, that is distinct from their being self-moving. And many readers think that the extra feature that they have must be something like human sense perception and reason, or at least some extra thing, beyond motion, that is necessary to generate something like those. Besides their names, this reading is encouraged by Cavendish's frequent characterization of them in very anthropomorphic terms.

I do not think this is the case, however. Rather, Cavendish holds that self-moving matter is all that is necessary to generate human sense perception and reason, just like it generates all other creaturely phenomena. What, then, makes matter either 'sensitive' or 'rational'? And what should we make of Cavendish's frequent descriptions of these in terms of these anthropomorphic functions?

Let us consider Cavendish's argument in the *Grounds* that these two degrees of matter exist. There, she distinguishes sensitive and rational matter from one another only inasmuch as they are differently 'burdened' with inanimate matter:

> Neither can there be more than two sorts of Matter, namely, that sort which is Self-moving, and that which is not Self-Moving. Also, there can be but two sorts of the Self-Moving Parts; as, that sort that moves intirely without Burden, and that sort that moves with the Burdens of those Parts that are not Self-moving: So that there can be but these three sorts; Those parts that are not moving, those that move free, and those that move with those parts that are not moving of themselves: Which degrees are (in my opinion) the Rational Parts, the Sensitive Parts, and the Inanimate Parts.
>
> (GNP 1 3)

In the last sentence, Cavendish is naming the kinds of matter, not telling us that the kinds of matter have further properties of sensation or rationality. That is a little more obvious in the 1663 edition of her *Opinions*, where she proposes naming the first kind 'Rational or Radical' (PPO2 1 3, 4) and the second kind 'Sensitive or Vital' (PPO2 1 3). The label 'radical' suggests the root or source of life, which is not necessarily reason; it is a term that Van Helmont also uses, and not to imply anything rational in the familiar sense. And to be 'vital' is simply to be self-moving—a point that is argued further in Section 5.9. Cavendish often describes the difference in the burdens of each kind of matter as their relative 'freedom', which she relates to some further broadly mechanistic properties of matter, including fineness, agility, and purity (PPO2 1 3). Rational matter is freer than sensitive matter.

In light of all this, I propose that the distinction between sensitive and rational matter entirely concerns their relative encumbrance. The other ways that Cavendish characterizes the two can be understood in these terms. Rational matter is freer and more 'penetrating' because it is not being mixed with and therefore limited by inanimate matter, so it can move in a wider variety of ways: 'The rational perception, being more general, is also more perfect than the sensitive; and the reason is, because it is more free, and not encumbered with the burdens of other parts' (OEP 166, see also 175, 181).

Cavendish tells us that self-motion 'makes the only difference between animate and inanimate matter' (OEP 192, my emphasis). She also frequently claims that sense and reason follow immediately on self-motion ('wherever there is Self-motion, there is Sense and Reason' (OEP 169)) and that sense and reason simply are self-motion ('Sense and Reason, which is self-motion' (PL 1 10; see also PPO2 6 23 and OEP 178)).

Cavendish often characterizes the distinction between rational, sensitive, and inanimate matter in terms of a building metaphor: rational matter is the architect, sensitive matter is the laborer, and inanimate matter is the raw materials from which, say, a house is built. This metaphor has led many readers to think that the distinction among the three degrees of matter must be irreducibly anthropomorphic and hierarchical, and must require that rational matter, say, sets its own ends. While Cavendish is certainly illustrating for us the role of rational matter, this does not mean that this metaphor irreducibly characterizes the distinction between the three degrees. In fact, it makes a lot of sense given the account of rational and sensitive matter as differentially burdened by inanimate matter. Both the architect and the builder are self-moving and thereby participate in creating, say, a house. The sensitive parts of matter are laborers inasmuch as they 'bear the grosser Materials about them, which are the Inanimate Parts' (GNP 1 5). The architect, being unencumbered, is simply freer in his self-motions. Moreover, just as self-motion is the ultimate source of all the variety of forms and all change, an architect is the ultimate source of the form of the house and the motions toward building it. Cavendish describes inanimate matter as the timber. It plays the role of passive principle, just as does Aristotelian hûle, or timber.

So we need not grant rational or sensitive matter some additional properties or capacities over and above self-motion. Despite their names, there is no reason to think that each has a fundamental ability to have sensory representations or rational representations or that they have some panpsychic or protopanpsychic properties. This does not mean that they do not have the ability to have sensory or rational perceptions. They must, because sensory and rational perceptions are made by matter. This helps to explain why Cavendish names them 'sensory' and 'rational', even though they are not intrinsically sensory and rational in the way that, say, human minds are. They are the kind of matter—viz., self-moving—that allows for sensation and reason. In that sense, self-motion is the 'Life and Soul of all Creatures' (PL 4 33).

In claiming that self-moving matter is sensitive and rational, Cavendish is claiming that self-moving matter has the ability to play all the roles of the Aristotelian sensitive and rational souls. During Cavendish's time, it was common for anti-materialists to describe matter as 'stupid', 'senseless', and 'dumb'; as Charles Wolfe writes, 'This theme of the "stupidity" of matter reaches something of a fever point in the seventeenth and early eighteenth centuries' (Wolfe 2016: 7). Against this background, the polemical power of these names is clear without committing Cavendish to the view that any bit of matter intrinsically has anything like animal sense perception or rational insight. The names insist on Cavendish's claim that all of that can be explained by self-moving matter:

> All parts of nature are living, knowing, and perceptive, because all are self-moving; for self-motion is the cause of all particular effects, figures, actions, varieties, changes, lives, knowledges, perceptions, etc. in nature, and makes the only difference between animate and inanimate matter.
>
> (OEP 191–192)

And Cavendish describes sense and reason as *actions* of matter (OEP 128) rather than as intrinsic or essential characteristics of it.

I do not expect that this non-anthropomorphic reading of the distinction between rational and sensitive matter will yet be obviously preferable to the anthropomorphic (or panpsychic) reading, from a textual perspective. The arguments of Chapters 6, 7, and 9 will, I hope, further motivate this account of rational and sensitive matter.

Section 4.9   How do the constituents constitute matter?

The degrees of matter have entirely different natures and cannot be transformed into one another: 'The nature of each must remain as it is; or else if it could be thus, then the animate part might become inanimate, and the rational, the sensitive, etc. which is impossible' (OEP 26; see also PL 4 33).[7]

At the same time, Cavendish writes; 'my meaning is not, that infinite nature is made up of two finite parts, but that she consists out of a commixture of animate and inanimate matter, which although they be of two degrees or parts, (call them what you will) yet they are not separated parts, but make one infinite body' (OEP 207). Nature's body is 'entire and whole in itself, as not composed of several different parts or substances' (OEP 47). This means, as we have seen, that 'not the least part (if least could be)…was without this commixture' and that 'wheresoever was inanimate, there was also animate matter' (OEP 34–35), but it is consistent with natural matter being 'in it self and its own essence simple and homogeneous' (OEP 199). The animate and inanimate parts, Cavendish argues, 'cannot so much as be conceived apart'.

To explain this, Cavendish appeals to the notion of a total or perfect mixture. A true mixture (mixis), as defined by Aristotle, is a substance made up of other substances but nonetheless 'homeomerous', which means that its parts are like the whole. So a mixture is not constituted of its components in the way that a whole is made up of its integral parts; it is a different way of combining substances. To many philosophers, it has not been clear that such a thing is even possible. As Aristotle put the problem, it seems to require both that the original constituents survive in the mixture—otherwise it would not be a mixture, but a simple substance—and be destroyed in the mixture—otherwise the resultant mixture would not be homeomerous. For Cavendish, the challenge is to explain how matter can be perfectly homeomerous inasmuch as it is all self-moving, but constituted out of animate and inanimate matter in this way.

---

7   The three mixing to form the matter of our nature is not the same as one degree becoming another degree. But Cavendish's claim that 'each must remain as it is' may seem to contradict the claim that nature is a perfect mixture. It is not true, though, that the natures of the degrees are lost in the mixture. That may seem a bit paradoxical, but that is precisely the paradox that a perfect mixture is supposed to embody.

The Stoics also took on the problem of mixture, setting themselves against Aristotle, and the influence of their view on Cavendish's is plausible. While Aristotle was concerned with the mixture of elements like earth, air, fire, and water, the Stoics, like Cavendish, were primarily concerned with the mixture of active and passive matter, their 'first principles'. Besides Thomas Stanley's History, Cavendish also would have been acquainted with theories of mixture as assimilated by Charleton and Van Helmont. According to Chryssipus, the complete mixture of active and passive matter meant that every spatial part of the cosmos contained both principles. Similarly, Cavendish holds that every effective part of nature contains all three degrees of matter.

However, there are some important differences between Cavendish's picture of mixture and that of the Stoics. Centrally, Cavendish does not accept Chrysippus's characterization of mixture as a problem to be solved with an analysis of spatial extension, and her claim that every effective part of nature contains all three constituents does not entail anything about the relationship between those constituents and spatial parts. Moreover, the Stoic theory of mixture also reached Cavendish not directly but through the work of chemical philosophers. I think this influence is at least as important for understanding Cavendish's view as the Stoic one—especially the influence of Van Helmont's Oriatrike.

According to Van Helmont, there is one element, water, from which everything in nature is made. But just as Cavendish concludes from the variety of self-moving matter's effects that it must be in some sense heterogeneous, Van Helmont posits that water contains mercury, sulphur, and salt—the tria prima of the chemists—as principles. He clarifies that these are not 'principles of composition', which means that they are not components into which water can ever in fact be analysed. Even less does this imply that water contains any spatial heterogeneity. Rather, these are 'principles of heterogenity', and they are manifest only by water's activity (Newman and Principe 2005: 64). It is in virtue of being constituted by these three principles that water can in turn serve as the ultimate source of activity and life.[8]

---

8   'Principles of composition' and 'principles of heterogeneity' are Newman and Principe's translations of Van Helmont's claim in the Latin edition that the

The parallel with Cavendish's triumvirate is clear. While matter is homogeneous and is everywhere self-moving, we can infer from its activity that it contains three 'principles of heterogeneity'. But these are not 'principles of composition', to borrow Van Helmont's distinction: matter is not strictly speaking built out of them, and there is no sense in which these principles can be analyzed out of the self-moving matter of our world. While I have not found a place in either Van Helmont or his influence, Galen, where the *tria prima* is called a triumvirate, John Donne describes the heart, liver, and brain, which in Galenic medicine govern all the processes in the body, as the 'triumvirate' (Mueller 2018: 273).[9] And Van Helmont refers to the stomach and the spleen, which are the seat of the Archeus and act as one to govern the life functions of the body, as the 'Duumvirate'. It is only in the 1663 PPO that Cavendish refers to the 'triumvirate', after the publication of Van Helmont's *Oriatrike* was published in London in 1662. Van Helmont's Archeus is the 'inner efficient cause' and 'inward director' of generation and motion and the source of all life (1662: 26); he also frequently calls it the 'chief' or 'Master Workman' (1662: 35). He also uses the word 'radical' to describe the Archeus, which is an alternative name that Cavendish gives rational matter in early work.

Cavendish writes that the degrees are

> so closely intermixt in the body of nature, that they cannot be separated from each other, but by the power of God; neverthe-less, sense and reason may perceive that they are distinct degrees, by their distinct and different actions, and may distinguish them so far, that one part is not another part, and that the actions of one degree are not the actions of the other.
>
> (OEP 33)

Cavendish's comment that the degrees can be separated from each other only by the power of God certainly seems to evoke the real

---

'*tria prima chymicorum principia*' are not a '*tria compositionis*' but a '*tria heterogeneitatis*'. The translation Cavendish would have read says that the 'first Principles of the Chymists' are 'not the Three of composition…but the Three things of Heterogeniety or diversity of kind' (Van Helmont 1662: 470).

9   Many thanks to Boris Demarest for pointing me to this reference.

distinction, and Shaheen (2021) argues that Cavendish does think that the constituents are distinct substances. Despite what she writes here, however, Cavendish does not in fact think that God can separate inanimate and animate natural matter. God cannot do anything to matter, as it actually is in nature. Cavendish leaves open the possibility that God could have created a world (although not a nature) made entirely of inanimate matter or entirely of animate matter, but I do not think that she positively holds that this is possible, in keeping with her denial that we can know anything outside of nature. So we are not licensed to conclude from Cavendish's 'separability' claim, as from a Cartesian separability claim, that inanimate and inanimate matter, blended as we find them in nature, are separate substances.

Describing the irreducibly various effects of nature, Cavendish writes that it is

> no consequence, that, because the effects are different, they must also have different principles: For first, all effects of nature are material; which proves, they have but one principle, which is the only infinite matter. Next, they are all self-moving; which proves, that this material principle has self-motion; for without self-motion, there would be no variety or change of figures, it being the nature of self-motion to be perpetually acting.
>
> (OEP 239)

Here, Cavenidsh confirms that, properly speaking, there are not two principles, but only 'principles of heterogeneity' within the one actual principle, which is self-moving matter.

Section 4.10 The relationship between matter and self-motion

The difference between inanimate and animate matter is that animate matter is self-moving and inanimate matter is not. I have argued that this means simply that animate matter acts and inanimate matter does not. The fact that animate matter acts is deep and perhaps even essential: 'By Animate motion, I understand the Intern and Essential motion, properly Inherent in the Nature and Substance of the Animate matter' (PPO2 Preface).

Does this undermine the claim that matter is not a kind of stuff, but simply stuff? After all, it now looks like we have two kinds of stuff: animate matter, which is stuff that acts, and another kind of stuff that doesn't act. Cavendish does not see it that way. She does not see self-motion as a mode or property or whatever of matter, which is part of why she often insists that matter is 'but one thing' with self-motion 'and could not so much as be conceived differently' (OEP 35; see also OEP 211). There is nothing more to say about animate matter than that it moves itself.

Some readers of Cavendish, sensitive to her claims that everything that exists is matter, conclude that motion must *be* matter—specifically, animate matter (e.g. Shaheen 2021). The idea seems to be that it is a fact that some matter moves itself, and this fact must be made true by the existence of something, which is self-motion, so self-motion must be matter. This reasoning is similar to the reasoning behind the 'inflationist somatology' interpretation of Cavendishian accidents: since they are real and have effects, they must be matter.

My first reply to this, to borrow a Cavendishian idiom, is that I have no idea what these authors mean when they say that either change or the cause of change *is* matter. To reify self-motion runs counter to Cavendish's refusal to multiply entities to gain explanatory resources, even if those entities are matter. And Cavendish herself seems explicitly to reject this view in the Argumental Discourse. To distinguish between matter and motion is not to distinguish between entities:

> The latter [thoughts] said, How can motion be corporeal, and yet one thing with body? Certainly, if body be material, and motion too, they must needs be two several substances.
>
> The former answered, that motion and body were not two several substances; but motion and matter made one self-moving body; and so was place, colour, figure, etc. all one and the same with body.
>
> The latter replied, that a man, and his action, were not one and the same, but two different things.
>
> The former answered, that a man, and his actions, were no more different, than a man was different from himself; for, said they, although a man may have many different actions; yet, were

not that man existent, the same actions would not be: for, though many men have the like actions, yet they are not the same.

(OEP 37)

Similarly, Cavendish writes later in the *Observations* that 'matter might subsist without motion but not motion without matter: for, there is no such thing as an immaterial motion, but motion must necessarily be of something' (OEP 230). Cavendish's claim that motion must be of something sounds like an affirmation that acting is what matter does, not some matter joined with the matter that acts. Cavendish's claims that self-motion is one and the same with matter mean that self-motion is one with the matter that acts, which is to say, no matter over and above the matter that acts, just as a man's action is no further entity beyond the man. The action of a thing is just the thing, acting.

Section 4.11 Conclusion

We now have in place all of the building blocks of Cavendish's metaphysics. There is matter; matter has structure which is parthood structure; matter itself causes the changes in that structure. These represent the minimal posits that Cavendish takes to be necessary to explain nature as we find it. These posits resonate with a call that Bacon, an important influence on Cavendish as well as on mechanical philosophy, made in his *Novum Organum*:

We should study matter, and its structure, and structural change, and pure act, and the law of act or motion, for forms are figments of the human mind.

(Bacon 2000 [1620]: 45)

Cavendish describes matter and self-motion as the principles of her philosophy (or, self-moving matter as the principle). It is out of these principles that 'all other creatures are made or produced' (OEP 205). As Georgescu (2021) urges, Cavendish takes great care to remind us not to confuse principles with effects. In this book, we are about to treat a huge variety of complex phenomena, but it is no consequence, that, because the effects are different, they must also have different principles: For first, all effects of nature are material; which proves, they have but one principle, which is the only infinite matter. Next, they are all self-moving; which proves, that this material principle has self-motion; for without self-motion, there would be no variety or change of figures, it being the nature of self-motion to be perpetually acting. Thus matter and self-motion being inseparably united in one infinite body, which is self-moving material nature, is the only cause of all the infinite effects that are produced in nature.

(OEP 239)

Neglecting these principles, and inferring instead all manner of causes from the great variety of creaturely natures, will cause us to 'make infinite principles, and so confound principles with effects… which will lead our sense and reason into a horrid confusion and labyrinth of ignorance' (OEP 239, see also 83). In the rest of the book, if it sometimes seems that I go to great lengths to avoid positing a new fundamental, it is because I take this seriously.[10]

The particularities of the natural changes that we observe inspire Cavendish, after much thought and internal debate, to posit the so-called triumvirate of matter: inanimate, sensitive, and rational matter. As I've argued, this distinction is more essentially a distinction between animate and inanimate matter, although the mixture of the two requires that we posit sensitive matter. Sensitive and rational matter are not intrinsically sensing and reasoning; rather, they are the principles of creaturely sense and reason. But ultimately, all sense and reason is so much self-motion of matter.

While the foundation is in place, the house is far from finished. In the next chapter, we will see how Cavendish explains the great variety of creatures and motions in terms of the principles thus far. After that, we must grapple with Cavendish's claims that perception and knowledge are ubiquitous. This will help us see why Cavendish does not hold that the parts of matter are fundamentally or intrinsically

---

10 Many thanks to Laura Georgescu for helping me to make the guiding spirit of my interpretation more explicit. Georgescu (2021) articulates a similar interpretive spirit.

mental, allowing us to appreciate Cavendish's beautiful and radical account of creaturely perception and knowledge and of our place among perceptive and knowing creatures. We will consider what this tells us about the prospects of our knowledge of nature. And with all that in place, we will be in a position to understand how Cavendish thinks of natural order. Finally, we will step back to investigate Cavendish's method: given what nature is like and our place in it, how should we go about doing natural philosophy?

Further reading

Adams, Marcus P. 2021. 'Motion as an Accident of Matter: Margaret Cavendish and Thomas Hobbes on Motion and Rest.' *The Southern Journal of Philosophy* 59(4).

Boyle, Deborah. 2018. Chapter 3 in *The Well-Ordered Universe: The Philosophy of Margaret Cavendish*. New York, NY: Oxford University Press.

Chamberlain, Colin. 2024. 'Move Your Body! Margaret Cavendish on Self-Motion.' In *Powers and Abilities in Early Modern Philosophy*, edited by S. Bender and D. Perler. New York: Routledge.

Cunning, David. 2016. Chapter 4 in *Cavendish*. New York: Routledge.

James, Susan. 1999. 'The Philosophical Innovations of Margaret Cavendish.' *British Journal for the History of Philosophy* 7(2): 219–244. doi: https://doi.org/10.1080/09608789908571026.

Peterman, Alison. 2019. 'Margaret Cavendish on Motion and Mereology.' *Journal of the History of Philosophy* 57(3): 471–499.

Lascano, Marcy. 2023. Chapter 3 in *The Metaphysics of Margaret Cavendish and Anne Conway*. New York: Oxford University Press.

Shaheen, Jonathan L. 2021. 'The Life of the Thrice Sensitive, Rational and Wise Animate Matter: Cavendish's Animism.' *HOPOS* 11(2): 621–641.

Five
Creatures

When several figured atoms well agreeing
Do join, they give another figure being.
For as those figures join in several ways,
So they the fabric of each creature raise.
(P&F The Joining of Several Figured Atoms Make Other Figures)

Cavendish calls everything that we encounter, or could encounter, in nature 'creatures', including human beings; other animals, plants, and minerals; the parts or features of things, like diseases (OEP 244); and artifacts, like ships and mirrors. All of these are parts of nature and effects of self-moving matter and are thereby all natural. Cavendish also holds that because they are all self-moving, the distinction between animate and inanimate creatures is 'useless' (OEP 112).

The collapse of the distinction between animate and inanimate is central to understanding Cavendish's account of creatures. On the one hand, it represents Cavendish's commitment to explaining everything in nature in terms of self-moving matter, which is also a commitment to explaining it in terms of structures and changes in those structures. To explain living things, we don't need anything beyond that, be it Aristotelian souls, Morean immaterial spirits, or the Archeus of Van Helmont. Cavendish shares this with mechanical philosophers like Hobbes and Descartes, who provide accounts of animal and plant bodies in terms of matter and its motion, though Descartes, of course, denies that this can be done in the case of the human mind.

On the other hand, Cavendish differs from most mechanical philosophers on two very important points, which make her principles

DOI: 10.4324/9781003107255-6

more apt to explain plant and animal life. The first is that Cavendishian matter is self-moving, so she is not faced with explaining the apparent self-motion of animals in terms of inert matter. The second is that fundamental structure, for Cavendish, is not spatial structure, and dynamics and kinematics are not fundamentally collisions and trajectories. Rather, fundamental structure is that of nested and overlapping composites, which organize themselves by dividing and composing. That structure is reflected at the level of creatures, all of which Cavendish sees not as machines but as organisms: they are naturally generated, self-moving, and self-sustaining; they grow, act and interact, flourish and get sick, and die. Her model systems are organic ones, not mechanical ones.

In this chapter, we will see how Cavendish accounts for the vast variety of creatures with their vast variety of characteristics and actions while still maintaining that all these creatures are so much self-moving matter. Our ability to understand the specifics of the infinite kinds of productions, alterations, and actions is very limited by our own finitude, but Cavendish does give us some general guidelines about how these may be explained by so much dividing and composing. Finally, we will consider why, despite this and despite her insistence on the continuity between humans and other creatures, Cavendish seems to make so much of the distinction between the artificial and the natural.

Section 5.1 Figure

Let us take as our starting point the question of how creatures and their features can change in the ways that they do. In the broadly Aristotelian framework upon which Cavendish builds, there are three kinds of change. In creation and annihilation, something comes into being *ex nihilo*, or something that exists is reduced to nothing. As we know, along with Aristotle and with the vast majority of philosophers, Cavendish holds that true creation and annihilation, at least in the natural world, is impossible, a claim which she relates to matter's eternity. That leaves two kinds of creaturely change. In generation and corruption, a new substance comes to be, but not *ex nihilo*: a baby bird is generated out of pre-existent organic material, and when it dies, its matter is incorporated into a hungry coyote or a nascent plant. In alteration, no new substance comes to be, but a substance is changed in some respect, as when a cat is warmed by the sun. Cavendish holds that baby birds come to be and that cats are warmed, but she denies the Aristotelian analyses of these in terms of matter joining with, respectively, either substantial or accidental forms.

Of the early philosophers who precede the development of hylomorphism, Aristotle credits only Democritus with giving serious thought to how to explain these different kinds of natural change. As Aristotle writes, Democritus 'postulate[s] "figures" [as it would have been translated at Cavendish's time], and make[s] "alteration" and coming to be result from them' (*On Generation and Corruption* Book 1 Part 2).[1] Many of Cavendish's contemporaries who were influenced by the Democritean tradition also take what they called 'figure' to be important both to distinguishing creatures from one another and accounting for the nature of creatures, and thus an important weapon in their battles against forms. For mechanical philosophers like Descartes, Boyle, and Hobbes, 'figure' most of the time means geometrical shape, especially when it is explicitly characterized as fundamental feature of bodies like a mechanical affection (e.g. Boyle 1666: 9–10). But sometimes, in Hobbes and Boyle as well as in Digby, it seems to serve as a stand-in for the general physical nature of a thing or to refer to individualizable things.

Cavendish uses figures and figurative motions to do the work of Aristotelian forms. Creatures are 'discerned from each other' by their 'limited and circumscribed figures' (OEP 31), and Cavendish constantly describes both the essential and nonessential features of things as 'figures'. Sometimes Cavendish describes them instead as 'corporeal figurative motions', indicating the fundamentality of figure to natural philosophical explanations, alongside matter and self-motion.

By 'figure', Cavendish means the compositional structure of a creature. This has more in common, then, with the mechanistic

---

1   See also Anaxagoras, echoing Parmenides: 'no thing comes to be or passes away, but is mixed together and separated from the things that are. And thus it is correct to call coming-to-be a mixing-together and passing-away a separating-apart.'

and ultimately Democritean conception of an 'arrangement' of parts (sometimes translated from '*figuratio*') rather than geometrical shape, or some other intrinsic feature of bodies. Descartes and Boyle sometimes include such arrangements in their lists of primary features of bodies, and they sometimes do not. For example, Descartes attributes the forms of bodies to the 'arrangement of their parts' and Boyle includes among the primary qualities of bodies the 'contrivances of their own Parts' (Boyle 1666) and the 'disposition of parts' (Boyle 1669). Again, we see the ambivalent relationship of the mechanical philosophy to the fundamentality of compositional characterizations alongside geometrical and spatial ones. For Cavendish, there is no such ambivalence: figure is compositional structure so that the nature of a thing is determined by its parts, composed.

This is evident, first, from the frequency with which Cavendish associates figure with compositional notions. She often uses the phrase 'composed figure' instead of simply 'figure' (e.g. OEP 34, 38, 80; GNP 3 1), assimilates 'composed parts' with 'figures' (e.g. OEP 133), and elides the distinction between the 'composition' of a creature and its form (e.g. GNP 5 4, 11 13). She describes changes of figure as compositions and dissolutions (e.g. OEP 26, 29, 31, 35, 127, 130, 139), identifies 'alteration of figures' with 'change of parts' (OEP 81), and assimilates the production of creatures with 'Associations of Self-moving Parts' (GNP 3 1).

Second, it is clear that what Cavendish calls 'patterns' are a species of figure (e.g. OEP 33, 51). We will learn more about patterns in Chapter 6. What is important here is that patterns are compositions and that changes of patterns require an 'alteration of parts' (OEP 76).

Third, Cavendish holds that 'there's no figure but is composed of parts' (OEP 194). This could be because only extended things have geometrical figures and extended things must have parts. In fact, much of the previous evidence is consistent with reading 'figure' as geometrical. But while these passages are consistent with that reading, there is no good reason for it, other than an assumption that Cavendish is using it like the mechanical philosophers are. She sometimes talks about figures that are shapes. But that is consistent with the primary of compositional structure, and Cavendish is usually focused, in these contexts, specifically on exterior figures (e.g. OEP 86). And again, it is not just that Cavendish holds that all figures have parts, but that she seems to hold that because of a deeper identity between figures and compositional structures. For example, she writes that

> composition and division of parts are general motions, and some figures may be more composed than others, that is, consist of more or fewer parts than others; yet there is none that hath not a composition of parts.
>
> (OEP 234)

Here, Cavendish seems to appeal to the generality of composition and division to motivate the claim that figures must be composed of parts.

As we have already seen, Cavendish cuts out the spatial middlemen between matter and compositional concepts. We know that it is a deep feature of nature that it is structured by parthood and composition, and we know that the fundamental actions of matter are dividing and composing. So it should be no surprise that nature 'works natural matter into…various figures' (OEP 71) by dividing and composing, and that those figures are compositional structures.

Section 5.2 Generation and corruption I: societies of parts

We now consider generation. How, on Cavendish's view, does a creature come to be or pass away?

In keeping with her characterization of figures as compositions, Cavendish's answer is that generation and death are 'just some sorts of Compositions and Divisions' of creatures (OEP 176). In this she follows Democritus, who, as Aristotle puts it 'explain[s] coming-to-be and passing-away by…dissocation and association' (*On Generation and Corruption*, Book II Part 1). Besides the frequent explicit identification of generation and production with composition and death with dissolution, especially in the *Observations*, this interpretation of generation is supported by Cavendish's descriptions of creatures as 'societies of parts'. Cavendish frequently describes creatures in this way, comparing, for example, the way that the parts of an eye compose it to how congregants compose a church (OEP

159). The production of a creature, like the production of a society, is done by the agreement or the consent of its parts:

> Composition is made by a mutual agreement of parts. (OEP 119)
>
> Production is only a Society of particular Parts, that join into particular Figures, or Creatures. (GNP 3 2)
>
> all Natural Creatures are produced by the consent and agreement of many Self-moving Parts, or Corporeal Motions. (OEP 31, see also 145)

Many readers of Cavendish have taken these analogies to indicate that composition must be understood in irreducibly anthropomorphic terms, so that the parts are like people and their consent is like the consent of agents. Lascano and Schliesser have described this as a 'political' account of creatures—and it is, inasmuch as the same principles govern the cohesion of communities, states, and churches as govern the cohesion of a stone, an oak, or a human being. But let us hold off on taking this metaphor too literally and assuming that the comparison is meant to explain creatures in terms of human institutions. After all, the concept of a law of nature draws on a metaphor with a human institution, but few think that it thereby relies on the concept of a lawmaker. And we should definitely hesitate to conclude that this 'social account of creaturely unity…reflects Cavendish's panpsychism' (Shaheen 2021: 636).[2] It is a reason to be suspicious that Cavendish is trying to explain compositions in terms of societies rather than vice versa that she calls politics a 'deceiving Profession' that is 'more craft than wisdom' (PL 1 13), and argues that we should think of political bodies first as natural compositions:

> if men do not naturally agree, Art cannot make unity amongst them, or associate them into one Politick Body and so rule them; But man thinks he governs, when as it is Nature that doth it… Thus it is not the artificial form that governs men in a Politick Government, but a natural power.
>
> (PL 1 13)

---

2 For another thoroughly political interpretation of creatures, see Sarasohn (2010), Chapter 5.

Cavendish's claim that natural power rather than artifice is what unites men suggests that we should not think even of human societies, no less other compositions, in terms of human agency.

In Chapter 3, I argued that composition, for Cavendish, is brute: there is nothing in virtue of which some parts form a composite. They just do (or do not). Is this undermined by Cavendish's claim that compositions require parts to agree to join?

I do not think it is; in fact, I think it strengthens that interpretation. For what, exactly, is the nature of this agreement, other than that the parts do indeed act to join together? The agential language can be seen precisely as highlighting that the joining is not grounded in any further facts. You might reply that agential actions like agreements are determined by mental states like desires and intentions. Even if this is true, those would be better candidates for causes of the agreement than grounds of the agreement. In any case, I don't think that Cavendish holds that the parts of an eye have anything like beliefs or desires, as Chapters 6 and 7 will argue. That is not what the language of agreement is meant to convey.

Besides the bruteness and spontaneity of composition, Cavendish's comparison between creatures and societies makes explicit her resistance to the Aristotelian tenet that a creature requires something over and above a composition of parts to unite it—something that is distinct from the parts and is itself simple, or a *unum per se*. Leibniz, writing several decades after Cavendish, will share with her the notion that the organic is fundamental, inasmuch as he holds that animals and plants as well as tiny creatures we will never see are all organized, self-moving collections of parts. But Leibniz holds that organisms can only exist when their components are united by a form which is itself a true unity; without that, a collection of parts is a mere aggregate and since not a unity, not a thing (Leibniz 2007: 17). For Cavendish, in contrast, organisms are *exactly* like armies. This does not mean that Cavendish accepts Leibniz's characterization of these as mere aggregates. On the contrary, as composites, they are genuinely one—as well as genuinely many. This reflects that composition is much more metaphysically meaty for Cavendish than it is for Leibniz.

So there is no reason to hold that agreement is some further state of some parts or relationship between parts that is distinct from and more fundamental than their composition. And there is, moreover, reason to reject this reading, which is that Cavendish is quite clear that agreement is not prior to composition. In some places, she even suggests that agreement depends upon composition, as when she writes that 'agreement and friendship is made by composition [and] disagreement is made by division' (OEP 145). But when it comes to the agreement to compose, specifically, that agreement and the composition are simply the same thing: 'friendly and amiable associations are nothing else but composing motions' (OEP 72).

Besides agreement and friendship, Cavendish sometimes writes that there is sympathy, sympathetical agreement, love, or sympathetic love between the parts of a creature, leading some readers to take sympathy or love to ground the fact that the parts are composed. Among Cavendish's influences and contemporaries, sympathetic action is the effect or influence of one thing on another because of some antecedent sameness with it. This sameness could be one of two kinds: it could be a similarity or sameness of type, or it could be a sameness of token, a unity that results from the two things being parts of the same whole. This tradition is reflected in Cavendish's conception of sympathy. She identifies sympathy between things that are similar: she describes sympathy as the result of a 'likeness of interior motions' (OEP 144) and gives as examples the thawing of ice by water (OEP 117) and the healing of a burn by heat (OEP 118). She also identifies sympathy between parts of one composition, as we shall see. Either way, sympathy was commonly understood to result from this sameness or connection, not to be an independent ground or cause of sameness or connection. That means that it is not responsible for grounding the fact of that sameness or connection. We will return to the role of sympathy in holding or keeping things together once they are joined, in Section 5.4.[3]

Finally, Cavendish holds that perceptions between parts, like sympathies between parts, result from and so do not ground the agreement that parts make to compose themselves: 'perception, or

---

3 For a detailed treatment of the history of sympathy, see Schliesser (2015), and especially the introduction, for an excellent overview.

perceptive knowledge, is only between parts' (OEP 172). Similarly, Cavendish writes that what causes 'acquaintance' among parts is

> their Uniting and Association: That which loses acquaintance of other Parts, is the Divisions and Alterations: for, as Self-compositions cause particular Knowledges, or Acquaintances: So Self-divisions cause particular Ignorances, or Forgetfulnesses: for, as all kinds and sorts of Creatures are produced, nourished, and encreased by the Association of Parts; so are all kinds and sorts of Perceptions; and according as their Associations, or their Compositions do last, so doth their Acquaintance.
>
> (GNP 5 2)

Now, this does not mean that there is no perceptual relationship between two parts before they become some particular whole. Two potential parts of the animal must perceive one another to join together as parts of that animal, just as two future fellow congregants must perceive each other at, say, the grocery store for one to recruit the other. That perception is different from the perception of each other as fellow congregants, but it still depends upon their being part of a particular whole, like the animal's environment.

Section 5.3 Generation and corruption II: matter's creative potential

Cavendish often reminds us that there are many kinds of generations, or productions, as she often puts it. Nature is 'too diversely various, to be tied to one way of acting in all productions' (OEP 67, see also 115). Does this undermine the claim that all production is composition?

No. On the contrary, it supports it. To see why, consider Cavendish's critique of the Aristotelian view that 'seminal principles' like seeds or eggs are always required for natural production, exemplified by William Harvey's declaration 'ex ovo omnia [everything from an egg]'. The debate over seminal principles was part of a long history of theorizing about animal generation, driven by the question: how can a brand new creature, like a rose, arise from matter which seemingly has nothing of that creature in it, like manure and soil? The Aristotelian answer to this question was that it cannot. The generative potential of matter can only be actualized by the addition of something actual: a form, of course. The forms are stored in seeds and eggs which, as Cavendish quotes him in the *Observations*, Robert Hooke characterizes as 'the cabinet[s] of Nature, wherein are laid up her jewels' (OEP 67).

Cavendish replies to Hooke that she 'cannot conceive, what jewels Nature has, nor in what cabinet she preserves them' (OEP 69). Here and in her critiques of *Harvey* in the Letters, Cavendish's target is the claim that some parts of matter are 'prime or principal' as opposed to others (OEP 69). No bit of matter is intrinsically different from any other, no bit of matter can be the special repository of creaturely information, and no bit of matter is bound to any way of acting. Just as matter does not have to be clayey to make clay, it does not have to contain the seeds of particular creatures to generate those creatures. It is enough to make the variety of creatures that matter can divide and compose itself into an infinite variety of forms. It is precisely the simplicity of the principle that is self-moving matter that generates the variety of its possible actions.

This is clear from Cavendish's otherwise potentially confusing claims that matter contains all potentialities; for example, that 'seeds are buried in life…for what is not in present act, we may call buried, entombed, or inured in the power of life' (OEP 69). But this just reflects her belief that self-moving matter has the potential to create the infinite variety of creatures that there are. Similarly, when Cavendish writes that the 'former form or figure' of a man who has died is 'buried in its dissolution, and yet liveth in the compositions of other parts', she means only that he has 'the life of some other creature he is transformed into' and that each of his former particles 'have life, by reason it has motion' (OEP 69). And when she writes that when a rope that has ceased its previous shaking still contains the former shaking motion, Cavendish clarifies that she means simply that 'the ceasing of such a motion is not the ceasing of self-moving matter form all motions' and that the rope's 'natural and inherent power to move is not lessened' (PL 1 5; see also PL 4 4). Of course, Cavendish's temptation to describe things this way betrays discomfort with the notion of the purely potential; as we saw in the last chapter, her attempt to address this can be seen as a central target of the metaphysics of the triumvirate. But ultimately, as we saw there, the only puzzle is the potential for matter to act quickly or slowly, not for it to act in certain specific ways. The specific ways can all be explained by the ways that matter is divided or composed.

Section 5.4 Survival

Some creatures, like some clubs and churches, last longer than others. Cavendish attributes at least some instances of the 'keeping or holding together' of parts to what she calls 'retentive motions' (OEP 55). 'By retentive motions', Cavendish writes,

> I do not only mean such as keep barely the parts of the composed figures together; but, all those that belong to the preservation and continuance of them; under which are comprehended digestive motion, which place and displace parts; attractive motions, which draw nourishment into those parts; expulsive motions, which expel superfluous and hurtful part: and many the like: for, there are numerous sorts of retentive motions, or such as belong to the preservation and continuance of a composed figure, as well as there are of creating or producing motions.
>
> (OEP 162–163)

In the examples here, retentive motions are simply all those complex motions that contribute to the survival of a creature. The processes that Cavendish lists as examples, which include nourishment and excretion, are not very surprising. They suggest that the keeping together of a complex creature is a function of all the many complementary motions of and among its parts. This is affirmed by Cavendish's insistence that since self-motion is equally responsible for composing as it is dividing, the cohesion of a complex creature is not due to a lack of motion. In fact, Cavendish writes, '[t]he truth is, the harder, denser, and firmer bodies are, the stronger are their motions; for it requires more strength to keep and hold parts together, than to dissolve and separate them' (OEP 131).

So it does not look like there is any need, at least at the level of complex creatures, to posit some additional 'glue' to keep, say, my heart and spleen working together. However, some readers of Cavendish have interpreted her claim that there is sympathy between the parts of a creature to imply that sympathy is a kind of additional glue—a fundamental force that is responsible for keeping the parts of an organism together. As we saw above, sympathy is not the cause of the initial agreement of parts to join together, because sympathy results from the fact that the parts are together. But once it is established between the parts, does it contribute to the survival of a creature?

The answer is yes. But sympathy is not a new feature of matter or force between parts, or something over and above the principles already established.

First of all, as with retentive motions, Cavendish often characterizes sympathies as sympathetic *motions*, including them in lists of the particular actions of nature, alongside respiration, digestion, and pressure (OEP 139). And she writes that there is no sympathy or antipathy 'but by Change of Motion' (PPO2 Preface). This makes it sounds like sympathetic motions are pretty much just retentive motions, and indeed Cavendish identifies as least some sympathetical motions with retentive motions, as when she claims that the 'sympathetical agreement of parts' is involved in the preservation of a creature (OEP 245). So we can explain the sticking-together of a creature's parts by these motions, which result from the composite structure of the thing.

That said, we can say a little bit more about why some motions are sympathetic. As we saw in the last chapter, the actions of a composite creature are actions resulting from the fact that it has the composite structure that is does. Part of the concept of sympathy that Cavendish inherited is that it is a kind of attractive force that results from the fact that things are already similar or part of one whole. In evoking the history of this concept, Cavendish makes clear that the continued agreement of parts to stay together is a result of their already being together. We may think of this agreement as a kind of 'compositional inertia': composites tend, all things considered, to remain composed. The role of sympathy in the survival of a composition highlights that existing sameness or connection tends to support further sameness or connection. That does not require that sympathy is some further force generated by the composition or its parts.

Compositional inertia follows simply from Cavendish's conception of composition. For imagine a conception of composition that did not tend at all to continued composition, and would therefore call for some additional glue to hold the parts together. This sounds a lot like the atomist conception of composition, where the parts are intrinsically independent and unconnected with one another and where their cohesion requires explanation. It does not sound like Cavendish's conception of composition, where there are no single parts or parts that do not depend on the other parts.[4]

Just as we should not see Cavendishian sympathy as a mysterious new force that is required to hold things together, neither should we see love, self-love, or affection that way. In earlier work, Cavendish does characterize the continued survival of a creature as love or affection between its parts. (By the *Observations*, Cavendish never appeals to love or affection to describe any non-human phenomena.) But like sympathy, it results from the existing acquaintance or union between parts. Cavendish writes, for example, that 'Societies and Conjunction...cause a perceptive Acquaintance, and an united Love' among the parts (GNP 3 5), that 'Regular Societies beget an united Love, by Regular Agreements' (GNP 9 12), and that 'the Self-moving Parts of a Human Creature, being associated, love one another, and therefore do endeavour to keep their Society from dissolving' (GNP 6 5). Parts love the ones they are with.[5]

This all suggests that sympathy and love between parts are just alternative ways of describing compositional inertia, or the tendency that a composition has to remain together. In that sense, sympathy and love between parts is a cause of a creature's survival but not a fundamental glue.

If parts stay together as a result of being together, why do creatures ever die? There are three main reasons: first, the parts of creatures are themselves complex; second, parts are often involved in multiple compositions; and third, the creatures themselves are a part

---

4   Lascano and Schliesser also point out that sympathy is a function of existing unity. I am not sure whether for them it is something 'over and above' the unity itself. Moreover, they put more weight on the anthropomorphic metaphor, arguing that creaturely compositions like humans are hierarchical and that the parts of creatures strive to do particular kinds of deeds. See also Lascano (2023: 79–81).

5   For defenses of a more robust role for self-love and sympathy, see Boyle (2018: 92–95) and Borscherding (2021).

of a larger composition. The liver, considered only as a part of the body, wants to stick together with the heart and other organs. But the matter that makes up the liver may have other relationships; for example, with oxygen, which has its own external entanglements, resulting in the production of free radicals (I don't know, I am not a biologist). The human being is in turn part of a society, which may send him to war, ultimately undermining the liver's endeavor to remain with the body. We will examine these kinds of creaturely complexity in the next section.

Section 5.5 Composition and complexity

We have explained how a creature comes to be. But have we explained how it comes to be the specific kind of creature that it is? It might seem that we have not. After all, consider a philosophy seminar with 15 students, and imagine that these same 15 students also have a yacht club together.[6] Aren't the seminar and the yacht club distinct societies with the same parts? How can we account for that difference without introducing new facts about what kind of thing they decide to constitute or about how they compose, rather than just about whether they compose?

There are a few ways to respond to this. One is to point out that there are many other facts involved in the students' forming a seminar and in their forming a yacht club than just their agreeing to compose. In the first case, there is a complex seminar scenario that involves their agreement to join, but it also involves 15 desks and some texts, as well as many kinds of compositional motions, like motions in their brains that constitute philosophizing. The next week, a very similar scenario will compose, though not exactly the same. It does not seem particularly important that one thing, a Philosophy Seminar, survives, even less that that thing is constituted only by the agreement of 15 students.

---

6   This example and question was suggested to me by Baron Reed and the students in his seminar on the history of skepticism at Northwestern University. I'm not sure why it was a yacht club of all things but perhaps it is because Northwestern, being on Lake Michigan, has a sailing club. Anyway, I like it.

It is consistent with this to admit that exactly these 15 people do form a composite and that that composite is the very same in the seminar scenario as in the yacht-club scenario: call it the 'these 15 people hanging out' composite. But because this composite is overlapping with many other composites, it results in a very different overall scenario. It may also be that these 15 people do not form a composite. I suspect that for Cavendish we are not very good at limning the compositional structure of the world around us. We will see the grounds and extent of Cavendish's skepticism about our abilities to know about particular creatures in Chapter 8, but here is a glimpse:

> The variation of the corporeal figurative motions blindeth our particular senses, that we cannot perceive them, they being too subtle to be discerned either by art or human perception. The truth is, if we could see the corporeal figurative motions of natural creatures, and the association and division of all their parts, we should soon find out the causes which make them to be such or such particular natural effects; but nature is too wise to be so easily known by her particulars.
>
> (OEP 236)

It is both the subtlety and complexity of natural figures that eludes our senses, as well as the fact that they are constantly in flux:

> There are numerous corporeal figures or figurative motions of one particular creature, which lie one within another. (OEP 226)
>
> There are continual and perpetual generations and productions in nature, as well as there are perpetual dissolutions. (OEP 67)

So what happens if one person leaves the yacht club but remains in the seminar? We need not fear the sudden collapse of the yacht club—or, at least, not the death of our dreams of collective yachting. Holding everything else fixed, 'these 15 people hanging out' remains (they still hang out at the seminar), and the seminar scenario remains. We might say that the yacht club composition is dissolved, but I think I'd rather say that there is dissolution (and hence change) in the yacht club scenario, which is made up of a lot of overlapping compositions. There may not be one precise composition that is the

Yacht Club, just as there may not be one precise composition that is the Philosophy Seminar, as long as there are some people similarly doing their thing on boats.

What begins to emerge is a picture of nature filled with not just nested but overlapping compositions. The Aristotelian idea that substances are what seem like unities to us, like plants and animals, are in fact the most important or fundamental compositions, is wrong. So is the idea that these creatures are distinct substances. In Cavendish's system, there is no reason to think that a human being is A Creature any more than a spleen. On the Aristotelian view, there is, because the spleen depends upon the human being for its function. But for Cavendish, the spleen also depends on the environment for its function, as well as on its own components, and the human being depends upon its environment for its function, as well as on its own components.

This interpretation of creatures makes sense of an ambiguity in Cavendish's treatment of survival. Sometimes, Cavendish writes or implies that in order to count as the same creature, all the very same parts must be composed (e.g. OEP 41; GNP Appendix). This makes a lot of sense given Cavendish's insistence that form cannot be abstracted from matter. In Chapter 3, we said that the compositional structure of something is nothing but some parts, composed. So strictly speaking, the structure of a thing should not be abstracted from the parts.

Other times, however, Cavendish writes things that capture the obvious fact that the creatures of our acquaintance survive the departure of many of their parts. For example, she claims that 'although some parts of a figure do disjoin from each other, and join with others; yet the structure of the Creature may nevertheless continue' (OEP 130; see also GNP 4 8).

The tension between this account of creaturely identity and the one on which all the parts are essential is eased by considering that the creatures of our acquaintance, like animals, do not have to be single composites. They may be societies of societies, which are in turn united with other parts of the creature's environment. We need not identify the one composition whose survival is necessary and sufficient for the survival of the creature. We need not find something to replace the Aristotelian substantial form. If we could isolate a single composite with exactly the same parts, then that composite could not survive the departure of any of those parts. But such an entity is an impossible abstraction. In reality, a composite always has very complex parts and is itself part of multiple wider wholes. Indeed, while Cavendish occasionally talks about the figure of a creature, she more commonly describes one creature as having many figures, which reflects the complexity of all creatures. As we will see, many of the creatures that we think of as each one creature are in fact many, including a person, who 'may have numerous souls, as well as he has numerous parts and particles' and whose parts 'retain life and soul' even when the human being is dissolved' (OEP 91). Cavendish's claims that there is 'no such thing as death in nature' also reaffirm this picture. What is death is just so many motions, and while it does make sense to speak of certain compositions coming into being and going out of being, Cavendish does not seem motivated to decide which comings and goings count as deaths and which do not.[7]

Section 5.6 Alteration

We have considered how Cavendish analyses generation and corruption. What about the third kind of Aristotelian change, alteration? In alteration, a substance has not come to be or ceased to be, rather it has 'come to be so-and-so' or 'ceased to be so-and-so', where 'so-and-so' might be a certain 'quantity or quality or…a relation, time, or place' (Physics i.7). It is easy for an Aristotelian to distinguish between generation and alteration by identifying generation as the reception of a substantial form and alteration as the reception of an accidental form. Cavendish, of course, denies that there are such forms and so cannot distinguish between generation and alteration in that way.

There are two options for Cavendish here, both of which are represented in the Democritean tradition. The first involves making the distinction between generation and alteration in some other way. Aristotle attributes to Democritus and Leucippus the view that generation and corruption are association and division, while alteration is change of 'grouping' and 'position' of parts. Some of what Cavendish writes suggests that she takes this path, for example, when she occasionally contrasts compositional changes with what she calls changes of 'postures'.

---

7 As Georgescu (2023: 706) also puts nicely and in more detail.

Ultimately, however, I think that she takes the second option, which is to deny that there is a very deep metaphysical distinction between generation and corruption on the one hand and alteration on the other. This is arguably the position of Descartes and Boyle, with Boyle writing, for example, that '[g]eneration, alteration and corruption are nothing but the names given to transformations of matter in motion' (Boyle 1666: 35). Similarly, Cavendish claims that 'all the varieties and changes of natural productions proceed only from the various changes of motion' (OEP 9) and, perhaps even more strikingly, that 'any thing may be called new, when it is altered from one figure into another' (PL 3 5).

To deny that the distinction between generation and alteration, for Cavendish, is as fundamental as it is in the Aristotelian system is not to deny that we can make no interesting distinction between more and less generation-like changes. It is just to deny that this distinction is unanalysable in terms of the actions of self-moving matter.

One way that Cavendish sometimes distinguishes between changes in which a creature is created or destroyed and ones in which one is only changed is in terms of what she calls the 'exterior' figure and motions of a creature from its 'interior' figure and motions. While she sometimes gives examples that suggest that interior motions are those that are inside a creature's body rather than on the surface, like a human spleen and liver (e.g. OEP 70), the distinction between interior and exterior is not, ultimately, the distinction between what is inside a body and what is on the surface. We will investigate Cavendish's distinction between interior and exterior figures and motions in more detail in the next chapter, because it turns out to be constitutively tied up with Cavendish's account of perception. For now, we need only appreciate that interior figures and motions are those that play some of the roles of the substantial form. The 'interior, natural, figurative *motions*' of a creature are those that 'cause it to be such or such a part or creature' (OEP 162, see also 52, 70). In other words, they are those that are essential, or at least more essential than others, to the nature of that creature. Cavendish argues, for example, that snow, ice, and hail differ only in their exterior figures, since each can be recovered from the other (OEP 110). Here, she uses the distinction between interior and exterior figure to classify a change as an alteration rather than a generation or corruption.

Given the picture of creatures that we painted in the last section, it would not make sense for there to be absolutely interior or exterior motions or figures, or for one creature to have one essential internal figure or motion. Rather, a creature has a variety of figures and motions, some of which are more essential to its survival—and to its powers to act—than others.

Section 5.7 Creaturely actions

A question, however, remains. Cavendish does seem to posit something like a fundamental distinction between generation and corruption, on the one hand, and alteration, on the other. That is because she distinguishes between two different kinds of agreements among parts. Parts can agree to form a society, which is to say, generate a new creature. Once they form that society, they can agree to perform particular actions. After agreeing to form a church, congregants can have a bake sale; similarly, the parts of an eye can agree to see, or pattern, some particular object.

That Cavendish distinguishes between agreements to compose and agreements to perform particular actions is clear because they have different relationships to perception. While the agreement to compose is a condition of parts perceiving each other, parts cannot agree to act in some way 'without perception or knowledge of each other' (OEP 172); parts that 'are concerned in the same action' cannot perform those actions 'without perception of each other' (OEP 15-16). It is only once congregants join the church that they can work with others to put on the bake sale, and only once the tendons and goo form an eye that they work together to see an object. As Cavendish writes:

> it is evident, how in one and the same organ of the eye, some motions or parts may work to the act of perception, properly so called, which is made by patterning out the figure of an exterior object; and other motions or parts may work to the retention of the eye, and preserving it in its being: others again may work to its shutting and opening; and others to its respiration, that is, venting of superfluous, and receiving of nourishing parts; which motions are properly subservient to the retentive motions.

(OEP 174)

Again, how can we explain this with just compositional facts, rather than being forced to add facts about how societies decide to act?

The answer is that while all the actions of the parts of the eye are ultimately dividings and composings, they are not all dividings and composings *of the eye*. The respiration of the eye may involve some specific parts of the eye dividing and composing with parts of the environment. Why do those parts agree to do that, and how do they know that that is a good thing to do for the eye? Cavendish's claim that the parts agree to act in tandem when they are composed together can be read as the claim that the parts of a creature act as they do as a result of the compositional structure of the creature. By putting self-moving matter into that compositional structure, the fact that the parts compose themselves determines the further action of the creature (alongside what is going on outside of it). When Cavendish writes that there is a 'general agreement of all the parts of a composed figure, in the execution of such actions as belong to it' (OEP 39, 81), she means that by agreeing to join in into a certain composed figure, 'by their Association…all agree in proper actions, as action proper to their Compositions' (GNP 2 1). The motions or actions of a creature are those that are proper to its composition or proper to its figure (PL 2 17, OEP 159) because 'matter is and Works in all Kind of Creatures the Same, yet Different ways, according to their Different Shapes, Figures, and Interior nature' (PPO2 xxxii). Note in the passage about the eye that all its actions are 'subservient to', or depend upon, the retentive motions, because those retentive motions are those that retain the figure.

So there is no mystery to what it means for the parts to decide to perform some action once they are a society. Their actions are dictated by the figure of their society, and the fact that they act is the self-motion of matter acting though that structure. There is certainly no need to attribute wishes or desires to the parts. This is again consistent with Cavendish's core commitment that all the ways that matter is, along with what it does, is due to its structure. She puts it very forcefully in a point about perception, but this applies to any actions:

> those parts that are composed into the figure of an animal, make perceptions proper to that which figures corporeal, interior, nat-ural motions: but, if they be dissolved from the animal figure,

and composed into vegetables, they make such perceptions as are proper for vegetables; and being again dissolved and composed into minerals, they make perceptions proper to minerals, etc. so that no part is tied or bound to one particular kind of perception, no more than it is bound to one particular kind of figure... the perceptions vary according to their objects, and according to the changes and compositions of their own parts.

(OEP 166)

In emphasizing that 'no part is tied or bound to one particular kind of perception,' Cavendish explicitly contrasts the dependence of the creaturely action of perception on its compositional structure with the dependence of it on some feature of matter that is independent of its compositional structure.[8]

Section 5.8 Kinds and sorts

Cavendish observes that while creatures are infinitely various, they tend to cluster into 'kinds and sorts.' These include the familiar genuses like animal, vegetable, and mineral, and their sub-kinds like owls, oaks, and ores. But they also include different sorts of motions, which account, for example, for different kinds of liquids (OEP 95) and different kinds of heats or colds (OEP 115). Cavendish often explains the characteristics, capacities, and behaviors of matter, including creatures, by pointing to their kinds.

While Cavendish often appeals to kinds and sorts in explanations, we should not think of those as fundamental explanations. She does not reify these kinds in the way that Aristotle does. They may be useful to natural philosophical explanation, but they are not indispensable. Cavendish often reminds us that kinds and sorts are overlapping, violable, and superficial—not sharp, fixed, and deep. Not every creature belongs to a species (GNP 3 5). Two members of one species might

---

8 Cavendish often writes that what determines how a creature acts is its knowledge or 'knowledges', which includes both its self-knowledges and its perceptions (OEP 163). This may seem to undermine the claim that actions are determined by structure. But as Chapter 7 will argue, knowledge, in this context, is just a kind of structure.

differ very much and very significantly from one another, while two individuals from distinct species might resemble each other quite a bit. For example, 'although all men have flesh and blood, and are of one particular kind; yet their interior natures and dispositions are so different...that it is a wonder to see two men just alike' (OEP 85); meanwhile, 'man's flesh, and the flesh of some other animals, doth so much resemble, as it can hardly be distinguished' (OEP 85). Cavendish also acknowledges mixed forms, like the mouse-bird and the cat-bird, better known to us as bats and owls:

> There are many several Creatures, which seem to be of a Mix'd Kind, as a Bat seems to be betwixt a Beast and a Bird, having a Body like a Mouse, and Wings like a Bird, and an Owl seems somewhat like a Cat, and hath the Nature of a Cat, to catch Mice.
> (GNP 11 8)

The existence of these mixed kinds is further evidence that species kinds are not deep and inviolable.

An additional way that Cavendish weakens the coherence of species kinds is by denying that reproduction is always specific: 'the generations and productions of insects are so various, as not only the same kind of creature may be produced from several kinds of ways, but the very same creature may produce several kinds' (OEP 68). This is important for understanding how Cavendish thinks about creaturely generation more generally, and about the distinction between the natural and the artificial, which will be the concerns of Section 5.10.

Section 5.9 Life

Cavendish uses the word 'life' in a few different ways. Sometimes she seems to identify it with self-motion, as when she describes motion as 'the life and soul of nature, and of all her parts' (OEP 72). From this perspective, 'there are no parts of nature, how little soever, which are not living and self-moving bodies' (OEP 246). While an 'animal life' is different from 'mineral life' (OEP 246; PL 133–134), they are all equally lives, and Cavendish has little patience with the chauvinism of philosophers who 'think that nothing is animate, or has life in nature, but animals and vegetables' (OEP 16). Even the carcasses of animals, or parts separated from an animal body, have a 'natural life…according to the nature of the figure into which they did change' (OEP 11, see also 72, 224; PL 342).

Sometimes, however, Cavendish seems to have a different reason for holding that all the parts of matter have life: she sometimes groups 'life' in with 'self-knowledge' (OEP 20), attributing it to all matter independently of self-motion (OEP 39) and claiming that even the inanimate degree of matter 'has not an active life' but still as life 'as well as the animate part' (OEP 39, see also 157; GNP 1 7). Here, too, Cavendish argues as a consequence that 'all the parts of nature have life, each according to the propriety of its figure' (OEP 224). In this sense, Cavendish seems to mean by life simply something like 'being', identifying the life of a composed figure, for example, simply with the survival of that figure (OEP 224), and the life of a creature in general with its 'life according to the nature of [its] figure' (OEP 111, see also 224).

In an excellent treatment of Cavendish's conception of life (or, it turns out, the lack thereof), Georgescu (2023) argues that Cavendish is not ambiguous on this point but changes her mind, ultimately settling by the *Observations* to the view that everything is 'alive simply because it exists' (697). Georgescu argues on that basis that 'life' is not a meaningful term in Cavendish's ontology, because it is not possible to say which thing or kind of thing it is, and it does not make a difference. I like this argument a lot, as it reflects Cavendish's resistance to positing new principles to explain natural phenomena and to identifying matter as a particular kind of substance with creaturely qualities. I would add only that Cavendish's ambivalence (or evolution) on the question of the connection between self-motion and life does reflect something significant, which is the centrality of self-motion to Cavendish's natural philosophy. While it is true that Cavendish writes that inanimate matter has a life, as we have seen, we cannot really imagine what that life is like. For all the lives, which is to say existences, that there actually are in nature, a creature's life and its activity are inextricably joined, and these are the only lives that we can understand.[9]

---

9   Similarly, Georgescu's claim that Cavendish is not a vitalist is a corrective to the tendency to imagine that something like a 'vital principle' is at the center of her philosophy, or that she 'problematize[s] life and the living' (2023: 713), or that matter is 'infused' with vital properties (714). If it simply means that Cavendish

Given the further connection that Cavendish makes between the self-moving and the natural, and to the extent that Cavendish identifies living with being made of self-moving matter, we have some reason to think that Cavendish also holds that every part of nature, which is to say every creature, is natural. And yet, unlike the distinction between the living and the nonliving, the distinction between the natural and the artificial seems to play a surprisingly important role in parts of her philosophy. As we shall see, while the distinction is an important one for us humans, the creatures who create artificial objects and give them significance, it is not a deep metaphysical distinction.

Section 5.10 The natural and the artificial

I claimed in the introduction that all compositions are natural creatures, including ships and looking glasses. Cavendish does include ships and looking glasses on lists of creatures, and while she does not often appeal to artifacts as examples of creatures, that can be explained by the fact that she is simply more interested in things that are not man-made rather than by the fact that she doesn't count them as creatures. More importantly, there seems to be no reason, based on the theory of creatures developed in this chapter, that ships and looking glasses should not count. After all, a natural creature is simply a part of nature, which is to say self-moving matter in particular compositions, and that describes ships and looking glasses just as well as it describes plants and animals. Cavendish herself recognizes that artifacts are natural inasmuch as they are parts of nature and are 'Natural Corporeal Figurative Motions' (GNP 13 12). Artifacts, she writes, 'can no more be excluded from Nature, than any ordinary effect or creature of Nature' (OEP 197), having 'life and knowledge [sic]…according to the different proprieties of their Figures' (PL 2 13).

---

holds that all natural matter and all natural creatures are self-moving, that is OK, I guess, and is a potentially useful way of distinguishing Cavendish from many of her contemporaries. As Georgescu points out, Detlefsen (2007) and Wolfe (2023) also raise compelling problems for labeling Cavendish a vitalist. In general, labeling a philosopher with some kind of -ism is often more hurtful than helpful to understanding.

Despite all this, Cavendish often appeals to the distinction between artificial and natural things in ways that very much echo the distinction as it is drawn in Aristotle and among medieval Aristotelians. And this distinction seems to do real argumentative work for her in important contexts, like the right explanation of organic growth and generation, the practice of medicine, and the prospects of creations, alchemical and otherwise. It also has polemical significance, as Cavendish describes artificial things as 'deformed and defective' (OEP 53) and as less good, lasting, useful, and true than natural things (OEP 9, 51, 87, 96, 105–106, 178).

As we will see in Chapter 8, one important application of the distinction is in Cavendish's critiques of other philosophers. The instruments of experimental philosophers deform our experience because they are artificial, and the applied mathematics of the mechanical philosophers are also mere inventions, which do not have the relationship with nature that many mechanical philosophers claimed they have. The syllogistic logic and invented jargon of the Aristotelians 'put [the] brain on the rack' (OEP 45), deforming our natural cognitive relationship with nature and hence misleading us. Alchemists' attempts to generate natural forms are futile, and Cavendish argues that art can at best generate superficial imitations of natural things, acting as 'Nature's Emulating Ape' (OEP 59). Cavendish borrows this phrase from Van Helmont, who holds that though it is difficult, chymistry does sometimes succeed at becoming 'the Misstriss of nature' (1662: 202). Cavendish denies that art can ever play that role (PL 362).

These critiques mirror an influential attack on 12th-century alchemists by Avicenna, an important Aristotelian. Targeting their pretensions to the transmutation of metallic species, Avicenna argued that human beings neither have the power nor the knowledge to create natural forms like gold. Similarly, in response to the question, 'Whether there can be an artificial Life, or a Life made by Art?', Cavendish answers:

> Life is natural, and not artificial; and thus the several parts of a watch may have sense and reason according to the nature of their natural figure, which is steel, but not as they have an artificial shape, for Art cannot put Life into the watch, Life being onely natural, not artificial.

(PL 1 45)

Cavendish's acknowledgment that the steel, but not the watch itself, is natural reflects the position of Aristotelians like Aquinas: while artifacts may be natural in virtue of their matter, they are not natural in virtue of their form. But it is unclear, given Cavendish's metaphysics, why any shape should be less natural than any other.

The examples that Cavendish gives of artifacts are things that human beings produce, including concrete objects like paintings, microscopes, and watches but also abstract constructs like logic, mathematics, and language. But it is neither necessary nor sufficient for something to count as an artifact that it is produced by human beings. Humans produce babies, which are natural, and birds produce nests, which plausibly count as artifacts. Cavendish tries a number of ways of drawing the distinction between the natural and the artificial, all of which have Aristotelian roots.

One difference between a baby and a microscope is that the former and not the latter is born, and indeed Aristotelians commonly took it to be a mark of natural beings as opposed to artifacts that they are not just produced but reproduced. Cavendish may have this in mind when she writes that natural productions like babies 'are produced from the Producer's own Parts' while artifacts are 'produced by composing, or joyning, or mixing several Forrein Parts' (GNP 13 12). But is this really the relevant difference between a baby and, say, a model car? Gross as it would be, I could build a model car out of my own body parts.[10]

Perhaps more essential to reproduction, and to hence to naturalness, is that the production is relevantly like the producer. Cavendish writes that an animal, vegetable, or mineral is produced by a 'constant action' of nature, operating 'after one and the same manner or way' to produce similar creatures: human beings produce human beings and dandelions produce dandelions. But as we saw in Section 5.8, Cavendish does not think that these categories are hard, fast, and deep. And she explicitly allows that 'there are productions of and from creatures of quite different kinds; as for example, that

---

10 Lascano (2023: 78–79) offers reasons to think that this is important to animal generation, for Cavendish, and that this represents a distinct kind of causation from occasional causation.

vegetables can and do breed animals, and animals, minerals and vegetables, and so forth' (OEP 66–67), such as 'Maggots out of Cheese, other Worms out of Roots, Fruits, and the like' (GNP 3 5). Not every creature comes in a species (GNP 3 5), and Cavendish explains the similarity that there is between a creature and its offspring as a result of the nature of the existing composition rather than participation in a common species (GNP 3 5). Finally, Cavendish sometimes elides the distinction between reproduction and other kinds of production. For example, to Van Helmont's claim that 'dead things do want roots whereby they may produce,' Cavendish replies that 'dead things, in my opinion, are the most active producers, at least they produce more numerously and variously then those we name living things; for example, a dead Horse will produce more several Animals, besides other Creatures, then a living Horse can do' (PL 3 27).

Cavendish sometimes suggests that natural forms are more permanent than artificial ones: unlike artificial kinds, natural kinds 'are and have been eternally in Nature' (OEP 203). But *every* form has been eternally in nature, including those of artifacts like houses (PL 1 17, 21; OEP 241). 'I do not understand,' Cavendish writes, 'how man, or any other creature, should have the power of making or introducing new forms, if those forms were not already in nature' (OEP 212). Of chemists' pretentions to produce new forms, Cavendish writes that the forms 'are not new in nature; for all that is material, has been existent in nature from all eternity; so that the combination of parts cannot produce anything that is not already in nature' (OEP 236–237). She goes on to invite chemists to

> consider their own particular persons, as, whether they were generated anew, or had been in nature before they were got of their parents; if they had not been pre-existent in nature, they would not be natural, but supernatural creatures, because they would not subsist of the same matter as other creatures do.
>
> (OEP 237)

Here, far from distinguishing between a baby and an artifact, Cavendish compares the production of a chemist by his parents to the chemist's production of an allegedly new form. And she goes on to write, of claims by some chemists to produce glass out of vegetables, that the 'glass was as much pre-existent in the matter of those vegetable, and the fire, and in the power of their corporeal figurative motions, otherwise it would never have been produced' (OEP 238). That all these forms preexist, of course, just means that they are 'in the power of corporeal, figurative self-motion' (OEP 238).

In some of Cavendish's other claims about the failures of art, it is harder to tell whether it is specific to art or concerns the operation of any finite creature. For example, she claims that art can put parts together but 'cannot make those parts move or work, so as to alter their proper figures, or interior natures, or to be the cause of changing and altering their own, or other parts, any otherwise than they are by their natures' (OEP 84). She also writes that while a man can build a house, he cannot produce the materials, so while artists may 'dissolve and compose several parts several ways, but yet they cannot make the matter of those parts' (OEP 241). Let us take seriously for the moment that art might be worse than other kinds of production. Why might that be?

We have yet to consider the most obvious difference between the ways that a baby and a microscope are produced: a microscope is produced by an intentional action, guided by cognitive states, while a baby is not. According to Aristotle, while the forms of natural things come from nature, the forms of artifacts come from the 'wise contrivance' of rational minds. Cavendish doesn't put things this way, but the examples of artifacts that she chooses—specifically, the ones that come in for criticism—are for the most part the products of human intentional action.

Now, for Cavendish, human intentional action is just so much activity of matter. A human being builds a house using, in part, her sense organs and brain, while she produces a baby in her womb. Cavendish vividly illustrates this by playing on the polysemy of the word 'conception.' The brain's productions are not fundamentally different from those of the womb nor even the gut; wise contrivance is just one a way of acting on the world alongside reproduction, digestion, photosynthesis, gravitation, or impact. There is no reason that the difference between intentional action and non-intentional action should be any deeper than between any two kinds of non-intentional actions.

Jonathan Shaheen has proposed that art's inability to work on the matter of artifacts is in fact a difference in kind, arguing that for Cavendish, nature and not human beings can produce sympathy or love between parts. So while the parts of natural things work together toward the survival of the creature, the parts of artifacts, 'lacking any serious longer term commitment to their union…are just playing around' (Shaheen 2022: 12). Since human beings can put stuff together and take it apart, this means that 'the step from division to dissolution, like the step from composition to production, is small, but extant' (Shaheen 2022: 8).

But even if art is particularly bad at altering the 'interior natures' (OEP 84) of things, there is no need to attribute that lack of control to our inability to manufacture special sympathy stuff. Cavendish has told us that human sense perception can only access the exterior figures of creatures. Along with rational perception, which does not do much better than sense perception with respect to interior figures, sense perception is the only source of our knowledge of external bodies. So it makes perfect sense that the kinds of human actions that require cognition (unlike, say, respiring or growing a baby) can only affect the exterior figures of things. As for the claim that artifacts may last less long than other things, this can be explained by the lack of our intentional control over matter. And Cavendish tells us explicitly that the reason that some creatures last longer than others is their figures and the strength of their figure and motions, and not some special glue that must be added to the matter: 'some sorts of Compositions are stronger than others; not through the degrees of innate Strength…but, through the manner and form of their Compositions, or Productions' (GNP 1 15, see also 11 13).

So Cavendish can agree with Avicenna that the natures of most creatures are determined at a level too deep for human beings to perceive, know, or manipulate, without holding that this means that there are metaphysically bulletproof natural forms, or a fundamental force of holding-together like sympathy. We may never build a supercollider powerful enough to limn the fundamental structure of the physical world, but that does not mean that that structure is in principle different from more accessible kinds of structure. Since Cavendish thinks that nature is infinitely complex, it would be pretty surprising if any human knife could carve nature at its joints.

This explains the limits of art. But it doesn't explain why Cavendish seems to think that art is bad. The answer is that she is not critical of artifacts but of how we regard them. This is clear from the fact that Cavendish has no problem with houses. What she has a problem with are microscopes and math. As we will see in Chapter 8, that is not because of some intrinsic problem with microscopes and math but with the idea that they give us more power over nature, and objective insight into it, as if we were divine. Similarly, chemists, in trying to create natural forms, 'strive to imitate nature' (OEP 240), which they cannot do. Cavendish tellingly compares the 'monstrous' productions of chemists that result from this hubris with a 'painter, who drew a rose instead of a lion' (OEP 240). There is nothing wrong with a rose—it is, unquestionably, an example of a natural thing. But it is a failure as an emulation of a rose, just as chemists' productions are failures as emulations of nature. And it does not have the powers that we think it has. Good luck trying to sic a rose on a charging ibyx.[11]

Section 5.11 Anti-anthropocentrism and anti-anthropomorphism

Not only do people think that art is much more powerful than it is, but they also have a lamentable tendency to imagine that all other production happens the way that art does. But, Cavendish tells us, we should not imagine

> that as a builder erects a house according to his conception in the brain, the same happens in all other natural productions or generations…if all Animals should be produced by meer fancies, [then] a Man and a Woman should beget by fancying themselves together in copulation.
>
> (PL 4.2)

Here, Cavendish tells us precisely what the difference is between the literal and metaphorical builder. While a human builder erects a house 'according to a conception in the brain,' rational and sensitive

---

11 For a detailed and extremely informative study of Cavendish's distinction between nature and art, and especially her claim that artifacts are 'hermaphroditical mixtures', see James (2018).

matter does not. This should be a further warning against anthropo-morphizing nature, creatures, and matter, and particularly against imagining that natural actions must all involve anything like inten-tional action.

The implication of the last few chapters, and specifically Cavendish's account of creatures, is that human beings are not special. That does not mean that we do not have unique features, although we share many of them with other animals. Whether a characteristic is unique just to humans or to animals more generally, however, it in no way makes us better than other creatures. It is hard to overstate how cen-tral this is to Cavendish's philosophy and how wide-ranging are its implications. We will see more of those implications in the next three chapters, when we explore Cavendish's philosophy of mind and her epistemology.

Many readers take Cavendish's anti-anthropocentrism to motivate one or another kind of anthropomorphism. The idea is that, since we are not above other creatures, we should attribute to other creatures some of the features that we jealously guard for ourselves. Cavendish does indeed argue like this often. She argues that it is chauvinistic to imagine that only we and other living things are self-moving and capable of free action, that only we and other animals have perception and knowledge, and that only we worship and are valued by God. This leads to the view, articulated by Detlefsen and many others, that Cavendish is an 'anthropomorphic naturalist' (Detlefsen 2007: 181).

I do not think this is the best way to read Cavendish. The argument for this will take most of the rest of the book, and Chapters 6 and 7 in particular will explain how Cavendish understands perception and knowledge, and how human sense perception and cognition relate to other kinds of perception and knowledge. But as a general principle, Cavendish sees anthropomorphic and anthropocentric thinking as mutually reinforcing. We think we are very important, and so we imagine that other things must function like we do; when they do not, we conclude that their differences are defects. On the other hand, there is a great deal that we share in common with other creatures: as this chapter describes, we are all self-moving composites of material parts, and we are all in turn parts of our wider environments and ultimately of nature. The challenge is to determine where the line is between what we correctly understand to be the features we share with other creatures and what we illegitimately project onto them. Where does our continuity with other creatures end and our conceited prerogative begin?

Answering these questions is made all the more complicated by the fact that Cavendish also holds that it is impossible for us, in some sense, to avoid thinking anthropomorphically. That is because we are, after all, human beings, and we can only think as human beings. This is a reason to treat with care what look like anthropomorphic descriptions of other creatures. If we are sometimes forced to describe other creatures in anthropomorphic ways, we may at least be able to remain aware of their limits.

Section 5.12 Conclusion

We have now seen how Cavendish explains the vast variety of natural creatures, and their changes and behaviors, from her parsimonious principles. She does so without adding any more principles to the fundamental level, such as life, sympathies, forms, or natural kinds. It helps that Cavendish holds that matter is self-moving and that, as a result of the nature of compositional structure, the parts of nature are responsive to each other. It is fine to think of her, as she is often thought of, as a vitalist or an organicist, if that means that she holds that all matter is self-moving, that all creatures are organic in the sense of being made of self-moving matter, having parts that depend upon each other, and being parts of many environments.

In principle, we have explained all the characteristics and actions of human beings alongside all other creatures. Of course, we would like to know how Cavendish explains specifically mental phenomena and what implications her account of the mind has for epistemology. As we are about to see, just as she explains living creatures without adding a vital principle, she explains the mind without adding mental principles. The mind, like everything else, is 'matter moved', and thoughts are 'nothing else but corporeal motions' (OEP 53).

Further reading

Borscherding, Julia. 2021. '"I Wish My Speech Were like a Loadstone": Cavendish on Love and Self-Love.' *Proceedings of the Aristotelian Society* 121(23): 381–409.

Chao, Tien-yi. 2012. '"Between Nature and Art"—The Alchemical Underpinnings of Margaret Cavendish's Observations upon Experimental Philosophy and The Blazing World.' *EurAmerica* 42(1): 45–82.

Clucas, Stephen. 2011. 'Margaret Cavendish's Materialist Critique of Van Helmontian Chymistry.' *Ambix* 58(1): 1–12.

Georgescu, Laura. 2023. 'Cavendish on Life.' *Notes and Records of the Royal Society of London* 77: 697–715.

James, Susan. 2018. '"Hermaphroditical Mixtures": Margaret Cavendish on Nature and Art.' In *Early Modern Women on Metaphysics*, edited by E. Thomas. Cambridge: Cambridge University Press.

Schliesser, Eric, and Marcy Lascano. 2022. 'Margaret Cavendish on Human Beings.' Pp. 168–195 in *Human Beings*, edited by K. Hübner. Oxford: Oxford University Press.

Shaheen, Jonathan L. 2022. 'A Vitalist Shoal in the Mechanist Tide: Art, Nature, and 17th-Century Science.' *Philosophies* 7(5): 111.

Wolfe, Charles T. 2023. 'The Life of Matter: Early Modern Vital Matter Theories.' *Notes and Records the Royal Society Journal of the History of Science* 77(4): 673–675.

Six
Perception

> Just like as in a nest of boxes round
> Degrees of sizes in each box are found,
> So in this world, may many worlds more be,
> Thinner and less, and less still by degree.
> Although they are not subject to our sense,
> A world may be no bigger than twopence.
> Nature is curious, and such works may shape
> Which our dull senses easily escape.
> (P&F Of Many Worlds in This World)

Cavendish holds that all creatures perceive and know, because they must for nature to be orderly. It will take the next two chapters, and Chapter 9, to understand what she means by this: we must understand what perception is, what knowledge is, and what order is. We begin in this chapter with perception.

Cavendish often talks of 'perception and knowledge', which makes it sound like these are two different things. But in fact, perception is a species of knowledge: it is 'exterior knowledge', that is, knowledge of 'exterior parts and actions'. It would be nice to begin by explaining the genus before the species. But it is difficult to understand and to motivate the surprising meaning of knowledge, for Cavendish, without first understanding the surprising meaning of perception.

What will be surprising is that by 'perception' and 'knowledge' Cavendish does not mean something essentially cognitive or mental. Human beings and other animals with sense organs and brains have among their particular modes of perceiving and knowing states and

DOI: 10.4324/9781003107255-7

processes that we would call cognitive or mental, but these represent an infinitesimally tiny fraction of perceptions and knowledges in general.

Similarly, it would be nice to begin by explaining perception in general before the particular case of animal sense perception. But understanding the specific case will help us to understand the general case, and it will help us to avoid overgeneralizing from animal sense perception to other kinds of perception. So we begin by looking at how Cavendish explains animal sense perception, and how her account aims to explain its unique features while still maintaining its continuity with nonmental perceptions.

Section 6.1   Patterning and the naturalistic challenge

Like all other creatures, animals perceive in a variety of ways. Among those ways are the 'perceptions of its exterior senses, as Seeing, Hearing, Tasting, Touching, Smelling' (OEP 15). These five kinds of perception are 'properly made by way of patterning and imitation, by the innate, figurative motions of those Animal Creatures' (OEP 15). Patterning is simply a kind of corporeal figurative (self-) motion, which Cavendish sometimes calls 'figuring' in this context; specifically, it is figuring that in some manner 'imitates…the figure, motion, or action' of an external object (OEP 150, 169, 173).

This patterning happens in 'the exterior parts, Man names the *Sensitive Organs*' (GNP 5 9). In vision, for example, the matter of the eye patterns out the figure, motion, or action of something outside the seeing animal's body. Each sense organ has 'many particular knowledges or perceptions as there are objects presented to them' (OEP 46).

'Now', Cavendish writes, 'if there be such variety of several knowledges, not only in one creature, but in one sort of sense…what may there be in all the parts of nature?' (OEP 46). It turns out that there are many other animal perceptions besides sense perceptions, for there are 'not only the five organs in an animal, but every part and particle of his body, that has a peculiar knowledge and perception' (OEP 140). In this category, Cavendish includes processes like digestion and respiration. But it is not only animals that perceive, nor even just animals and plants, but also objects like stones, which perceive men as much as men perceive them (even if differently; OEP 141, 171). Perception is an action of self-moving matter, and every part of a body has knowledge and perception simply 'because it consists of self-moving matter' (OEP 140). Like any other creaturely action, a creature has the kinds of perceptions that it does 'according to the nature and property of such a kind or sort of Composition' (GNP 1 9, see also 5 20 and OEP 167).

We will see in the next section what all the kinds of perception have in common. What they do not have in common is patterning. One other kind of animal perception, rational perception, involves patterning external objects (OEP 33,55), and we will discuss this further in Section 6.8. But other than that, Cavendish writes,

> There are as many different sorts of perceptions, as there are of motions...and though, in a composed figure or Creature, some motions may work to the patterning out of exterior objects, yet all the rest may not do so, and be nevertheless, perceptive: For, as a man, or any other animal creature, is not altogether composed of eyes, ears, noses, or the like sensitive organs: so, not all perceptive motions are imitating or patterning...
>
> (OEP 173, see also 15)

While Cavendish sometimes writes only that we don't know whether other perceptions are patterings, she means that we have no reason at all to attribute this kind of perceiving to other things, not that we should be 50/50 on the question. This is consistent with Cavendish's repeated exhortations that we are not to assume that other kinds of perception are like animal sense modalities, including, as we will see, several places where she specifically seems to warn against overgeneralizing patterning. It is also consistent with the fact that Cavendish associates patterning perceptions with specific parts of animal bodies.

Cavendish describes the patterns that are made by the sense organs as copies, pictures, prints, and imitations, all of which suggest some kind of resemblance or isomorphism between the object perceived and an internal state of the perceiver. So it is quite plausible to suppose that with her theory of patterning, Cavendish is trying to capture the fact that one important way that animals interact with the world around them is by mapping different parts or aspects of it in their bodies. Moreover, these patterns can go on to be re-patterned in other parts of the body, including the brain, and they can be made more 'general' with the help of those parts.

So it is natural to interpret patterns as something like representational or semantic states: states of a perceiver's body that resemble or otherwise correspond to the external world, that can be evaluated as true or false, and that can play a role in reasoning. Given that Cavendish holds that everything we know of the other parts of nature is through perception (e.g. OEP 41), patterning could provide her with a solid and fertile foundation for an epistemology of finite creatures. I will call this the correspondence view of patterning, according to which patterns are supposed to ground the fact that we can have perceptual knowledge of finite creatures outside of us.

However, the correspondence view of patterning has some problems. For one thing, while patterning is a specific kind of perception, it is still a perception. And when we come to understand what perceptions in general are, it becomes difficult to see how a perception can involve a straightforward replication of an external form. As we will see, Cavendish emphasizes the partial and relational nature of perception; she associates the idea that we have objective insight into the natures of things with a picture of ourselves as little divinities, rather than finite parts of nature. And she takes a quite skeptical stance regarding what we can know about other parts of nature by sense experience.

So a central challenge for Cavendish's view of perception is how it can describe animal sense and rational perception as just one among many kinds of perception, while accounting for the seemingly quite special features of that kind of perception. This is far from a problem unique to Cavendish; it is a version of the perennial, and perennially difficult, question of how to naturalize the philosophy of mind and epistemology. We will do our best to resolve these tensions, but the tensions that remain are evidence, I think, of how seriously Cavendish takes this challenge.

Section 6.2 Matter's perceptiveness

As we know, perception is exterior knowledge. That tells us, at least, that a creature's perceptions somehow concern external creatures. But we don't know yet what knowledge is, and Cavendish does not define it.

It would be easy to assume that knowledge always involves a creature's having something like a belief state and that perception always involves one creature's having something (even remotely like) a belief state about the other. This is how many readers interpret it, and they explain Cavendish's claim that perception is necessary for order as the claim that creatures must internally represent information about each other to know how to act.

But as we saw in the last section, if Cavendish's account of patterning is indeed an attempt to capture something like internal representational or informational states, then she denies this to creatures other than animals. The next chapter will argue that knowledge in general is not cognitive or mental and does not involve anything like representational or semantic states, and it will defend the positive claim that a creature's knowledge is simply what allows it to act in the ways that it does. A creature's self-knowledge are the internal conditions of its actions, and its perceptions are the conditions of its actions that involve external parts. And these are all just so many material compositions and motions. Like Cavendish, many of us would be happy to describe the pancreas as knowing how to produce insulin; like us, Cavendish does not mean that it does so by having anything like mental states about the nature of insulin or about anything else.

Cavendish's reason for attributing knowledge and perception to all creatures is that nature is orderly. Focusing on perception, Cavendish argues that it is probable that creatures have an 'exterior perception of other figures or parts, and their actions; by reason there is a perpetual commerce and intercourse between parts and parts' (OEP 140). To say that perception is necessary to explain the 'perpetual commerce and intercourse between parts and parts' is, minimally, to say that perception is necessary for parts to be responsive to each other. There is no reason to assume that the only thing that could serve this purpose is something akin to the sense perceptual states of animals. Most philosophers, and people, think that there are interactions between bodies without bodies having sense perceptual knowledge of each other.[1]

---

1   I take Michaelian to be making a similar point when he writes, 'To the extent that the activity of a thing involves other things, then, it is perceptive: perception

So what must perception be for it to serve this purpose? Well, it must be something that relates one thing to another and allows it to act responsively to it. We already saw, in Section 3.9, that Cavendish grounds relations in compositional facts. Two distinct parts are related just by being composed into one composite. As we will see throughout this chapter and the next, perception and knowledge are inextricably linked to parthood and composition. 'As a union or combination of parts makes knowledge,' Cavendish writes, 'so a division or separation of parts, makes ignorance' (OEP 20). But to be two parts of one composition is precisely to be both united and separated, and so to be both ignorant of one another and knowing.

This is exactly how Cavendish characterizes perception. Perception is the result of the fact that two parts have an ignorance between them because they are distinct parts (they are 'sensible of their division' (OEP 139)), but they also share knowledge between them because they are composed. The essence of perception is this simultaneous knowledge and ignorance that results from the fact that two parts are both united and distinct. 'All knowledge of exterior parts, comes by perception', Cavendish writes, and 'as there is an ignorance between parts, so there is also an acquaintance (especially in the parts of one composed creature' (OEP 38–39).

When we consider knowledge and ignorance this way, we see that perceptual knowledge should be thought of like an acquaintance between parts, which parts have as a result of their composition. It should not be thought of as an internal state of one thing that represents another thing. As Georgescu (2021:630) puts it, perception is 'a relation of knowledge between parts; it is not strictly what one part knows about other parts.' Just as for us to be friends is not for me to know a list of facts about you, for one part to perceive another is not for it to know a list of facts about the other. It is for the parts to be acquainted while still being distinct. On this model of knowledge, to know a thing perfectly would be to be only united with, and not in any sense divided from, that thing: it would

---

is a precondition of orderly action. But an activity can be perceptive in this sense without being the activity of perception (of patterning out)' (2009: 41). I don't think that all 'activities of perception' are patternings-out, though.

be to become that thing. Georgescu, again: ignorance is a 'difference maker in perceptive knowledge: without it, no particular knowledge could be picked out as being the knowledge about that particular rather than about any other particular' (2021: 629). Perception is inherently perspectival and asymmetrical: it is always knowledge of one thing by another. This is because self-knowledge is ultimately the ground of perception, so that a part first knows itself and then perceives another as a result of their composition.

Perception (and knowledge more generally, as we will see) is a metaphysical phenomenon first and what we would think of as an epistemological one only after. It is a way of describing the relationships that the parts of matter have in virtue of being distinct parts that are composed. This is reflected in the fact that Cavendish sometimes characterizes perception with no reference to knowledge at all; for example, as an 'exterior action' which is 'occasioned by an object that is without the perceiving parts' (OEP 171).

Section 6.3   Creaturely perception in general

The fact that perception involves knowledge and ignorance and is perspectival is fundamental to it. The directionality of perception is due to perception's fundamental nature. But like other actions of matter, Cavendish explains the way that this tendency manifests, in complex creatures, in terms of that creature's figure and motions: 'No part of nature can have an absolute knowledge, yet neither it is absolutely ignorant; but it has a particular knowledge, and particular perceptions, according to the nature of its own innate and interior figure' (OEP 143).

In creatures, Cavendish explains the difference between one creature's perception and another's by the fact that a perceiver perceives with her interior parts and perceives exterior parts. That is why my perceptions of my cat are mine and are different from my cat's: because she perceives my exterior parts with her interior parts, and vice versa.[2]

When Cavendish claims that all creatures are perceptive, then, she means that all creatures, being made up of parts as well as being

---

2   I take Lascano (2023: 115–116) to make a similar point.

parts of nature themselves, act in complex ways that reflect their internal structures but also are sensitive to the world around them. That is why there is an 'intercourse and commerce' between all creatures. And Cavendish makes clear that given the dependence of perceptions on a creature's structure, she is in no way committed to saying that this means that all creatures perceive in anything like the sense that animals do. Just because a stone does not feel pain or withdraw itself from a cart wheel, Cavendish writes, does not mean that the stone does not perceive the cart wheel according to its structure and that the stone does not respond accordingly to its interior structure—by, say, supporting the cart (OEP 222; see also PL).

Cavendish also suggests a bit more directly that natural perception in general does not involve anything like internalizing a representation of an external form, the way that we might imagine animal sense perception does. She asks:

> Q. 14 How is it possible that any perception of an outward object, can be made by patterning, since pattering doth follow perception? For, how can anyone pattern out that which he has no perception of?
>
> (OEP 178)

The thought here is that perception is supposed to be responsible for the orderly 'intercourse and commerce' between creatures. But successfully patterning an external thing requires orderly intercourse and commerce. So the parts of the eye must perceive to perceive, since they have to be sensitive to the external world to pattern it. Here is Cavendish's reply:

> I answer: Natural actions are not like artificial; for art is but gross and dull in comparison to nature: and, although I allege the comparison of a painter, yet it is but to make my meaning more intelligible to weaker capacities: for, though a painter must see or know first what he intends to draw or copy out; yet the natural perception of exterior objects is not altogether after the same manner; but, in those perceptions which are made by patterning, the action of patterning, and the perception, are one and the same.
>
> (OEP 178)

Cavendish warns us not to be misled by anthropomorphic analogy into thinking that, like a painter, an eye must gain some information about the pattern it makes before making it. In visual perception, perception just *is* the making of the pattern. Not all kinds of perception involve internalizing information about the external world the way that a painter does.[3]

Further evidence for a non-mental reading of creaturely perception in general is provided by the fact that Francis Bacon, an important influence on Cavendish, uses the term in a similar way and also holds that it is ubiquitous. Bacon argues that

> it is certain that all bodies whatsoever, thought they have no sense, yet they have perception…And sometimes this Perception, in some Kinde of Bodies, is far more Subtle than the Sense…a Weather-Glass, will find the least difference of the Weather, in Heat, or Cold, when Men find it not.
>
> (Bacon 1627: 171)

Perception is a kind of sensitivity or reactivity of one body to another, which is especially apt to explain action at a distance, as when a lodestone attracts iron or when wool suspended above water becomes moist. Despite Bacon's agential language—and despite the fact that, as Dana Jalobeanu points out, he sometimes uses the word 'sense' in these contexts in place of 'perception'[4]—Bacon does not think that perceiving bodies are sentient.

As Jalobeanu observes, 'Bacon does not give a natural philosophical definition of perception; and he is silent when it comes to its mechanisms of operation' (2021:614). While Cavendish does not exactly specify a mechanism of perception (except in the case of patterning), she does

---

3 Note that this includes sight! Cavendish warns us not to think even of human sense perceptions on the model of how a complex human creature uses sense perceptions. In making this point, Cavendish is warning against making what is sometimes called the homuncular fallacy. See note 11 in Section 6.6, which returns to this point.

4 '…as, for example, when explained that air senses the variations in heat, or the weather-glass is sensible to the modifications of the surrounding air with respect to heat etc.' (Jalobeanu 2021: 614).

tell us more about the grounds of its operation than does Bacon. Perception happens in a great variety of ways, but we can say more to characterise perception in general. For Cavendish, it involves the basic compositional structure of matter.

Section 6.4 Animal sense perception as creaturely perception

In many ways, the nature of sense perception reflects the nature of perception in general. Sight, hearing, and so on are actions of a creature, in a direct relationship with an external object (e.g. GNP 1 9, 5 11). The object of a sense perception is an external material object that exists and is in some sense present to a perceiver (OEP 77, 171). Cavendish's alternative definition of perception in the *Grounds* is that it is 'a sort of Knowledg, that hath reference to Objects; that is, Some Parts to know other Parts' (GNP 1 9). She consistently uses 'object' to mean 'object of perception' rather than 'thing', reflecting the usage of the term at the time to mean something presented to perception. But this should not cause us to go back to thinking that perceptions are all like sense perceptions, because objects must be something like intentional objects. Cavendish identifies air, for example, as the proper object of respiration just as colour is the proper object of sight (GNP 13 14).

So a hallucination is not a sense perception; rather, a visual hallucination, for example, is merely a seeming-to-see (GNP 9 11, 1 9; OEP 190). It is not a seeing, and it does not have an object.[5] Cavendish explains hallucinations as motions in the eye that are similar to motions made when the animal actually perceives an object so that they can play a similar role to actual perceivings by occasioning

---

5 Objection: a seeming-to-see is a perceptive process, or a process that involves perceptions, just like a genuine sense perception of an object. So it must have an object. Two part response: the seeming-to-see is a perception only inasmuch as it is acting in response to external objects. It is, because every part is always connected to external objects. So the seeming-to-see does have some external influences, which is to say objects. But most of the 'perceptiveness' of the process is internal to the process and to the body. So it is not in one relationship with one external object as a sense perception is. And it is not a patterning.

similar further motions, as when a fevered and hallucinating man acts as if what he seems to see is real (OEP 189).

Cavendish tells us that a particular sense perception, like visual perception, happens entirely in the relevant sense organ, like the eye. There is no need for what happens in a man's eye to be passed along to the brain or otherwise processed for seeing to occur, although perceptions do usually occasion other things to happen in the man's brain and the rest of his body (OEP 151, 154, 175). This does not, however, mean that to say that an animal sees something is synonymous with saying that an eye patterns something. If we could manage to force an eye to pattern something while it was detached from the rest of the body, it would not count as a seeing. This is reflected by Cavendish's description of sense perception as a kind of animal perception, since what makes it an animal perception can only be that it is happening in the context of a whole animal. And it is reaffirmed by the fact that Cavendish holds that there are other kinds of patterning that are not animal perceptions. Echoes, reflections, and pictures are patterns, 'made by the self-moving matter, by way of patterning and copying out'. But that does not mean that reflecting glass or echoing walls have anything like an animal's perception of a reflected object or sound. 'I cannot guess what their perceptions are,' Cavendish writes, 'onely this I may say, that the air hath an elemental, and the glass a mineral, but not an animal perception' (PL 1 24).

These are perceptions and perceptive motions in that they involve activities that relate a thing to others, as would be the perceptions of the detached eye, but they are not animal perceptions and in that sense are very unlike visual perception. So while Cavendish is very clear that 'the action of patterning, and the perception, are one and the same' (OEP 178), that does not mean that the mere fact that a pattern of an external thing is contained in a part of our body is identical with the fact that we visually perceive something. It is, rather, the fact that part of the body responds to an external thing in a certain way in the context of the whole body.

This is further suggested by how insistent Cavendish is upon the dependence of a perception on the interior nature of the perceiver, as opposed to on the exterior nature of the object.

> [A] man, a tree, and a stone, may all have perceptions of one object, but yet their perceptions are not alike: for, the tree has

not an animal or mineral, but a vegetative perception; and so has the man, not a vegetative or mineral, but an animal perception; and the stone, not an animal or a vegetative, but a mineral perception; each according to the interior nature of its own figure.

(OEP 167, see also 141)

Almost any perceptual theorist will admit that perceptions depend in some way upon the nature of the perceiver. But there are reasons to think that this fact is much more important for Cavendish and that it has implications for how we think about patterns.

Consider, to begin, Cavendish's emphasis on the ignorance that every creature has of the perceptions of other creatures. A man 'only knows what he feels, or sees, or hears, or smells, or tasteth, but knows not what sense or perception' other animals or plants or stones have, 'nay, he is so far from that, that even one part of his body doth not know the sense and perception of another part of his body' (OEP 142). Similarly, 'the eye doth not know what the ear knows, nor the ear what the nose knows'—not because they have different objects, but 'because they are composed differently' (OEP 185). So we should not think of patterns as something that can be easily abstracted from their specific perceptual context. This is true even in very similar systems, like the eyes of two different humans (GNP 6 9).

Similarly, Cavendish acknowledges that our senses afford us perceptions of different 'proprieties or attributes of one body' (OEP 193): 'Sight may pattern out the figure and light of a candle; touch may pattern out its weight, hardness or smoothness; the nose may pattern out its smell; the ears may pattern out its sparkling noise, etc.' (OEP 177). But she takes our perception of diverse qualities to be evidence of diversity in and of perceivers more than of diversity in the object. That diversity proves

> that perception is an effect of knowledge in the sentient, and not in the external object; or else there would be but one knowledge in all parts, and not several knowledges in several parts; whereof sense and reason inform us otherwise, viz. that particular figures have a variety of knowledges, according to the difference and variety of their corporeal figurative motions.
>
> (OEP 177)

And similarity between perceptual experiences is evidence of similarity between perceptual capacities at least as much as it is evidence of similarity of perceptual objects:

> even one and the same attribute or propriety of a body may be patterned out by several senses; for example, magnitude or shape of body may be patterned out both by sight and touch, which proves, that there is a near affinity or alliance betwixt the several senses; and that touch is, as it were a general sense, which may imitate some other sensitive perceptions.
>
> (OEP 177)

So in cases where perceptual modalities are not totally ignorant of one another's perceptions, for example, when a blind man can feel a colour, that is because of similarities in those modalities rather than in the objects.

Cavendish also uses the fact that one object may be perceived in many ways to argue that objects do not cause our perception of them: 'Neither is any perception made by exterior objects, but by interior, corporeal, figurative motions; for the object doth not print or act any way upon the eye, but it is the sensitive motions in the eye which pattern out the figure of the object' (OEP 79; see also GNP 5 9, PPO2 1 27). If objects were the cause of our perceptions of them, our perceptions would all be the same:

> But there are Infinite several manners and ways of Perception; which proves, That the Objects are not the Cause: for, every several kind and sort of Creatures, have several kinds and sorts of Perception, according to the nature and property of such a kind or sort of Composition, as makes such a kind or sort of Creature.
>
> (GNP 9 8)

Now, we already know that objects do not cause perceptions, strictly speaking, because there is no transeunt causation. But we also know that objects do *occasion* perceptions, which is a kind of influence similar to causation, including in its counterfactual nature. So the fact that a similar figure can be made in the absence of the object that normally occasions it does not show that the object does not influence or determine the perception *at all*. What it shows, at minimum, is that the object cannot be the *sole active* contributor to the pattern.[6]

Cavendish deploys this kind of argument specifically against Hobbes' claim that all sense perception requires pressure on the sense organs. In the case of vision, for example, 'neither do all eyes pattern out all objects exactly; which proves that the perception of sight is not made by pressure and reaction, otherwise there would be no difference, but all eyes would see alike' (PL 1 25).

As Adams (2016) acknowledges, such arguments indicate that Cavendish does not think that the complexity of sense perceptions can be accounted for with the simple mechanism of pressure and reaction, while her account of internal self-motions of a perceiver can. But this reflects a deeper fact about Cavendish's theory of perception. The reason that all eyes don't see alike is that all eyes are not alike, and given that perceivers are active and not passive in perception, perceptions reflect those differences.

The fact that Cavendish so frequently concludes, from the diversity of our perceptions, that we perceive diversely rather than that we perceive diverse things should make us wary of assuming that sense perception simply reproduces patterns that exist out there in the external world. This can be a tempting view if you think that Cavendish is trying to capture the Aristotelian notion that sense perception involves taking on a form of an external thing without the matter. Now, Cavendish explicitly argues against theories that involve the assimilation of a form-like entity, whether that be an Aristotelian form or 'species' or whether it be an abstract object, like a Platonic form, or a mental object, like a Cartesian idea (OEP 174, 145–146, 148, 174). Just as she offers other arguments targeting the details of mechanistic theories,[7] Cavendish offers arguments against the details of form-assimilation theories. For example, if perception were made

---

6   As Marcus Adams (2016) discusses, Cavendish may have in mind here the Hobbesian notion of a *causa integra*, or entire cause, which occurs when the agent and patient are both necessary and sufficient to produce the effect. See also O'Neill in OEP: xxxiii, Michaelian 2009: 40, and Lascano 2023.

7   For example, she offers a number of objections to the claim that perceptions are caused by the impact of the object on the sense organs, either immediately or mediated by light, air, or particles of matter, and the resultant motions in the

by 'the ideas of exterior objects entering into the organs of the sentient', we would in fact be perceiving features of ideas and not of bodies (OEP 145–146), and if this process were mediated by the forms of things being imprinted on air, there would be so many such prints necessary to account for all of our perceptions that it would cause 'a notable confusion' (OEP 146).

But, you might think, maybe she wants to preserve the intuition that perception involves internal replication of external forms, but give it a respectable metaphysical foundation? It certainly might sound like she is doing something like that here:

> [an] original is one thing, and the copy another: the picture of a house of stone, is not made of natural stone, nor the picture of a tree, a natural tree; for if it were so, painters would do more than chemists by fire and furnace.
>
> (OEP 179)

It would be easy to interpret this to mean that a perception of a tree involves the internalization of the form of the tree (or the form of some quality of the tree) without the matter. If we were to do that, we could appeal to the fact that Cavendish tells us that in sense perception, the interior motions of the eye, say, are those of the eye, and they only pattern the exterior figures and motions of the tree or house. While this is a good place to start, it turns out that by replacing the form/matter distinction with the interior/exterior distinction, Cavendish takes her perceptual theory very far from the Aristotelian one. Let's take a look at that distinction.

Section 6.5 Exterior figures and sense perception

The proposal that we are entertaining now is that in sense perceptions, patterns resemble, at least in some sense, the exterior figures of external things. So while Cavendish does not think that we can replicate the deeper, interior natures of things through

---

sense organs, including that this would cause too much damage to our sense organs (OEP 79; PL 1 4).

perception, because it 'goes no further than the exterior parts of the object presented' (OEP 50), we can replicate some of its more superficial features. I do not, however, think that this captures Cavendish's distinction between interior and exterior figures and motions. A thing's exterior figures are not superficial features that it has independently of sense perception. They are the ways that things can be sense perceived by a variety of objects, and they are essentially relational.[8]

For one thing, while Cavendish sometimes writes that rational perception, being more 'subtle and active' than sensitive, 'may have also some perceptions of some interior parts and actions of other creatures' (OEP 41, see also 100), she is clearly tempted by the idea that interior figures and actions are necessarily imperceivable. She continues: 'yet it cannot have an infallible and thorough perception of all their interior parts and motions' (OEP 41, see also 100) and also that 'perception has but only a respect to the exterior figures and actions of other parts' (OEP 41). Just a few paragraphs later, she writes that 'perception extends but to adjoining parts, and their exterior figures and actions', so that 'if [the rational parts] know anything of their interior parts, figures or motions, it is only by guess, or probable conclusions, taken from the exterior actions' (OEP 41). Later, Cavendish writes that by this method they merely 'may chance to hit the truth' (OEP 100, see also 175), and in the *Grounds*, that there can be no perception, sensitive or rational, of the interior parts of another creature (GNP 2 7, see also 5 5 and 12 31).

We will return to the questions this raises about rational perception in Section 6.8 and Chapter 7. But for now, we can simply ask: why is Cavendish tempted by the idea that interior figures are always imperceivable? It is not because they happen to be imperceivable because they are hidden under the skin. Though our own eyes might see though a transparent body, Cavendish writes, 'yet it cannot perceive what that transparent body's figurative motions are, or what is the true cause of its transparentness' (OEP 59). This is consistent with the interpretation in the last chapter of interior motions as the more fundamental motions that cause exterior figures and motions.

---

8   Boyle 2015: 442 defends a similar interpretation of interior vs. exterior figure.

And it is further supported by arguments that Cavendish makes about the limits of experimental philosophy. She begins her critique of microscopy by summarily dismissing the possibility that microscopes are 'able to discover the interior natural motions of any part or creature of nature' (OEP 50). But if interior motions and figures merely happened to be inaccessible to our unaided perception, how do we know that microscopes couldn't help us discover the more fundamental, interior motions of things? We should not think of the distinction between exterior and interior figures as a distinction of kind or as an absolute distinction. Rather, the distinction between exterior and interior is relative and a matter of degree.

This reflects Cavendish's repeated claim that

> To see the effects, belongs to the perception of sense; but to judge of the cause, belongs only to reason; and since there is an ignorance as well as a perceptive knowledge in nature, no creature can absolutely know, or have a thorough perception of all things, but according as the corporeal figurative motions are, so are the perceptions.
>
> (OEP 242)

Cavendish connects the partiality of perception here to the fact that we can only perceive effects and not causes. The point is not that we can only perceive the effects of things on us. What we cannot perceive is the ultimate causes of the ways that things appear to us; the causes of those interactions, abstracted from the interaction itself. To perceive the interior motions of a thing would be to perceive the intrinsic and non-relational facts about that thing rather than to have an interaction that reflects the nature of ourselves as well as the object. Our perceptions are always interactions, so they cannot simply deliver nonrelational facts about external things to us. Exterior parts are by definition interfaces; they have an essential connection to perception and not an incidental one.[9]

---

9 I am trying very hard not to say that we cannot perceive things 'in themselves', but I do think something like that is right.

Finally, Cavendish often writes that things are perceived 'as they are presented' (e.g. OEP 50). In one example discussed by several interpreters of Cavendish, she tells us that the eye patterns out an object

> as it is visibly presented to the corporeal motions in the eye; for according as the object is presented, the pattern is made, if the motions be regular: For example; a fired end of a stick, if you move it in a circular figure, the sensitive corporeal motions in the eye pattern out the figure of fire, together with the exterior or circular motion, and apprehend it as a fiery circle…so that the sensitive pattern is made according to the exterior corporeal figurative motion of the object, and not according to its interior figure or motions.
>
> (PL 4 28)

Michaelian (2009) writes that the eye in this case produces an 'inaccurate (because incomplete) copy', because it does not pattern the interior motions. As we have seen and as Lascano (2023: 110) points out, we never pattern the interior motions of things, and Lascano concludes that the fiery circle is a 'true perception of the phenomena'. I think I agree with that, if by true perception we mean that it reflects the response of the eye of a creature like me to a whirling flaming stick. That does not mean that it successfully produces 'adequate copies' of some nonrelational feature of anything external to me (as in Lascano 2021a: 417). In the *Grounds*, Cavendish revisits the same example, writing that it is a case where 'Sense and Reason are but partly mistaken': they are 'not deceived' in that 'a fired end of a Stick, by a swift exterior Circular Motion, appears a Circle of fire', but they are 'mistaken, to conceive the Exterior Figurative Action to be the proper natural Figure' (GNP 6 1). I read this as a warning not to mistake a good (natural) perceptual interaction for something that presents to us a 'proper natural Figure'.

When Cavendish writes that the eye and other sense organs pattern 'according as the object is presented' to those organs, she is pointing to the relationality of sense perception. To pattern an exterior figure is not to produce a copy of a feature that an external object has in itself. There are no absolute exterior figures, independent of how objects are perceived, which is to say, related to. And while this sense perception is not incomplete in the sense of failing as a sense perception in any way, perceptions are in a sense incomplete in their very essence: they are a poise between knowledge and ignorance and, for that reason, cannot reach to the intrinsic features of external things.

The claim that perception cannot access interior motions and figures is not just about animal patterning perceptions. Consider the perceptual processes of circulation, digestion, and vision. Circulation is primarily interior inasmuch as the parts of the circulatory system usually interact directly only with other parts of the body. That doesn't mean that the parts of the circulatory system don't perceive. They perceive all the time, but they mostly perceive other parts of the body. In contrast, digestion is largely interior, inasmuch as most of the interactions of parts of the digestive system are with other parts of the body. But some parts of it directly interact with the outside world, like when we eat. Finally, the visual system does much more interacting with things outside the human creature, and so it is more 'external' than the others in that respect. 'Interior' and 'exterior' is a spectrum, not a binary, and 'exteriority' is not absolute but relative to a creature. The circulatory system is not any more 'interior' in absolute terms than is the visual system, it is just more interior to the human body. They are both equally interior to the whole of nature, for example.

Section 6.6 Naturalness, usefulness, accuracy

Notice that in considering sense perceptions from this perspective, we have said nothing about the 'character' of perceptual experience or the relationship of that character to either the pattern or to the object. To say that a perceiver must be in a direct relationship with an object to perceive it does not entail that her internal state resembles the external object, whether that resemblance is introspectable or not. Cavendish does, however, distinguish between better and worse perceptions and even sometimes truer and falser ones (though the latter is surprisingly rare). If not in terms of accuracy to their objects, how does Cavendish understand the normativity of perception?

To answer this, we return to Cavendish's evaluation of microscopy. After dismissing the possibility that microscopes give us knowledge of interior figures and motions, Cavendish considers the more difficult question of 'whether it can represent yet the exterior shapes and motions so exactly, as naturally they are' (OEP 50). If what we have already said is right, by asking whether we can perceive exterior figures and motions 'as they naturally are', Cavendish is not asking whether we replicate some inherent feature of an exterior part in our own matter. And this is indeed reflected in the arguments that Cavendish gives.

She argues that it is better to observe nature with a healthy human eye than with 'optic glasses, [which] may, and do oftentimes present falsely the picture of an exterior object' (OEP 49–50). But it is better, she writes, because the eye and not the microscope presents things in a way that is not useful. For example, if a painter

> should draw a louse as big as a crab, and of that shape as the microscope presents, can anybody imagine that a beggar would believe it to be true? but if he did, what advantage would it be to the beggar? for it does neither instruct him how to avoid breeding them, or how to catch them, or to hinder them from biting.
>
> (OEP 52)

Similarly, other animals' perceptions are tuned for their good. The different species of birds, for example, are 'better discerned by those that eat their flesh, than by micrographers that look upon their colours and exterior figures through a magnifying glass' (OEP 52).

It may seem obvious that modified perceptions must be less useful because they are less accurate. But that does not seem to be what Cavendish is claiming when she writes that lenses present things as 'mis-shapen rather than natural' (OEP 51). In what sense is our natural visual representation of a louse correct, and why should natural human vision have a monopoly on accuracy? If 'a louse by the help of a magnifying glass appears like a lobster' (OEP 51), why is that a false representation? I do not think Cavendish is identifying better and natural perceptions with accuracy in this sense. This is clear from the following argument:

> If the edge of a knife, or point of a needle were naturally and really as the microscope presents them, they would never be so useful as they are; for, a flat or broad plain-edged knife would not cut, nor a blunt globe pierce so suddenly another body.
>
> (OEP 51)

This would be an entertaining but not a good argument if Cavendish meant that our ability to use the knife depends on our picking up some real absolute sharpness in the knife. But this is not her meaning. A good perception of the knife is one that allows me to use it, and human vision, combined with other human capacities, can tell us when a knife is sharp enough for some human purpose. To borrow a phrase from the 20th-century perceptual theorist J.J. Gibson, to perceive a knife's sharpness is to perceive 'an action possibility available in the environment' (Gibson 1979: 119).[10] Our abilities to perceive that action possibility are obscured by looking at the knife through the microscope.

Indeed, Cavendish is far more likely to characterize sense perceptions as natural or unnatural than to characterize them as true or false. This reflects that sense perceptions, Cavendish writes, are for the 'Subsistence, Consistence, and use of the Whole Man' (GNP 5 4), just like any other kind of animal perception, including digestion or respiration. It is a way that an animal can act in the world to help it survive.

I do not want to deny that, with patterning, Cavendish wants to account for our ability to represent things more and less truly. And there are some particular passages where she seems to imply that to pattern is to replicate some external form. For example, she tells us that at least some kinds of perceptions, like the different sense perceptual modalities, have proper objects that they perceive 'perfectly' (e.g. OEP 46–47) (though we might read 'perfectly', like 'naturally'). Other times, Cavendish treats a pattern as abstractable from its perceptual context. For example, she claims that when we see a reflection of an object, that object is patterned by the glass or water and that copy is pattered out by our vision, making another copy (OEP 147). She continues:

> the optic sense could not perceive either the original, or copy of an exterior object, if it did not make those figure in its own parts; and therefore figure and colour are both in the object, and the eye; and not, as they say, neither in the object, nor in the eye: for, though I grant that one thing cannot be in two places

---

10 Gibson 1979.

at once, yet there may be several copies made of one original, in several parts.

(OEP 147)

And she argues that the eye perceives objects by patterning because we can see tiny images of objects in the eye of another (OEP 174), which does make it sound like patterns are little pictures of external objects.[11]

And, after all, I started this chapter with the claim that patterning is precisely Cavendish's attempt to account for the unique features of animal sense perceptions, specifically that part of what enables animals to react to the world is that we create representations of it. If she doesn't think that, why describe this kind of perception as patterning at all?[12]

This is a hard question, but here are a few considerations that try to address it.

First, as Cavendish knows, we certainly imagine ourselves to have accurate pictures of things outside of us or independent of us. I think that ultimately the precise way that we think we have these

---

11 This latter argument is surprising because she seems to be falling prey to the homuncular fallacy we nowadays call the homuncular fallacy, which she seems very critical of in other contexts. A theory of mind is accused of this fallacy when it over-analogizes the mind's subsystems to full human minds or agents, for example, trying to explain vision by positing that something 'sees' the image of an external object in the eye. Such reasoning, which purports to naturalistically or mechanistically explain vision, in fact does no such thing, since the system that wants explaining—human vision—is just replicated mysteriously at the level of the sub-system. Consider the passage from Section 6.3 about the painter, where Cavendish warns against imagining that a patterning eye, like a painter, must itself see the thing it patterns. For a brief history of homuncular arguments, and an argument that the homuncular reasoning is not always fallacious, see Figdor 2018.

12 A similar worry, as perceptively raised by Alison Simmons in conversation, is that this account of sense perception makes the patterns 'explanatorily idle'. I think the patterns are doing work: patterning is part of what enables an animal to react to external things, in virtue of being joined with them as parts of nature. What it makes idle is resemblance between the patterns and the external world.

objective pictures is part of us imagining our minds as deities. But she agrees that because we are composed with and so are responsive to external objects, our internal states reflect those objects in some way. Patterning captures the metacognitive stories we tell ourselves about our perceptions, but the details of how it works make clear that we should take those stories with a grain of salt.

Second, it helps to focus on Cavendish's descriptions of patterning as imitations, and to think of sense perceptions as imitative actions. While imitating something does involve acting in a similar way, it does not necessarily involve producing a copy of anything. There are many different ways to evoke the nature and actions of another creature. The creature that we imitate does not have to be much different from us for imitation to become pretty impressionistic, so that isolating some precise sense in which our actions are a copy of another creature's seems not to the point of imitation. If asked to imitate a bird, someone might flap her arms or tweet or sing or sit with her legs tucked under her or build a nest or do a bird-themed interpretive dance. Birds are in fact pretty similar to us in the grand scheme of creatures, and it will be even less obvious what counts as a 'correct' imitation of a creature who is much more different from us, including things that we like to think we perceive accurately, like mugs and napkins. We could try to characterize all these imitative acts in terms of discrete productions of copies of features of the other creature, but this would be getting things the wrong way around.

Finally, situating Cavendish's account of perception against the background of sympathy goes some way toward explaining why the kind of relationship that perception is can result in some similarity between the perceived and the perceiver. As Chapter 5 explained, 'sympathy' names the fact that one thing may influence another because they are similar or because they are joined as one. That influence is one that tends to reinforce the similarity or union between the two things. In Cavendish's case, we already know that if one thing is influencing another, they are joined by composition. So it makes sense that for Cavendish, joining can result in similarity. This allows us to resuscitate a bit of the intuition that drives Cavendish's account of patterning. While it is common to all perceptions, Cavendish may hold the quite reasonable position that the structure of the eyes is more apt to convey similarities than the structure of the pancreas, which is a different kind of perception.

Section 6.7 Against naïve realism

What I do hope is clear enough from the previous considerations is that Cavendish does not think that our sense perceptions simply deliver to us the forms of things outside of us. However, some comments that Cavendish makes about our experiences of sensory qualities have (understandably) led readers to think otherwise. Most of these concern colour, specifically, and to a lesser extent, heat.

These comments usually occur when Cavendish is responding to the mechanistic account of certain sensory qualities. Boyle, Hobbes, and Descartes all deny that colour, heat, taste, smell, and sound are true qualities of matter. Rather, they are or reflect the effects that bodies have on us. Objects act on our bodies in mechanistically respectable ways. From there, Boyle and Descartes think that an immaterial mental process is initiated that is our experience of colour or heat.

The difference between the mechanistic and sensory qualities of bodies furnishes Descartes with an argument that sensory qualities are not caused by bodies but instead occasioned by them: external objects 'give the mind occasion to form "sensory ideas" by means of the faculty innate to it' (Descartes 1985: 304). Cavendish, too, insists that sense perceptions are occasioned and not caused by external objects. This generates some additional support for the claim that Cavendish's insistence that perceptions are occasioned rather than caused is in part driven by her resistance to the idea that sense perception involves the bare reception of forms or qualities. Unlike Descartes, of course, Cavendish does not think that a mental faculty generates sense perceptions; sense perceptions must be actions of self-moving matter.

Cavendish takes issue with the claim that colour and heat are not in the perceived objects. For example, she recount's Hobbes's argument that heat cannot be in a hot coal because felt heat is identical to a pleasure or pain, and there can be no such thing in a coal. Cavendish replies:

> They are so far in the right, that the heat we feel, is made by the perceptive motions of, and in our own parts, and not by the fire's parts acting upon us: but yet, if the fire were not really such a thing as it is, that is, a hot and burning body, our sense

would not so readily figure it out, as it does: which proves it is a real copy of a real object, and not a mere phantasm, or bare imparted motion from the object to the sentient, made by pressure and reaction.

(OEP 148)

The first part of this passage reminds us that perceptions are self-motions, and I have argued that part of why Cavendish is so insistent that perceptions are self-motions is to undermine the picture of perception as passive reception of forms. But Cavendish goes on to deny that this means that sensory qualities are not in the objects themselves. Similarly, she rejects the opinion that colour and sound are not 'really inherent' in the objects perceived (OEP 147) because if they were not in the objects they could not be patterned.

As we have already seen, it is certainly true that no perception of any quality is possible without the object being there. To perceive fire appropriately, it must be 'such a thing as it is, that is, a hot and burning body.' If fire weren't the way it is, our perceptions of it wouldn't be the way they are. But Cavendish does not tell us is what it means to be 'hot and burning.' Similarly, when she balks at the notion that 'were there no men to perceive such or such a colour, figure or sound…that object would have no colour, figure, nor sound at all' (OEP 148), she does not tell us what it is for an object to have a particular colour, figure, or sound. So these passages do not show that Cavendish is a realist about the phenomenal, introspectable, or qualitative character of perceptual objects. They do not make clear what real colour and heat are. In the absence of that, all we know is that when we perceive colour or heat, there must be something real that we are in a direct relationship with.

Some readers go further. Colin Chamberlain proposes that Cavendish holds that '[g]rass is green in precisely the way it visually appears to be' and that 'sensuous color' is a real property of matter—and, more than that, as fundamental and essential to matter as figure, self-knowledge, and self-motion (Chamberlain 2019). And Daniel Whiting argues that Cavendish is what he calls a 'naïve realist' about sensory qualities more generally, holding that 'perceptual acquaintance with the mug is (partially) constitutive of how the mug is presented to me in my experience or of the ways in which that experience warrants judgments concerning the mug and its features' (2024: 232).[13] Both Chamberlain and Whiting hold that Cavendish thinks that our phenomenal experience of colour (and perhaps other qualities) resembles real properties of objects.

However, some of the very arguments for realism that Cavendish makes are problematic when they are read as concerning sensuous colour, but they are perfectly fine otherwise. The argument that colour must be in the object for our optic sense to perceive it is equally applicable to any perceptual modality and any feature of matter perceived by it, by any creature whatsoever. That is not a problem if we understand it to establish direct realism in general: that just means that everything that is genuinely perceived requires both the perceiver and the perceived thing to be in a certain way. But if it concerns sensuous colour, it seems to multiply sensuous qualities all over the shop.[14]

Chamberlain's arguments that colour is not only real but fundamental to matter draw on Cavendish's claims that 'Matter, Colour, Figure, and Place, is but one thing, as one and the same Body' (GNP 12 29) and that a colourless body is inconceivable (OEP 86, 88). Cavendish's claim that a colourless body is inconceivable, however,

---

13 While Chamberlain and Whiting agree on the so-called 'naïveté' of at least some of our experiences of sensory qualities, their accounts differ in their attribution of 'directness' to Cavendishian perception. Whiting holds that Cavendish is a naïve direct realist, while some of Chamberlain's arguments seem to depend on a representationalist view of perception, inasmuch as they depend upon resemblances between experienced states of the perceiver and features of the perceived objects (specifically, their colours). (In conversation, Chamberlain has expressed that he now holds that Cavendish is a direct sensuous colour realist.) Whiting can hold that Cavendish is a naïve realist despite denying that perception involves any representational states because he maintains that perception, for Cavendish, involves taking on the forms of things without their matter (Whiting 2024: 8). I have argued that given her thoroughgoing rejection of the form–matter distinction, Cavendish cannot (and does not) hold this.

14 Whiting is fine with this, but he does not seem to think that Cavendish's denial of the form-matter distinction and Cavendish's eliminativism about accidents is as important as I do. As in the case of Chamberlain's interpretation, where texts about perception are ambiguous, I think my view squares better than either of these with Cavendish's metaphysics.

plausibly just means that human beings perceive or conceive of perceiving a body without colour. And Cavendish's claims that some thing or another is 'all one thing' with matter can have a variety of different meanings. Ultimately, everything can be said to be all one thing with matter, since matter is all there is. That includes matter's effects or actions, not just fundamental or inherent features of matter.

And there is plenty of evidence that Cavendish takes colour to be an effect of matter, which requires structural complexity and motion, rather than a fundamental feature of matter. 'Several colours,' Cavendish writes, 'are of several figures...and...the change of colours proceeds from the alteration of their figures' (OEP 83–84). Colours 'are made by the figurative corporeal motions, and that they are as various and different as all other creatures; and when they appear either more or less, it is by the variation of their parts' (OEP 85, see also 81). Colour can change just as 'a man may put his body into several postures, and have several actions, and yet without any change of the substance of his body' (OEP 38). Cavendish is unsurprised by Boyle's report of a blind man who can distinguish between colours by touch, because 'colours are corporeal figurative motions' (OEP 83). And consider her speculation that 'that which makes a Lilly white, may also be the cause of the whiteness of Snow, that is, such a figure as makes a white colour' (PL 4 14). If it be objected that by 'figure' Cavendish means primitive sensuous colour rather than something structural, consider that she continues:

> different figures, in my opinion, are the cause of different colours...Nature by contraction of lines draws such or such a Figure, which is such or such a Colour; as such a Figure is red, and such a Figure is green, and so of all the rest: But the Palest colours, and so white, are the loosest and slackest figures; Indeed, white, which is the nearest colour to light, is the smoothest, evenest and straightest figure, and composed of the smallest lines: As for example; suppose the figure of 8. were the colour of Red, and the figure of 1. the colour of White; or suppose the figure of Red to be a z. and the figure of an r. to be the figure of Green, and a straight l. the figure of White.
>
> (PL 4 14)

These are explicitly structural analyses of colours.[15]

Elsewhere, Cavendish defends her colour realism by writing that we have no more reason to say that the whiteness of snow is not an inherent and natural colour than we do to say 'that blood is not blood, or flesh is not flesh in the dark, if our eye doth not perceive it' (OEP 85–86). But blood and flesh are uncontroversially effective parts of matter and not fundamental features of it. In addition to these textual reasons for rejecting realism about fundamental sensuous colour, the doctrine runs afoul of a number of what I take to be Cavendish's deepest philosophical commitments.

First, it clashes on its face with Cavendish's unsparing eliminativism about forms and qualities, which reflects a deeper commitment to ontological parsimony. If sensuous colour is real, it sounds a lot like a quality of the sort she rejects. I have tried to explain how to think about matter's nature—that it is dividable and composable, and that it moves itself—without thinking of these as qualities of matter. I do not see how to do this for colour. Chamberlain has said to me in conversation that he suspects that Cavendish relates colour's essentiality to matter to the essentiality of spatial extension to matter. Even if that would help some, I don't think that spatial extension is essential to matter. Also, if Cavendish holds that colour is essential to matter alongside divisibility and self-knowledge, why does she only tell us that when she is writing directly about colour? In the places that she lays out her view of matter, like the brief statement of the principles of her natural philosophy in the *Observations*, or in the first chapter, or in the first chapter of the *Grounds* entitled 'Of Matter,' there is no mention of colour.

Second, sensuous colour realism badly violates Cavendish's anti-anthropocentrism. Only things with eyes, like human beings and some other animals, perceive colour in the relevant sense. Vision is just one sense modality for one kind of creature among infinite kinds of creatures. Even other animals with eyes perceive different colours than we do. Why should the fact that we perceive colour (or heat) indicate that those things are in the world as perceived, any

---

15 Allen (2019) also offers arguments that colours are not fundamental and considers them in Cavendish's context.

more than whatever ways earthworms or planets perceive things? Cavendish could respond that it does not and that the sensuous perceptions of earthworms or planets are in matter, too. But nothing suggests that Cavendish does think that, and if she did, she would *really* be multiplying forms and qualities.

Third, to hold that matter must be intrinsically coloured to be perceived as coloured is like holding that matter must be 'clayey' in order to make clay. After describing colours as 'but effects', Cavendish goes on to remind us that 'it is as great an error to believe effects for principles as to judge of the interior natures and motions of creatures by their exterior phenomena or appearances' (OEP 83). Matter is subject to all forms; there is 'no part or particle in nature which is not alterable' and 'nothing in Nature that can properly be called fixt' (OEP 233). While some effective parts of matter are 'more fixt than others,' that is just because 'no art has been found out as yet, which could alter their proper and particular figures' (OEP 233). We know that this applies to colour because Cavendish tells us specifically that no body is 'subject to one colour' (OEP 88). So if colour is inherent to matter, it would have to be colourfulness in general, which would be very hard to understand, especially in light of Cavendish's professed view that changes of colour are changes of parts (OEP 81).

Just as colours are corporeal figurative motions, the perceptions of colours are 'made and dissolved by the sensitive figurative motions' (OEP 80). If a hand were rearranged into the figure of an eye, it would see, presumably in colour, 'for perceptions are according to the composition of parts, and the changes of nature's self-motions' (OEP 186). Just as matter does not have to be clayey or intrinsically coloured to make clay or be coloured, the eye does not have to be made of special colour-perceiving matter to perceive colour.

Section 6.8 Rational perception

I said earlier that to imagine that we are able to represent nature objectively is to imagine ourselves as little deities. But Cavendish herself seems to acknowledge that though we are not deities, we do indeed have a knowledge that seems divine: 'so pure and subtle a knowledge, that many believe it to be immaterial, as if it were some

God' (OEP 47). It is not a God, of course; it is 'only a pure, fine, and subtle figurative motion or perception' (OEP 47). This purer knowledge or perception is rational knowledge and perception, and its purity and subtlety reflect the purity and subtlety of rational matter (OEP 180).

Reason, rational matter, rational knowledge, and rational perceptions are all Cavendish's way of accounting for the kinds of knowledge that we have that are not sense perceptions. Here, we will discuss rational perception, which will take us into the next chapter, which treats reason and the rational at greater length.

Cavendish usually characterizes rational perception as a kind of patterning (OEP 33, 55) that is made outside of the sense organs. As we have seen, Cavendish holds that sense 'deludes more than it gives a true information' (OEP) and should defer to and be guided by 'regular reason'. Rational perceptions are more 'penetrating' and 'general'; where Cavendish thinks of generality not in terms of abstraction but because the 'more easily make an united Perception, than the Sensitive; which is the reason the Rational parts can make a Whole Perception of a Whole Object: Whereas the Sensitive makes but Perceptions in part, of one and the same Object' (GNP 1 10; see also OEP 144, 180).

Cavendish describes 'thoughts' of objects as 'rational perceptions' (OEP 180) and 'thoughtful perceptions' (PL 1 35), which suggests that they are meant to capture our ability to think about things rather than just to have sense perceptions of them. Occasionally, and more commonly in earlier work, Cavendish seems tempted by the Aristotelian maxim that 'there is nothing in the understanding, that is not first in the senses', writing in *World's Olio*, for example, that 'the senses bring all the materials into the brain, and then the brain cuts and divides them, and gives them quite other forms, then the senses many times presented them' (WO Of the Senses and the Brain). Later, she more consistently holds that rational perception is independent of sense perception, though in a properly functioning animal, the rational and sensitive parts 'work to one and the same perception, and…as it were, by one act' (OEP 174) so that we have a 'double perception of one and the same object' (OEP 179). So while Cavendish is not an empiricist, she does seem to recognize the unique role that our sense perceptions play in our cognitive life.

(Cavendish also indicates that rational perception is responsible for the different senses' abilities to have 'some notion of each other' (OEP 83), reminiscent of the Aristotelian common sense.) While rational and sensitive perception can pattern the same object, the perceptions are very different.

Besides being more general than sensitive perception, Cavendish sometimes characterizes rational perception as 'more perfect' than sensitive (OEP 180) and writes that it can

> judge better of objects than the sensitive, as being more knowing; and knows more, because it hath a more general perception, because it is more subtle and active; and is more subtle and active, because it is free, and not necessitated to labour on, or with any other parts.
>
> (OEP 181)

That said, it is possible (and common) for rational perceptions to be erroneous, especially if they are 'irregular' (e.g. OEP 226).

As we have seen, Cavendish is ambivalent as to whether the penetratingness of rational perceptions means that there can be rational perceptions of the interior figures of things. We can, however, have rational perceptions of things that we cannot perceive with our senses, like air (OEP 47). Cavendish also sometimes says that we can have a rational perception of God (OEP 47). As we will see in the next chapter, other times she characterizes our knowledge of God as non-perceptual. We will evaluate the latter claim in the next chapter, but the former is a bit of a nonstarter. The reasons that Cavendish gives that we cannot have sense perceptions of God—that he cannot be patterned, for example—would seem to rule out rational perceptions of God, too, since rational perception is patterning. And while Cavendish writes that the rational part of nature has the 'perfectest notions of God', she continues: 'I mean, so much as nature can possibly know of God' (OEP 47). Which is to say, nothing, strictly speaking.

Not all rational perceptions are what we would call cognitive or mental. There are 'infinite perceptions rational, as well as infinite perceptions sensitive: wherefore I cannot say, that all rational perceptions are like to human thoughts, otherwise, than in respect of purity' (OEP 179–180). Because rational matter is in all parts of the body, 'rational knowledge is not only in the head or brains, but in every part or particle of the body' (OEP 153). Similarly, it is not the case that sensitive perceptions or motions are always made by sensitive matter, or rational ones by rational matter; rather, 'there are different, sensitive and rational motions, which move differently in the different parts of one composed creature' (OEP 20).

The greater subtlety, purity, agility (GNP 1 10), and penetratingness (GNP 1 9) of the rational parts are manifestations of their greater liberty or freedom, which is related to the fact that they are not 'incubred with the Inanimate parts' as the sensitive parts are and thus are not as 'obstructed and retarded' (GNP 1 10; see also OEP 150). The way that this manifests in a particular creature depends, of course, on the structure of the creature. Cavendish sometimes describes certain effective parts of an animal as rational or sensitive, like the brain or eyes. These parts are made of all three constituents, but they may more or less reflect the properties of rational or sensitive matter. Those parts that make rational perceptions, like the brain, are less burdened with other parts than, say, the eyes. These features also make rational matter the 'most comfortable to truth' (OEP 17), although that does not mean that rational matter is never involved in error.

Before moving on to complicate matters in the next chapter, we close by observing that Cavendish often tells us that perceptions, in general, are our only knowledge of external things, and sensitive and rational perceptions are our only cognitive types of knowledge of external things. She writes that 'no man can naturally go beyond his rational and sensitive perception' (OEP 110), that 'parts can know no more of other parts, but by their own perceptions', and that every creature must 'content itself with such knowledge as is within the reach of its own perceptions' (OEP 41). If it's not a perception, it doesn't put us in touch with the external world.

Section 6.9 Conclusion

In this chapter, we examined one species of knowledge: perception, or exterior knowledge. I argued that certain kinds of animal perceptions, especially sense perceptions and certain rational perceptions, which are centered in the sense organs and brain, are responsible for all of our cognitive contact with the external world. Cavendish's claim that all creatures perceive, however, does not mean that all creatures have these kinds of perceptions. Perceptions more generally are creatures' diverse abilities to interact with their environments, of which cognitive perceptions are but a handful among countless.

In developing this interpretation, we mostly bracketed the question of what knowledge is. The fact that we were able to develop a plausible (I hope) interpretation of perception without addressing that question is significant: it points to or at the very least leaves open the possibility that knowledge itself can be characterized in non-cognitive terms. But since perception is a kind of knowledge, our account of perception will not be convincing until we discover what Cavendishian knowledge is. This is the goal of the next chapter.

Further reading

Adams, Marcus P. 2016. 'Visual Perception as Patterning: Cavendish against Hobbes on Sensation.' *History of Philosophy Quarterly* 33(26): 193–214.

Allen, Keith. 2019. 'Cavendish and Boyle on Color and Experimental Philosophy.' Pp. 58–80 in *Experiment, Speculation and Religion in Early Modern Philosophy*, edited by Alberto Vanzo and Peter R. Ansley. Routledge.

Boyle, Deborah. 2015. 'Margaret Cavendish on Perception, Self-Motion and Probable Opinion.' *Philosophy Compass*, 10(7): 438–450.

Boyle, Deborah. 2019. 'Informed by Sense and Reason: Margaret Cavendish's Theorizing About Perception.' Pp. 231–248 in *The Senses and History of Philosophy*, edited by Brian Glenney and José Silva. Routledge.

Chamberlain, Colin. 2019. 'Color in a Material World: Cavendish against the Early Modern Mechanists.' *Philosophical Review*, 128(3): 293–336.

Georgescu, Laura. 2021. 'Self-Knowledge, Perception, and Margaret Cavendish's Metaphysics of the Individual.' *Early Science and Medicine* 25(6): 618–639.

Lascano, Marcy. 2023. Chapter 5 in *The Metaphysics of Margaret Cavendish and Anne Conway: Monism, Vitalism, and Self-Motion*. New York: Oxford University Press.

Sharp, Brooke Willow. 2024. 'Veil of Light: The Role of Light in Cavendish's Visual Perception.' *Ergo (Ann Arbor, Mich.)* 10: 1471–1494.

West, Peter. 2022. Margaret Cavendish on Conceivability, Possibility, and the Case of Colors. *British Journal for the History of Philosophy* 30(3): 456–476.

Whiting, Daniel. 2024. 'Is Margaret Cavendish a Naïve Realist?' *European Journal of Philosophy* 32: 321–341.

Seven
Knowledge

Who knows, but birds which under th'azure skies
Do fly, know whence the blustring winds do rise?
May know what thunder is, which no man knows,
And what's a blazing star, or where it goes,
Whether it be a chip, fall'n from the sun,
And so goes out when aliment is done,
Or a sulphureous vapor drawn up high,
And when the sulphur's spent the flame doth die,
Or whether't be a jelly set on fire,
And wasting like a candle doth expire,
Or whether't be a star whole and entire;
the birds, perhaps, might tell, could we inquire.
(P&F Of Birds)

Knowledge is at the heart of Cavendish's philosophy—not just of her epistemology but also of her metaphysics. Knowledge, at its most general, is metaphysical: it is essentially connected, for Cavendish, with being and with the fact that to be, in nature, is to be both an individual, distinct from others, as well as to be joined with others. That does not mean that knowledge is not epistemic, although it is not all epistemic in the sense that we usually understand that word, which involves beliefs and justification. Knowledge's place at the heart of both epistemology and metaphysics is expressed in Cavendish's claim that 'natural knowledge and perception, is the ground and principle, not only of philosophy both speculative and experimental, but of all other arts and sciences, nay, of all the infinite particular actions of nature' (OEP 137).

DOI: 10.4324/9781003107255-8

The kind of knowledge that we think of as epistemic, if it exists or if anything like it exists, is something that particular creatures have—namely, humans and other animals. In the case of perception, it was much easier to start with the familiar concept of human and animal sense perception, because Cavendish's way of defining it is familiar, even if the theory itself is more complicated. In the case of human and animal non-perceptual knowledge, however, it is not easier to start with that, because her account of those, it turns out, is not a familiar one. So we start by considering the case of creaturely knowledge more generally, and we consider what human and animal knowledge must therefore be.

I will argue (controversially) that all nonperceptual kinds of knowledge are kinds of self-knowledge. But unlike 'perception', Cavendish uses 'self-knowledge' in two different senses. Creaturely self-knowledge, like creaturely perception, depends on the nature of particular creatures. But both creaturely self-knowledge and creaturely perception depend upon a principle that Cavendish also calls self-knowledge, which is intrinsic to all matter and independent of structure and motion.

The principle of self-knowledge is not something new. Cavendish's claim that matter is fundamentally self-knowing expresses the relationship between being and compositional structure. To know something perfectly, for Cavendish, is to join with it fully, which simply means: to become it. So self-knowledge as a principle is identity, in the context of Cavendish's compositional account of natural beings. The result of this, at the level of creatures, is an account of knowledge as a kind of assimilation: to know something is to become it, at least in part. (It is not, as we have seen, to become like it, in the sense of taking on the form of another thing.)

As for creaturely self-knowledge, it is, like perception, what allows a creature to act in the world. Self-knowledges are the conditions of action that are internal to the creature rather than those that involve its relationships with other things. Like perceptions, they depend on the structure of the self-moving matter in a creature. In fact, we will see that self-knowledge simply is a creature's structure (or rather: a creature, structured).

The naturalistic challenge for the kinds of knowledge that we would describe as cognitive is even more acute for the nonperceptual case than for the perceptual case. It is not obvious how so much swirling in the brain and other parts of the body get us the kind of knowledge of other things that we usually take ourselves to have. To some extent, Cavendish responds to this challenge by simply accepting that we do not have mental states that reflect the world in just the way we think they do. It will be the task of the next chapter to see what this means for the prospects of natural philosophy.

Section 7.1 Creaturely knowledge

Cavendish holds that all creatures are knowing. The knowledge of a creature is a very basic fact about it—maybe the most basic fact about it. Consider that the title of the first chapter of the part of the *Grounds* that is devoted to different kinds of creatures is 'On the different Knowledges, in different Kinds and Sorts of Creatures' (GNP 11 1).

That section goes on to establish that every kind of creature has its own special kind of knowledge, and no kind can be said to know more or less than another. 'A fish may be as knowing as man,' Cavendish writes, 'but man hath not a fishes knowledge, nor a fish a mans knowledge' (PPO2 4 14). Just as no creature has more or less knowledge than another, no creature's ways of knowing are better or worse than another's. This includes man, who 'may have a different Knowledg from Beasts, Birds, Fish, Flies, Worms, or the like; and yet be no wiser than those sorts of Animal-kinds' (GNP 11 1). In addition to having knowledge proper to it, every creature has multiple knowledges in its different parts. In animals, this includes the sense organs but also the heart and pancreas, as well as the special knowledges and sub-knowledges of 'Vegetables, Minerals, and Elements' (GNP 11 1). All the parts of animals

> are as sensible, and as rational, as those five sensitive organs; and the heart, liver, lungs, spleen, stomach, bowels, and the rest, know as well their office and functions, and are as sensible of their pains, diseases, constitutions, tempers, nourishments, etc. as the eyes, ears nostrils, tongue, etc. know their particular actions and perception.
>
> (OEP 151, see also PL 1 37)

We kind of already knew this, since all creatures are perceptive, and perception is a species of knowledge. What other sorts of creaturely knowledge are there? Well, if some knowledge is not knowledge of exterior parts, it can only be self-directed. We'll come back to this; for now, let us assume it. So our task now is to determine what creaturely self-knowledge is, and what creaturely knowledge is in general.

To understand creaturely perception, we started by considering the role that it played in an animal. It makes sense to do the same thing here. And Cavendish gives us license to do so, in an important passage from the *Letters*:

> In your last, you were pleased to express, that some men, who think themselves wise, did laugh in a scornful manner at my opinion, when I say that every Creature hath life and knowledg, sense and reason; counting it not onely ridiculous, but absurd; and asking, whether you did or could believe, a piece of wood, metal, or stone, had as much sense as a beast, or as much reason as a man, having neither brain, blood, heart, nor flesh; nor such organs, passages, parts, nor shapes as animals? To which, I answer: That it is not any of these mentioned things that makes life and knowledg, but life and knowledg is the cause of them, which life and knowledg is animate matter, and is in all parts of all Creatures: and Antimony, or the like, will act very wisely in Vomiting; and Opium will act very wisely in Sleeping; also Quicksilver or Mercury will act very wisely, as those that have the French disease [syphilis] can best witness: likewise the Loadstone acts very wisely, as Mariners or Navigators will tell you: Also Wine made of Fruit, and Ale of Malt, and distilled Aquavitæ will act very subtilly; ask the Drunkards, and they can inform you.
>
> (PL 4 30)

Cavendish's argument that everything is knowing is that everything acts in a certain way, namely, 'wisely', like we do. Here, it sounds like Cavendish means that things act in subtle, complex, and predictable ways, and concludes from this that all creatures must have knowledge. As we have already seen, Cavendish does not think that we can infer a difference of causes from a difference of effects. While she seems friendlier to the idea that we can infer similar causes from similar effects, as we will see in the next chapter, it is likely that our knowledge of the common cause involves some insight that is not drawn from particular effects. In any case, we know that reason tells us that animate matter is the cause of all nature's actions. And indeed, Cavendish writes explicitly here that life and knowledge, which is the cause of the actions of creatures, is animate matter.

This tells us that for a creature to have knowledge is for animate matter to be whatever way it must be to cause 'wise' actions, which include opium's soporific action and antimony's purgative action. Pretty much all the other examples that Cavendish gives of crea- turely knowledge are knowledge that a creature has of how to act. For example, in a human being

> those Parts that produce, or nourish the Bones, those of the Sinews, those of the Veins, those of the Flesh, those of the Brain, and the like, know all their several Works…the like, I believe, in Vegetables, Minerals, or Elements.
>
> (GNP 3 3)

More generally, Cavendish tells us, every part 'knows its own office, like as officers in a commonwealth' (GNP 5 5), 'knows his own Employment' (GNP 5 5), and 'knows itself, and its own actions' (OEP 39).

Michaelian (2009: 45) and others argue on this basis that creaturely knowledge, for Cavendish, is what contemporary epistemologists call 'knowledge-how' rather than 'knowledge-that'. This is an important insight, as far as it goes, but it still does not tell us what knowledge is, from a metaphysical standpoint.[1] As with perception, we should not jump to assume it is something like a belief state. And we are not forced to the conclusion, with Boyle and

---

1 Georgescu (2021) argues that calling Cavendishian knowledge 'knowledge-how' implies an overly inflationary account of Cavendishian knowledge. I do not intend that; by the claim that Cavendishian knowledge is knowledge-how, I simply mean that whatever it is, it determines how a creature acts. I will go on to give a deflationary account of this, which would be harder to do if one thought that Cavendishian knowledge was knowledge-that.

Detlefsen, that to know how to do something is to be responsive to norms.[2]

Instead, we ask: what is it in virtue of which creatures perform their actions? Well, Cavendish has told us: knowledge is animate matter. And like perception, the nature of a creature's knowledge depends upon the structure of the creature's body:

> Innate Figurative Motions of all Creatures, must of necessity alter the Life and Knowledge of that Creature. (GNP 11 7)

> [T]he Corporeal Motions moving after a different manner, is the cause there are different Knowledges, in different Creatures. (GNP 11 1)

> The Knowledg of every Part alters according as their Actions alter. (GNP 2 4)

In fact, Cavendish holds the even stronger position that there is no change in knowledge without a change in structure; in other words, knowledge supervenes on material structure. This follows easily from the arguments of Chapter 3, which establish that all structure is parthood structure and that there are no entities or distinctions that are not parts and parthood distinctions. But it is also more directly evidenced by passages like the following, which suggest that different figures make the only difference between kinds of knowledge:

> Though the Bell hath not an animal knowledge, yet it may have a mineral life and knowledg…and the Jack-in-a-box a vegetable knowledg…each in its own kind may have as much knowledg as an animal in his kind; onely they are different according to the different proprieties of their Figures.
>
> (PL 2 13)

Given that differences in material structures are both necessary and sufficient for differences in creaturely knowledges, we have two interpretive options. The first is to say that knowledge depends upon these structures but is something over and above them. The second

---

2 For defenses of these positions, see Boyle (2015, 2018) and Detlefsen (2007).

is to say that knowledge simply is these structures. But we know that Cavendish does not take the first route, because in nature there is only matter, divided and composed. So Cavendish should reject any account of knowledge that remotely threatens to make it a thing emergent from matter or a quasi-thing like a property. And nothing she tells us about creaturely knowledge, either in general or in her examples, gives us reason to question that her materialism applies here. All the examples that Cavendish gives of creatures acting with knowledge are examples of creatures acting in virtue of the arrangement of their matter. So we conclude that creaturely knowledge is simply matter, compositionally structured. This makes sense of the priority that Cavendish gives to creaturely knowledge when she sets out to give an account of the different kinds of creatures. Creatures are distinguished by their knowledges, which are just their material structure.

The proposal that Cavendish might describe such structures as 'knowledges', without intending to imply that they involve cognition, mentality, consciousness, or truth-evaluability, is sometimes met with incredulous stares. But Cavendish is, as always, working to remind us of the continuity between our own ways of being in the world and those of other creatures. We think that we are able to move in the world in a unique way afforded by a unique capacity we call 'knowledge'. But all creatures move in the world in the complex and responsive ways that we do. So why not call the tools that they use to do it 'knowledges'? The knowledge that a lodestone has of where to move is not propositional knowledge. And consider the claim that the human pancreas is more knowing than human mind-parts about how to appropriately produce insulin—an obvious fact to any Type 1 diabetic who has had to deploy their cognitive parts to do the work of an indolent pancreas (I know whereof I speak). The cognitive parts are just not that good at it, but that doesn't mean that the pancreas has anything remotely like the kind of knowledge of insulin than the scientists who first isolated it did. Cavendish illustrates this vividly if insensitively when she describes various irregularities in creatures as the results of certain parts being 'natural fools':

> if a Man be born Blind, then only his Eyes are Fools; if Deaf, than only his Ears are Fools…if a Man is born lame, his Leggs are

Fools; that is, those Parts have no knowledge of such Properties that belong to such Parts.

(GNP 6 13; see also PPO 2 7 17)

One might reply that these claims can only be true analogically. But there is no more reason to assume, if we do think of this as a simile, that eyes and legs are fools in the sense that human mind-parts are any more than Cavendish's similes between thoughts and pancakes in a pan or bread baking in an oven implies reductive materialism.

Some readers still find it just too hard to believe that Cavendish would use the word 'knowledge' to describe something that does not involve mental states. It helped to motivate Cavendish's noncognitive account of perception to point out that Bacon clearly uses the term in this way. I do not know of a similar precedent in the case of know-ledge, but that doesn't mean that 'knowledge' has always been used in a way that entails a mental state like belief. (Azzouni (2020), for example, argues that our own sense of 'knowledge' does not entail a mental state.) In the absence of a detailed philological investigation, the next section considers some philosophical reasons to reject not just the notion that knowledge is fundamentally mental or cognitive, but any view that puts the mental or cognitive at the fundamental level, for Cavendish.

Section 7.2 Against panpsychism

We have said that creaturely knowledge is not something distinct or emergent from self-moving matter, structured and acting as it does. The question remains, however, whether we must modify the con-ception that we have so far developed of matter itself in order to account for the fact that creatures have knowledges. Must matter have some further feature—knowledge itself, or proto-knowledge or some knowledgyness—that yields complex creaturely knowledge when it is put into compositional arrangements? The alternative is that know-ledge is simply matter, as we already know it, arranged in certain ways. It turns out that each is partly right (but mostly the former).

Much of what we have seen already supports the latter alterna-tive. We know that down to the smallest effective parts, knowledge can be completely destroyed or transformed by change of structure.

So while creaturely knowledges are composed of other creaturely knowledges, they are not ultimately so composed. There is no 'atom' of knowledge, just as there are no atoms of matter:

> If there can be no such thing as a single part in nature, there can neither be a single self-knowledge or perception…for knowledge, being material, consists of parts; and as it is impossible that there can be single parts, or parts subsisting by themselves, without reference to each other, or the body of nature; so it is impossible that there can be single knowledges.
>
> (OEP 160)

So if matter has some new fundamental property that underwrites creaturely knowledge, it is not creaturely knowledge itself. Creaturely knowledge, alongside perception and all of the features and actions of matter, is like clayeyness: it is contained in *potentia* by self-moving matter, but no particular bit of matter holds on to any particular creaturely knowledge, independent of its material structure:

> When I name *Humane sense and reason*, I mean such sensitive and rational perception and knowledge as is proper to the nature of Man; and when I say *Animal sense and reason*, I mean such as is proper to the nature of all Animals; for I do not mean that the sensitive and rational corporeal motions which do make a man, or any Animal, are bound to such figures eternally, but whilst they work and move in such or such figures, they make such perceptions as belong to the nature of those figures; but when those self-moving parts dissolve the figure of an Animal into a Vegetable or any other Creature, then they work according to the nature of that same figure, both exteriously and interiously.
>
> (PL 4 33)

That leaves open the possibility that composed creaturely knowledges require that matter has some feature that we have not yet considered—not creaturely knowledge itself, but proto-knowledge. But what, exactly, is this proto-knowledge, given that we have no reason to think that it is anything like creaturely knowledge? And if it is nothing like creaturely knowledge, what makes us think that we do in fact need anything further? The examples and descriptions that Cavendish gives of particular knowledges do not give us any clue as to what further *je ne sais quoi* would have to be added to structured matter to get knowledge. The explanations of creatures' knowing actions are entirely in terms of structured matter and its motions.

The idea that we need some extra *je ne sais quoi* does not, I think, come from internal pressures in Cavendish's system, but rather from foregrounding the question of whether Cavendish is a panpsychist. We have already seen lots of reasons to reject the notion that the mental or cognitive is ubiquitous and fundamental. But it is worth briefly taking on directly the frequent claim that Cavendish is a panpsychist. Just as Georgescu, Wolfe, and Detlefsen argue about the term 'vitalist', the application of 'panpsychist' to Cavendish obscures more than it illuminates. And because, like 'vitalist', 'panpsychist' can mean so many things, it is difficult and not necessarily useful to try to argue that Cavendish is not a panpsychist in any sense someone could come up with. But here is some reason to be wary of this label.

'Panpsychism' is a label borrowed from contemporary philosophers, most of whom are motivated by the thought that explaining some very unique feature of human mental life is impossible without the psychic being widespread and fundamental. Usually this feature is consciousness. But 'consciousness' is a word that Cavendish does not use.[3] And in the few places that she does seem to be focused on the distinction between conscious and unconscious perceptual states (e.g. OEP 150), she does not seem particularly troubled by it, but gives a straightforward explanation of it in materialist terms. So I see no reason to attribute to Cavendish the view that everything must be conscious to have perception and knowledge.

Are there other special features of human mental life that Cavendish might think are fundamental and widespread? Other obvious candidates include representational or semantic states. But the last

---

3 As a number of people have pointed out, 'consciousness' is not a term that Cavendish uses, probably because it seems that it was first used in the sense of 'awareness', like we use it nowadays, by Cudworth in 1678. But it doesn't mean that something like the concept was not around enough that Cavendish had the opportunity to be interested in it.

chapter argued at length that Cavendish does not take these to be widespread. Another candidate is something even more minimal, something like intentionality, in the sense of directedness toward an object. Cavendish does think that perception is directed toward an object. But while some philosophers think that directedness is essentially mental, Cavendish, as we have seen, does not.

Moreover, it misses something very important about Cavendish to think that, first, she is struck by the inexplicability of any special features of human mental life, and second, that she thinks that it would be a satisfying solution to this inexplicability to posit that these features are fundamental and widespread. Human mental life is a creaturely effect, and it is a 'very great error' to attribute to principles the features of particular effects. (I'll spare you another mention of clayeyness.) But this is especially important here, because it blocks attempts to describe and explain how the mind works by appealing to what kind of stuff it is made of. As we said in Chapter 3, Cavendish's materialism is not the claim that the mind is made of one kind of thing or another or has one kind of property or another. On the interpretation that I've been defending, I just do not think that Cavendish takes this to be part of a good explanation of any phenomenon.

It is especially anathema to Cavendish to attribute to principles the features of particular *human* effects. Some insist that it is possible to attribute to Cavendish the view that there is fundamental mentality everywhere in nature without anthropomorphism. I welcome a characterization of the 'psychic' that avoids this charge, but I haven't seen one. The kinds of panpsychism that we are considering now precisely involve discerning, usually by introspection, a particular feature of our own mental experience and arguing that it must be everywhere, which is anthropocentrism (or maybe just egocentrism).[4]

These considerations, again, do not rule out every possible version of panpsychism. For one, they are focused on versions of

---

4 Of course, were Cavendish to assign human mental life to other things, that would really be zoocentrism, since she thinks we share all that with other animals.

panpsychism according to which mentality is basic. For another, they involve a tiny fraction of the huge variety of ways there are of understanding the mental. To take just one recent example, Rovelli argues that contemporary physics vindicates a 'very mild form of panpsychism' inasmuch as

> it is not about how individual entities are by themselves. It is about how entities manifest themselves to one another...This implies that the most effective way of thinking about the world is not in terms of entities with properties, but rather in terms of systems that have properties in relation to other systems.
>
> (2021: 32)

This might sound a bit like Cavendish, but it does not sound like panpsychism. Like intentionality, Cavendish doesn't give us reason to think that relationality is essentially psychic.

The version of panpsychism that has the best chance of applying to Cavendish is one which interprets Cavendish's theory of mind along the lines of what are nowadays called biosemantic or teleofunctionalist accounts of the representational and the mental. Cavendish emphasizes the continuity between animal sense and rational perception and other kinds of perception, taking the animal cases to be a few among just so many ways that creatures have of interacting with and surviving in their environment. The object of a sense perception is an external object and the relationship between them is just like the relationship between any perception and an external object. If Cavendish were to take the mental or the representational to require only this kind of responsiveness relationship to an object, then every creature would indeed involve mentality or representation. Similarly, given how intent Cavendish is on naturalizing the mind, there may be senses of 'sensitivity' or 'responsiveness' or 'reflexivity', or 'information' on which everything counts as having those things. As I argued in the last chapter, I think that Cavendish's theory of patterning is an attempt to acknowledge the unique features of animal sense and rational perception, while still appreciating its continuity with other kinds of perception. So I am not particularly tempted to interpret her as a panpsychist in this sense, but I wouldn't be mad if somebody else did.

Finally, in conversation, Jonathan Shaheen has suggested an argument for panpsychism from Cavendish's claim that all creatures must have knowledge of God. I have argued that knowledge in general need not be cognitive. But I have done so (and will continue to do so in Section 7.7) without taking at face value Cavendish's claims that we have knowledge of God, interpreting some of them away and suggesting that the few that remain indicate that she herself is uncertain that knowledge of God can be captured her ontology. And it must be admitted that Cavendish seems to think it is important that all creatures have knowledge of God, and one might imagine that knowledge of God, specifically, requires that a creature is somehow mental. She also holds that creatures worship God and that they have equal values in the eyes of God, at least when it comes to their natural lives, and one might argue that worshiping or having value requires being somehow mental. This is all well worth taking seriously, but it will need lots of fleshing out. In doing so, I would urge attention to the question of in what precise sense, and why, knowledge of God (or worship, or value) requires mentality, and especially to any assumption that minded things must be more valuable than things without minds.

To deny that Cavendish is a panpsychist is not to deny that she has a visionary and a revisionary conception of matter, according to which it is everywhere responsive and worthy of wonder. And it is precisely to emphasize the deep continuity between human beings and other animals and other plants and all other things made of self-moving, self-organizing matter, especially the continuity between the cognitive and epistemic capacities of human beings and all other matter. Cavendish's account of perception and knowledge is not reductionist if reducing means ignoring the uniqueness and the power and importance of human and animal cognitive and sense-perceptual capacities. The power of these capacities is part of why Cavendish attributes perception and knowledge to all creatures, and in doing so, she clearly means to ennoble all creatures, not reduce humans and other creatures to machines, as Descartes (on some interpretations) does to animals. The point is just that we cannot know, from our perspective, anything about how other creatures organize their actions other than by the fact that they organize them by corporeal figurative motions.

Section 7.3 Creaturely self-knowledge

The last section argued that it is basically right that Cavendish does not think that we need to add anything to matter, as we are so far acquainted with it, to ground its capacity for creaturely knowledge. That said, I must now admit that Cavendish tells us straight out that creaturely knowledge, including perception, requires that matter have a certain 'principle' that we have yet to discuss in any detail. She usually calls this principle 'self-knowledge' (and less commonly just 'knowledge'). Unlike creaturely knowledges and perceptions, this kind of knowledge does not depend on self-motion (OEP 39), and so even the inanimate parts of nature have an 'innate and fixt self-knowledge' (OEP 19).[5] This kind of self-knowledge is 'every part and particle' of matter (OEP 163) and 'cannot be divided from its own nature' just as 'matter cannot be divided from being matter, or self-motion from being self-motion' (OEP 163). Self-knowledge in this sense, which does not depend on structure or motions, is rather 'the ground and principle of all particular knowledges, as self-motion is the ground and principle of all particular actions' (OEP 138, see also 156).

Sometimes, Cavendish seems to distinguish between self-knowledge and perception in a way that makes it sound as if all self-knowledge is this 'innate' principle while all complex creaturely knowledges are perceptions. She writes, for example, that 'a fixt and interior self-knowledge, may very well be without exterior perception' while 'perception presupposes an innate self-knowledge as its ground and principle' (OEP 39). But as 'fixt', 'interior', and 'innate' suggest, the focus here is on the principle of self-knowledge. And there are plenty of texts that make clear that there is, in addition, creaturely self-knowledge; to take just one example, Cavendish writes that 'there being infinite several Corporeal Figurative Motions, or Actions of Nature, there must of necessity be infinite several Self-knowledges and Perceptions' (GNP 5 5). Moreover, as we

---

5   As Marcy Lascano has pointed out in conversation, Cavendish sometimes uses 'fixt' and 'innate' to refer to figures, motions, or knowledges that are complex. But these ways of describing self-knowledge are suggestive when they are considered alongside the more decisive ways that Cavendish characterizes this kind of knowledge, and I think she sometimes uses them to indicate that she is talking about the principle of self-knowledge and not creaturely self-knowledge.

saw in Section 7.1, it is plausible to interpret creaturely knowledges that are not perceptions as the internal conditions of a creature's actions, which is to say, its internal compositional structure. So Cavendish uses 'self-knowledge' to refer to two different (but related) things: one, a kind of creaturely knowledge that is to be contrasted with perception, and the other, the innate self-knowledge of matter, which is the principle of those creaturely knowledges.

Given the complexity of creatures, which contain further compositional structures and overlap with others, all of a creature's parts are perceptive as well as self-knowing. Indeed, every effective part of nature is both perceptive and self-knowing. The fact that creatures are made of parts is also why our self-knowledge is not perfect. We might otherwise have wondered, with Cavendish's latter thoughts (OEP 38), why, if all creatures have self-knowledge, we are in fact ignorant of so much about ourselves. Cavendish's answer is that

> all creatures…are composed of many several parts, and every part has its own particular self-knowledge…which causes an ignorance between them; for, one part's knowledge is not another part's knowledge; nor does one part know what another knows… Nevertheless, each part knows itself, and its own actions.
>
> (OEP 38–39)

This does not mean that our self-knowledge is erroneous or incomplete, exactly. What is incomplete is the kind of perceptive knowledge that the parts of ourselves that are cognitive, which we wrongly identify with our whole selves, have of the other parts. My sense organs and certain parts of my brain do not have perfect knowledge of my pancreas, although they have some exterior knowledge of it, since they perceive it; neither does my pancreas have perfect knowledge of my brain: 'Truly, Madam, you may as well ask any one part of your body, how every other part of your body acts, as to ask me, who am but a small part of Infinite Matter, how Nature works' (PL 4 1).

Section 7.4 Self-knowledge as a principle

Now, we move to discussing self-knowledge as a principle. What, exactly, is this 'ground and foundation of all other particular knowledge and perceptions' (OEP 176) that is innate to 'every part and particle' of matter (OEP 163)?

Cavendish connects knowledge and ignorance very closely to composition and division. 'As a union or combination of parts, makes knowledge', she writes, 'so a division or separation of parts, makes ignorance' (OEP 20). But we have seen that we should not imagine knowledge to be some stuff that is intrinsic to and spread throughout matter, like the redness of red Legos, which divides and composes as we divide and compose the Legos. If this were the right way to think about knowledge, it would not make sense of Cavendish's claim that division is ignorance: division would just give us two lesser portions of knowledge.

In the last chapter, I argued that perceptual knowledge is the acquaintance between parts, and ignorance is the lack of knowledge that results from the fact that the parts are still distinct. If that is right, what would perfect knowledge be? Well, it would be to be joined and not divided from something. In other words, it would be for a knower to be identical with the known object.

Self-knowledge as a principle, then, is simply identity. In the impossibly abstract case of a sole bit of matter, this is straightforward: to know itself is simply to be itself. But since every part of matter is both divided and composed, things get a little more complicated when we consider the self-knowledge that creatures have. Creaturely self-knowledge is also identity: to know oneself as a creature is to be oneself. But to be a creature is to be a particular composite, with many parts. This results in ignorance between the parts and in the fact that all the parts of a creature (and hence everything) are perceptive as well as self-knowing.

Now, one might ask: isn't to know something perfectly not to become it but to have a perfect representation of it? In the Aristotelian paradigm that we mentioned in the last chapter, this would be to become perfectly like the object, rather than to perfectly become the object. As we have seen, this is not what Cavendish thinks perceptual knowledge does for us. Perceptual knowledge is essentially what puts us in touch with other things. Even if I could replicate the figure of something else in myself, in what sense, Cavendish might ask, would that count as acquaintance with another thing? If I magically became perfectly like my cat, but I am otherwise unrelated to her,

I'm still cat-like over here and she is still cat-like over there. Knowledge, for Cavendish, must be a genuine *connection* between parts.

So, in telling us that the (self-)knowledge that is intrinsic to all matter is the principle of creaturely knowledge and perception, Cavendish is telling us that the ability of parts to compose and divide with one another is what grounds the compositional structures that constitute creaturely knowledges. 'All creatures,' Cavendish writes,

> are composed of many several parts, and every part has its own particular self-knowledge, as well as self-motion, which causes an ignorance between them; for, one part's knowledge is not another part's knowledge; nor does one part know what another knows; but all knowledge of exterior parts, comes by perception: Nevertheless, each part knows itself, and its own actions. And as there is an ignorance between parts, so there is also an acquaintance (especially in the parts of one composed creature).
> (OEP 38–39)

So while all creaturely knowledges do require that matter has the principle of (self-)knowledge, this principle is just another name for something that we already knew about matter: that it is divided and composed.

In naming this principle 'self-knowledge,' Cavendish raises a question. It is supposed to underlie all creaturely knowledge, both self-knowledge and perception. So why should it be *self*-knowledge, rather than just knowledge, neutral between knowledge of self and other? To put a more explicitly metaphysical spin on it, does this undermine the claim that Cavendish privileges neither the parts nor the whole composite, suggesting that unity is prior to diversity?

Only if you assume that identity is prior to composition. But given that compositional structure is essential to matter, which is to say natural being, this is not the case. To be (and to be oneself) is to be composed; to be composed is to be. To return to the idiom of knowledge, perfect self-knowledge is an abstraction:

> The truth is, that nature being not only divisible, but also compoundable in her parts, it cannot be absolutely affirmed that there is either a total ignorance, or a universal knowledge in nature, so

as one finite part should know perfectly all other parts of nature: but as there is an ignorance amongst particulars, caused by the division of nature's parts, so there is also a knowledge amongst them, caused by the composition and union of her parts.

(OEP 214)

Cavendish's claim here that there is no universal knowledge only applies to the knowledge that one part has of other parts. But that is all the knowledge that is recognizably epistemic to us. Any 'particular life and knowledge' will be internally complex as well as related to other things and will so involve division and perception (OEP 20).

Finally, as this passage suggests, there is no such thing as ignorance or error when it comes to the principle of self-knowledge, since that is just identity (see also OEP 39, 40). What about creaturely self-knowledge? We have seen that it admits of ignorance because it is complex and so involves the ignorance that is entailed between parts. But what about error? Cavendish tells us that error and ignorance

proceeded not from interior self-knowledge, but either from want of exterior particular knowledges, or from the irregularity of motions; and ignorance was likewise a want not of interior, but exterior knowledge, otherwise called perceptive knowledge.

(OEP 40–41)

The suggestion in this paragraph is that errors in creaturely self-knowledge arise from 'irregularity of motions'. Reminding ourselves that thus far we are focused on creaturely knowledge in general (and not on cognitive kinds of knowledge), we can interpret this kind of error, for now, merely as a natural error. As we will see in Chapter 9, for motions to be irregular is just for them to conduce to the dissolution of a creature. There is a sort of failure here, but it is not yet clearly an epistemic failure.

Section 7.5 The mind I: material and multiple

Let us consider now the creaturely knowledges that make up what we think of as the mind. In many ways, Cavendish makes clear that these kinds of knowledge should be treated like any other creaturely knowledge. Cavendish seems to recognize such a class of such activities, which include 'Thoughts, Conceptions, Imaginations, Fancy, Understanding, Memory, Remembrance, and whatsoever motions are in the Head, or Brain' (PL 2 18). These thoughts, of course, are nothing else but corporeal figurative motions (PPO2 2 17; PL 1 35, 4 4; GNP 6 1, 6 2).[6] Cavendish characterizes them here in terms of their location in the body; in addition to writing that 'whatsoever' motions are in the head or brain are in this class, she versifies poeticizes:

> For had the Heele such quantity of Braine,
> Which doth the Head, and Skull therein containe;
> Then would such Thoughts, wich in the Braine dwell high,
> Descend downe low, and in the Heele would lye.
> (P&F The Reason why Thoughts are only in the Head)

Elsewhere Cavendish clarifies that it is absurd to imagine that 'the mind chiefly resides but in one part of the body' (OEP 154) or that 'one single part should be King of the whole Creature.' A creature is 'a Republic and not a Monarchy' (PL 3 24); indeed, 'every particular Creature hath numerous souls' (PL 4 3), souls which are moreover not very distinct from the souls of other creatures (PL 4 2). She does seem to think that the kinds of parts that make thoughts and so on are found mostly in the brain, take place mostly in the mind, but these parts don't have a special relationship with the identity or the 'soul' of a creature.

On the contrary, the multiplicity of the mind provides Cavendish with a further argument that it is material. She sometimes argues that the mind must have parts from her already established materialism:

> [T]he rational soul of every particular Creature is composed of parts (I mean parts of a material substance; for whatsoever is substanceless and incorporeal, belongs not to Nature)...not any

---

6 Cavendish sometimes tells us that human beings, and only human beings, have supernatural souls. But she also writes that this, like any other claim about the supernatural, 'no body is able naturally to know' (PL 3 22). And she certainly does not think that our immortal souls constitute, are part of, or influence our natural minds.

Creature can have a soul without parts...that which makes so many confusions and disputes amongst learned men is, that they conceive, first, there is no rational soul but only in man; next, that this rational soul in every man is individable. But if the rational soul is material, as certainly to all sense and reason it is, then it must not only be in all material Creatures, but be dividable too.

(PL 4 2)

But she also argues in the opposite direction, observing that the mind has many objects (PL 2 4) and many functions, including 'Understanding, Imagination, Conception, Memory, Remembrance, and the like' (PL 2 4); that it can have several perceptions such as smell and touch at the same time (PL 2 13); and that a man be of a divided mind about something (PL 2 15). The mind contains variety, and all variety is variety of material parts—so the mind is material. This kind of argument stands in stark contrast with a long philosophical history of arguments that the mind must be immaterial because it has a special kind of unity or simplicity that cannot be accounted for by divisible matter—a unity evidenced by conscious experience and necessary to ensure the survival of the soul after the death of the body.[7] While Cavendish agrees that the mind has a kind of unity, that unity can be accounted for by the unity of composed matter, just like the unity of any other creature (PL 2 13).[8]

Section 7.6 The mind II: Is there nonperceptual knowledge of exterior objects?

Cavendish sometimes calls thoughts, imaginations, and all the 'voluntary actions, both of sense and reason', 'conceptions', which she contrasts with perceptions (OEP 192). Both sense and reason can be involved in perceptions as well as voluntary motions like conceptions

---

7   For more on Cavendish's arguments from the complexity of the mind to its materiality, see Chamberlain (2024a).
8   Laura Georgescu has proposed in conversation that Cavendish might even have been motivated to make parthood and composition, rather than spatial structure, central to her metaphysics by the thought that it is a better account of mental structure. By being essentially compositional rather than spatial, Cavendishian matter thus generates a more plausible materialist analysis of the mind. I like this idea.

(e.g. GNP 5 11; OEP 33). But the sensitive parts don't work as well by rote as the rational parts, which is why hallucinations and dreams are misleading; their stronger connection with inanimate matter means that they are more suited to working in response to other things, that is, in perceptions. So it is reason that should be doing things by rote, and Cavendish associates conceptions in particular with the rational and not the sensitive.

We usually take conceptions, thoughts, memories, and so on to be at least sometimes about things outside of us. Does the claim that they are instances of self-knowledge mean that they cannot be? An initial answer to this is 'no'. A creature's self-knowledges are just the (relatively) internal structural conditions of its behavior, and that doesn't entail anything about what they are *about*—though the question of aboutness does not arise for any other kinds of self-knowledge.

The problem, however, is that in the case of perceptions, we said that they are about the external object that they are related to, and not about the internal pattern. And Cavendish tells us that the distinction between thoughts and other nonperceptual mental states, and perceptions, is precisely that thoughts do not put us into a relationship with an external object. Thoughts, conceptions, memories, and a number of other mental activities from perceptions, Cavendish tells us, are 'voluntary'. By this, she means that they are not patternings of external objects, or as she puts it, they are made 'by Rote, and not by Example' (GNP 5 11). This does not mean that they are entirely spontaneous in the sense of being completely unoccasioned. They may be occasioned by plenty of things, especially things internal to our bodies, and the fact that they involve actions of matter in response to parts external to that matter means they are in some sense perceptual. But they are animal perceptions, and they do not pattern what occasions them (OEP 19–20).

So can thoughts, conceptions, memories, and other cognitive kinds of animal knowledge be of exterior parts and creatures? I think that Cavendish genuinely worries about this question. In the following passage, she vacillates between claiming that thoughts are merely unoccasioned by external objects and claiming that they do not 'concern' foreign objects:

> [T]his is the difference between exterior perceptions, and interior voluntary actions:…perceptions *are properly concerning*

foreign parts, figures and actions, and are occasioned by them: but, the voluntary actions are not occasioned by any outward objects, but make figures of their own accord, without any imitation, patterns, or copies of foreign parts, or actions... the reason why I call the voluntary actions, interior, is, because they have no such respect to outward objects, **at least, are not occasioned by them, as perceptions are, but are the figurative actions of sense and reason, made by rote**; whereas perceptions do tend to exterior objects, and are made according to the presentation of their figures, parts or actions.

(OEP 170–171, my emphases)

The boldfaced portions of this passage suggest that conceptions might be about external parts even though they are not occasioned by them, while the italicized potions suggest that they also do not 'concern' or 'have respect to' foreign parts.

Further arguments can be marshalled for either interpretation. Let's start with the possibility that thoughts and so on are of or about exterior parts objects, even if they are not occasioned by them. For one: of course they are! Isn't that a central feature of our mental life that Cavendish is trying to capture here? Cavendish gives examples of these nonperceptual states that seem clearly to be about external things. Like perceptions, she seems to think they can be truer or falser, according as they are more regular or irregular.

On the other hand, Cavendish tells us a number of times that 'all knowledge of exterior parts, comes by perception' (OEP 39) and that 'no man can naturally go beyond his rational and sensitive perception' (OEP 110). As she puts it decisively in the Grounds, 'Notions, Imaginations, Conceptions, and the like, are such Actions of the Mind, as concern not Forrein Objects' (GNP 6 1). And as we saw, rational perception seems acknowledgment that knowledge of external things must be perceptual, as it is an attempt to carve out a nonsensory perceptual modality.[9] So that leaves less work for nonperceptual knowledge to do.

---

9   One possibility is that thoughts, memories, and the like are not knowledge of exterior parts, since they are not perceptions, but they are still about exterior parts. This might seem like a strange thing to argue if you think that Cavendish is trying to do justice to our intuitions about our mental states: why say they are about anything at all, then? If this is what she thinks, it makes the metacognitive account of patterning suggested in Section 6.6 more plausible.

Cavendish occasionally refers to something called 'interior knowledge', which we might imagine should be contrasted with 'exterior knowledge' in respect of lacking an external occasion but not in respect of lacking an external object. Michaelian, for example, argues that interior knowledge includes 'knowledge of external things that is not occasioned by the presence of those things' (2009: 45). But Cavendish uses this phrase very rarely, and when she does, it is almost always clear that she is referring to the principle of self-knowledge and not creaturely self-knowledge (e.g. OEP 20, 39, 40, 138), which is not, we have argued, the sort of thing that is about anything at all.[10] The only thing that Cavendish does claim that we have interior knowledge of is God who is, in any case, not an exterior object.

Section 7.7 The mind III: So what are conceptions of?

What, then, are our thoughts and conceptions of, if not exterior parts?

It is tempting to think that thoughts, conceptions, and so on, if they are not ways of knowing external parts, are ways of knowing things that are not external parts. One possibility is that these are ways of knowing interior parts. But I think we have completely described the sense in which these are interior, and it is not that they represent other parts of the body to us. (We will return to the relationship between these thoughts and the rest of the body.)

Every other possibility is that thoughts are of things that are not parts of nature. From a principled perspective, this is unacceptable. Cavendish does not think that we have any cognitive contact with anything outside of nature, writing that, just as in the case of perception, 'a corporeal cannot have a conception of that which in nature is not a body' (OEP 89). That said, it is worth briefly entertaining a few specific possibilities.

The first, of course, is God, of who Cavendish tells us that we can have some conception, and specifically that we have 'interior

---

10 Boyle (2015: 440) agrees that interior knowledge is self-knowledge, but I do not think she agrees that it is not about anything, nor that there is a distinction between the principle of self-knowledge and creaturely self-knowledges.

knowledge' of God and 'self-knowledge' of God. This is only slightly less problematic than the proposal that our knowledge of God is a rational perception. Cavendish's struggle to classify our knowledge of God reflects that she does not in fact think that we do have knowledge of God, at least when it comes to natural philosophy—or, at least, that she herself does not see how to accommodate it. As always, she follows her claim that we have interior knowledge of God with a hedge: this time, that it is really just knowledge that God exists, that nature depends upon God, and that God 'ought to be worshipped' (OEP 38). But as we know, 'what God is, cannot be known by any part' (OEP 90). The reasons for this apply to all immaterials, so thoughts are not of any of those.[11]

Another possibility is that while perceptions acquaint us with concrete particulars, thoughts and conceptions are more abstract and general. There is something right about this, but it's important to note that they do not do this by putting us in touch with abstract eternal truths or anything like that. Similarly, as we will see in Chapter 8, Cavendish does not think much of our purported knowledge of mathematics.

In fact, Cavendish seems quite happy to characterize thoughts, conceptions, and so on in entirely nonrepresentational terms. To take just one example from among many:

> When [the] Rational Parts...divide in divers sorts of Actions, Man names it, Arguing, or Disputing in the Mind. And when those divers sorts of Actions are at some strife, Man names it, A contradicting of himself. And if there be a weak strife, Man names it, Consideration...When all the Parts of the Mind move regularly, and sympathetically, Man names it, Wisdom.
>
> (GNP 6 2)

This reflects how deeply Cavendish identifies mental states with just so many organic activities. Conceiving, remembering, dreaming,

---

11 The fact that Cavendish feels pressure to classify our knowledge of God as self-knowledge is some evidence that external knowledge and self-knowledge exhaust the kinds of knowledge that there are.

arguing, and considering are first and foremost things that we do—specifically, with our brains—rather than relationships we have with content. Meanwhile, perceptions are things that we do in response to other concrete things.

Indeed, in the following passage, Cavendish contrasts conceptions and the like with perceptions by unhesitatingly lumping them in with nonmental interior motions:

> But it is well to be observed, that, besides those exterior perceptions of objects, there are some other interior actions both of sense and reason, which are made without the presentation of exterior objects, voluntarily, or by rote; and therefore are not actions of patterning, but voluntary actions of figuring: As for example, imaginations, fancies, conceptions, passions, and the like; are made by the rational, corporeal, figurative motions, without taking any copies of foreign objects; also, many generations, dissolutions, alterations, transformations, etc. are made by the sensitive motions, without any exterior patterns; for, the generation of maggot in a cheese, of a worm in the root of a tree, of a stone in the bladder, etc. are not made by patterning or imitation, because they are not like their producers, but merely by a voluntary figuring.
>
> (OEP 170)

As Boyle (2015) writes, with this kind of 'reasoning' Cavendish tries to capture everything that we do while we philosophize, but all that is still just so many figurative motions.

Perhaps the non-perceptual mental state that most interests Cavendish is imaginative world-creation. Man has the special ability, Cavendish writes, to 'enjoy Worlds of his own making' and to 'govern and command those Worlds; as also, dissolve and compose several Worlds, as he pleases' (GNP 6 4). But Cavendish is very much inclined to talk of these conceptions in the sense of begettings rather than in the sense of concepts, even playing on the word's polysemy (e.g. GNP 1 13 and PPO2 3 9, to remind us that conceptions are the offspring of brains. Finally, Cavendish describes desire and appetite as so many corporeal figurative motions (PL 2 15); they are actions of a body in virtue of its structure.

Now, this doesn't mean that memory, dreaming, and imagination aren't about anything. Cavendish does seem to attribute to many of these activities something like derivative content. For example, remembrances are not occasioned, but they do 'repeat some former actions' and so to that extent are connected with original patternings (GNP 6 2). Similarly, dreams are 'those Corporeal Motions of Sleep, [which] make the same pattern of that Object in Sleep, as when that Object was present' (GNP 7 4). While dreaming happens strictly speaking by rote,

> if the Self-moving Parts move after their own inventions, and not after the manner of Copying; or, if they move not after the manner of Human Perception, then a Man is as ignorant of his Dreams, or any Human Perception, as if he was in a [Swoon]; and then he says, he did not dream; and, that such Sleeps are like Death.
>
> (GNP 7 3)

My memory of Mount Rainier is not occasioned by Mount Rainier, but it is still occasioned by the other parts of my brain and body, whose current states reflect past interactions with Mount Rainier. To the extent to which Cavendish takes mental actions to be 'about' specific objects, she seems to have the hunch that such intentionality or content has its roots in perception, or in actual encounters with external objects, sensory or rational. While Cavendish says that thoughts are voluntary, that does not mean that they are unoccasioned. And it does not mean that thoughts are not in some sense perceptive. After all, they are motions of the brain and the body. In a sense we can think of a memory of Mount Rainier as very mediated perception that includes actual Mount Rainier at some point in the process.

Does my brain, in reminiscing about Mount Rainier, do some similar dances, as Cavendish describes perception, as when I first perceived Mount Rainier? Surely. Does that mean we should identify Mount Rainier as the object of a particular thought? I am not sure that is useful. Cavendish's way of thinking about the mind, which is firmly entrenched in descriptions of it as biological processes, takes us away from thinking about it in terms of the manipulation of symbols (or 'patterns') by essentially cognitive processes. That also makes it difficult to characterize errors in these kind of creaturely self-knowledge as failures to correspond to an object. Like every other error of this kind, it is natural error.[12]

Section 7.8 Reason and reasoning

Finally, we must consider what Cavendish has to say about reason. Cavendish identifies many or all of her philosophical views as rational conceptions, writes that rational conceptions are the source of the 'invention and delivery of arts and sciences' (OEP 171), and associates rational conceptions with 'musing and contemplating' (OEP 151). As we will see in the next chapter, while she takes 'sense and reason' to be the best guide to natural philosophy, she also holds that reason is 'above' sense, and should guide it. So reason is central to Cavendish's epistemology and method. How should we understand reason so that it can do all of this work, especially given what we have said about conceptions so far?

We have already learned about reason in two of its aspects: first, we know that there is rational perception alongside sensitive that is more general and more penetrating than the sensitive, and second, we know that the relative freedom of rational matter is responsible for this. But just as the sensitive is more suited to perception, the rational is more suited to conception, being less bound to inanimate matter and as a result less bound by external things. Like rational perception, rational conception is privileged but not infallible; it does not have an essential connection to truth or regularity. Cavendish notes

12 It is interesting to compare Cavendish's account of error with Spinoza's, especially with Jonathan Bennett's discussion of Spinoza's claim that falsity is 'nothing positive' and only a species of ignorance (Bennett 1986). As Bennett points out, Spinoza is driven to this conclusion by some broadly naturalistic commitments, which he shares with Cavendish. Bennett suggests that Spinoza might have done better with a naturalistic account of error like functionalism, which is something like what I suggest for Cavendish here. In that sense I think that Cavendish has a positive account of error though not a positive account of falsity. That is because her identification of being and knowing leads her, like Spinoza, to be suspicious of the idea that, as Bennett puts it, 'something that is real can be contrary to the true' (1986: 9).

for the reader at the beginning of the *Observations* that she sometimes uses the word 'rational' when she actually means 'regular', which is to say, when she invests 'rational' with a positive epistemic sense (OEP 16). But there can be irregular conceptions as well as regular ones (OEP 16), just as there can be irregular rational perceptions.

A second activity of reason is what Cavendish calls 'reasoning', which is better understood as an activity of matter rather than as a state.[13] Reasoning involves comparing things in the mind (PL 1 10) and it is discursive (PL 3 25); Cavendish classifies it as a variety of actions of creatures alongside digestion, dancing, and weeping (GNP 5 12), and sometimes seems to assimilate reasoning with having conceptions and thoughts. This characterization of reason's activity fits well with the interpretation of voluntary motions developed so far, because it makes sense of the claim that these activities are not about objects in the same sense that perceptions are. It also fits well with another claim that Cavendish makes: that reason is particularly concerned with discovering causes. 'To see the effects,' Cavendish writes, 'belongs to the perception of sense; but to judge of the cause, belongs only to reason' (OEP 242). These two points about reasoning suggest that perhaps reason involves inference, particularly inference from effects to causes. This is what allows reason to 'penetrate deeper' into the natures of things.

However, Cavendish does not seem to think that we can very successfully reason from effects to causes. And she does not give us guides for how to reason properly, which we might expect if we think of reason as a kind of inference. Cavendish's ambivalence on this point can be seen in a passage from the *Grounds*, where she writes that the rational parts of a creature can 'make Conceptions of the Interior Parts, but not Perception: for, neither the Sense, nor Reason, can perceive what is not present, but by rote, as after the manner of Conceptions, or Rememberances' (GNP 1 8). But in the very next section, she reminds us that creatures can only have knowledge by

---

13 Boyle (2015: 443) also appreciates this function of reason, although I am not sure that, as she argues, Cavendish sometimes assimilates it with rational perception. I might say instead that Cavendish is sometimes unsure whether some particular bit of knowledge should be counted as rational perception or as a result of reasoning, for reasons that will become clearer in the next chapter.

perception, 'which is the cause of Suppositions, or Imaginations, concerning Forrein Objects', wherein the rational parts 'may suppose, or presuppose' what the interior nature of another creature is. These, Cavendish writes, we name Conjectures'. This fits well, as we will see, with the account of reasoning from causes to effects given in the next chapter: reasoning, in this sense, is only probable conjecture.

Finally, in a passage from the *Letters* about Van Helmont, Cavendish seems to distinguish between something like reasoning and yet another activity or role of reason:

> But your *Author*, by his leave, confounds Reason, and Reasoning, which are two several and distinct things; for reasoning and arguing differs as much from Reason, as doubtfulness from certainty of knowledg, or a wavering mind from a constant mind; for Reasoning is the discoursive, and Reason the understanding part in Man.
>
> (PL 3 25)

She goes on to write that 'perfect Truth requires not reasoning or arguing, as whether it be so, or not; but yet it requires reason, as to confirm it to be so, or not so: for Reason is the confirmation of Truth, and Reasoning is but the Inquisition into Truth.' I think that the best way to read this passage is to identify 'reason' not with some particular kind of creaturely (indeed, human) activity, but with the innate self-knowledge of matter, which is a principle of all reasoning. For as the next chapter will argue further, it is not for human beings to have 'confirmation of Truth'. This reading is even more plausible if we consider the context: Cavendish is targeting Van Helmont's claim that reason is mortal and the intellect or understanding immortal, and the fact that he as a result 'slights and despises the Rational soul... making her no substance.' In reply, Cavendish tells us that reason is in fact the substance of reasoning, and is, of course, material.

Section 7.9 Conclusion

I have tried in this chapter to walk a line, with Cavendish, between accounting for some of the unique features of mental states, on the one hand, and understanding them in their nature as compositions of self-moving matter, on the other. We have seen that knowledge, at its most general, is a fundamental metaphysical principle, but it is not a new one. Self-knowledge as a principle reflects the deep connection that Cavendish makes between being and knowing.

Presumably, the kinds of knowledge that fill the *Observations*, *Grounds*, and Cavendish's other works can be explained this way as well. But so far, it is not clear how Cavendish will derive the epistemic resources to make the kinds of sweeping claims about nature that she does in those works. So in the next chapter, we will explore Cavendish's method, drawing on the lessons of these chapters as well as her explicit comments about the prospects of natural philosophy and how best to realize them.

Further reading

Several of the suggested readings from last chapter are relevant here as well, especially Boyle (2015), Michaelian (2009), and Georgescu (2021).

Cunning, David. 2016. Chapters 5 and 7. *Cavendish*. New York: Routledge.

Cunning, David. 2023. 'Cavendish and Strawson on Emergence, Mind, and Self.' Pp. 369–398 in *Oxford Studies in Philosophy of Mind* 3, edited by Uriah Kriegel. Oxford Academic.

Eight
Method

Wherefore I am in a maze, when I hear of such men, which pretend to know so much, as if they had plundered the Celestial Cabinet of the Omnipotent God.

(PL 2 33)

It is no accident that we consider Cavendish's method near the end of this book and not at the beginning. Cavendish is a metaphysics-first thinker. She is much more likely to argue from metaphysical first principles to epistemic claims than vice versa. Part of this is that Cavendish does not think that we have special access to our own mental states or our own selves, so the study of our minds is not nearer to us than the study of other material things.

Cavendish simply tells us what her method is:

neither my sensitive, nor my rational faculties could enable me to perceive a more substantial ground, or firmer foundation, than that of 'material nature'; not to follow a better method, than that of 'sense' and 'reason'.

(OEP 21)

As this passage reminds us, the ontological and the epistemic are tightly linked. Knowledge puts us in touch with nature in both senses. Similarly, 'sense and reason' describes both the nature of matter itself as well as complex epistemic phenomena.

DOI: 10.4324/9781003107255-9

'Go with your natural sense and reason', however, is a rather obscure directive when it comes to actual inquiry into natural philosophy. And when Cavendish is more specific about method, it is almost always critical. From one perspective, this is unsurprising. The philosophy of mind that we have seen, as well as what we know about knowledge and perception already, does not make it obvious how we can develop the kind of insight into causes that is the goal of natural philosophy. As we might expect from this, Cavendish does take a rather sceptical stance regarding a number of realms in which we take ourselves to have knowledge, and she even tells us sometimes that natural philosophy cannot achieve its goal of discovering causes at all.

Still, Cavendish also makes clear that there are better and worse methods, and she obviously thinks that we are (or at least she is) licensed to make claims about nature, both about particular creatures and about the deepest causes of natural phenomena. What justifies these claims? And how should we go about exploring infinite nature and her infinite parts and effects?

I do not think that Cavendish ultimately has a precise and detailed method. That makes sense from one perspective. Method is, arguably, artificial, and artifice obscures. (Cavendish herself implies this when she identifies the 'artificial and methodical' in the preface to the *Letters*.) But drawing on Cavendish's philosophical practice as well as her criticisms of other philosophers, we can say more about what it means to let our natural sense and reason lead.

Cavendish's central methodological guideline is that we must mind the distinction between causes and effects, and carefully avoid confusing them. It turns out, however, that almost all reasoning from effects to causes is subject to our tendency to confuse them, Cavendish identifies this as the dominant source of error in natural philosophy. A particularly tempting and pernicious species of this confusion occurs when we mistake human beings for causes, and this gives rise to Cavendish's frequent diagnoses of philosophical error as overreliance upon artifice.

The only way to avoid this is by reasoning from causes to effects, which requires that we have some independent insight into causes. This is the source of Cavendish's claim that speculative philosophy should guide experimental philosophy. The question, then, is how we can come to have such independent insight into causes, especially given the philosophy of mind that we have developed thus far. And that is not an easy question to answer.

In considering Cavendish's method, it helps to keep in mind the distinction between ontological and epistemic versions of anthropocentrism and anthropomorphism. As we will see, Cavendish takes philosophy, as we do it, to be an essentially human enterprise, even an essentially discursive one. To understand how philosophy depends on our particular natures is to help us to beware of the tendency to project ourselves onto infinite nature ourselves. If we can do that, Cavendish thinks, we can cultivate the proper wonder and humility in the face of the diversity of nature's actions, but also realize our goal of giving genuine natural philosophical explanations.

Section 8.1 Natural philosophy, causes, and effects

Cavendish understands natural philosophy in the way that her early modern contemporaries did, which traces back to Aristotle: it is the 'rational inquisition into the causes of natural effects' (OEP 158), which included, at Cavendish's time, much of what we call science. As Section 2.7 argued, this is all the inquiry that is open to us, at least if we want any hope of meaningful answers. The limits of natural philosophy are the limits of nature, and the claims of natural philosophy can be at best naturally necessary.[1]

How does one discover causes? A useful heuristic distinguishes between three possibilities.

First, we might simply perceive causes. We know from the last chapter that Cavendish does not think that we can do that, at least not when it comes to particular things. With rare exceptions, she tell us that even rational perception can only perceive exterior figures and motions, which is to say, effects.

Second, we might reason from perceived effects to their causes. Cavendish suggests that we can do that in a limited way. Though our exterior senses can 'go no further than the exterior figures of creatures', 'our reason may pierce deeper, and consider their inherent natures, and interior actions' (OEP 100). However, reason may only

---

1 With very few exceptions. One possible exception is if a proposition is explicitly contradictory, as I suggested in Chapter 2 is the case for 'immaterial substance'.

'probably guess at them, and may chance to hit the truth' (OEP 100). This does not take us very deep—certainly not to ultimate causes— and it is only a probable guess.

The third and final possibility is we have some other source of knowledge of natural causes, in a way that is not connected to perception at all. We saw in the last chapter that Cavendish seems to trace all the content of our possible knowledge to perceptions, which is to say encounters with nature. So if such knowledge is possible, we will want to know how, exactly.

These preliminaries seem to be leading us to a rather pessimistic view of the prospects of natural philosophy. And Cavendish does indeed often express such pessimism. For example, to the question '*Whether any truth may be had in Natural Philosophy*', she replies that 'Natural Philosophers cannot find out the absolute truth of Nature, or Natures ground-works, or the hidden causes of natural effects' (PL 4 27; this passage is worth visiting to read in full). However, she does follow this up with two important caveats. First, natural philosophical speculations are 'grounded upon probability', and probability, in turn 'is next to truth'. Second, though natural philosophers do not discover hidden causes, nevertheless it is worthwhile, because in their pursuit of causes 'they have found out many necessary and profitable Arts and Sciences, to benefit the life of man'.

This pragmatic assessment of natural philosophy is reflected in Cavendish's brief evaluation of scepticism in the *Observations*. There, she writes:

> When sceptics endeavour to prove, that not anything in nature can be truly and thoroughly known; they are, in my opinion, in the right way, as far as their meaning is, that not any particular creature can know the infinite parts of nature; for nature having both a divisible and compoundable sense and reason, causes ignorance, as well as knowledge, amongst particulars.

But, she continues,

> if their opinion be, that there is no true knowledge at all found amongst the parts of nature, then surely their doctrine is not

only unprofitable, but dangerous, as endeavouring to overthrow all useful and profitable knowledge.

(OEP 214)

Note that Cavendish does not add 'false' to her diagnosis of the sceptical stance as unprofitable and dangerous.

Cavendish is writing here of natural philosophy in general, and so seemingly of all possible knowledge of natural causes. Ultimately, we will see that there is a sliver of knowledge that may escape this analysis. However, when it comes to all knowledge that comes from reasoning from effects to causes, Cavendish is fairly consistent: the knowledge that we have in this way is merely probable guess, and it is does not in fact succeed at reaching causes. We look closer at each of these points in turn.

Section 8.2 Probabilism

Cavendish frequently characterizes opinions, including her own, as more or less probable, and she characterizes her quest as one for 'the probability of truth, according to that proportion of sense and reason nature has bestowed upon me' (OEP 9, see also e.g. 24, 30, 35). This applies both to our knowledge of metaphysical principles and to our knowledge of creatures. We focus on the latter here and return to the former in Section 8.8.

As we have seen, Cavendish writes that our inferences to particular causes are made 'by guess' and are merely 'probable conclusions' (OEP 41, see also 100). We might wonder at the equation of these two claims, especially if we think of the probabilities of our beliefs as quantifiable and objective. But when Cavendish writes that it is 'probable' that all natural creatures have pores, she does not mean that we can be, say, 60% certain that all natural creatures have pores. Rather, Cavendish thinks of what is probable as what has more reasons or considerations on its side than the alternative, and judgments of probability are required when there are compelling reasons on both sides. This is illustrated, for example, by the Argumental Discourse, where Cavendish presents considerations on both sides of a matter and describes the rational parts of her mind as 'inclined' to one opinion, 'which they thought much more probable' than the other (OEP 42).The ultimate determiner of probability is the judgment of an individual thinker upon considering these reasons, and Cavendish provides the reader with both sides of the argument so that she can assess what is probable for herself.

As Clucas (2003b) explains, Cavendish can be situated in a probabilist tradition in 17th-century England.[2] That tradition included Charleton, who aims at 'plausibly satisfactory' explanations in the face of man's inability to 'prætend to an exact or adæquate comprehension of nature'; Glanvill, who rejects the possibility of any 'certain Theory of Nature'; and Boyle, who describes the corpuscularianism of the *Origin* as 'a heap of bare Probabilities' (Clucas 2003b: 202). Consider that after his diagnosis of Cavendish's philosophy as 'ingenious and free' but not 'Apodictical', Charleton goes on to write that this

> can be no discredit to your Philosophy in particular, because common to all others: and he is a bold man, who dares to exempt the Physics of Aristotle himself, or of Democritus, or Epicurus, of Des Cartes, or Mr. Hobbs, or any other hitherto known. For my part, Seriously, I should be loath to affirm, that they are any other but ingenious Comments of Mens Wits upon the dark and inexplicable Text of the World; plausible Conjectures at best.
>
> (Clucas 2003b: 203–204, citing Charleton)

The probabilism of many of Cavendish's contemporaries was, like hers, influenced by classical scepticism but also by earlier Catholic theorizing that knowledge must be limited in light of God's complete knowledge. Some, like Charleton, attribute our epistemic imperfection to human fallenness. Cavendish very occasionally contrasts our limited knowledge with God's, mostly to mock the pretensions of some natural philosophers, who 'pretend to know so much, as if they had plundered the Celestial Cabinet of the Omnipotent God' (PL 2 33). But the proper contrast for our limited knowledge, for Cavendish, is not God's knowledge, but nature's infinite knowledge

---

2 Drawing on work by Barbara Shapiro (1983) and Henry G. van Leeuwen ([1970] 2013). For useful background, see Shapiro (1985), Chapter 1.

of herself. Our knowledge is limited not because we are fallen, but because we are finite, and there is no shame in that.

As Clucas highlights, Cavendish associates her probabilism with freedom of thought, writing that 'Opinion is but a guess of what may be a Truth; but men should be as free to Opinions as Opinions to them, to let them come and go at pleasure' (WO 127). Similarly, in the *Letters*, she writes:

> I would rather praise, then contradict any Person or Persons that are ingenious; but by reason Opinion is free, and may pass without a pass-port, I took the liberty to declare my own opinions as other Philosophers do…[and] have done that, which I would have done unto me; for I am as willing to have my opinions contradicted, as I do contradict others: for I love Reason so well, that whosoever can bring most rational and probable arguments, shall have my vote, although against my own opinion.
>
> (PL Preface to the Reader)

This passage hints that reason-giving is an essential part of the natural philosophical enterprise.

Shapiro explains that probability and opinion were anciently associated with rhetoric (1983: 37–38), and ultimately with authority, so that 'probability for many generations was associated as much with what was approved as with what was provable' (38). In the 17th-century, it largely lost this association, as probability but not authority was embraced by mechanical and experimental philosophers, and anti-Aristotelians more generally. Cavendish does not revere authority any more than these other philosophers do. She frequently emphasizes the newness of her own ideas and even accuses experimental philosophers of remixing ancient opinions despite their own claims to novelty (OEP 239). However, she also writes that we should not ignore the ancients and other philosophers who came before us, who have as much a share of sense and reason as we do (OEP 195). And she accuses experimental philosophers of relying on authority, too: their own. The are led by 'the bare authority of an experimental philosopher', rather than reason, 'as if they only had the infallible truth of nature, and engrossed all knowledge to themselves' (OEP 197). Here and elsewhere, it is clear that despite the fact that it is up to each thinker to assess probability for herself, the route to knowledge is not to isolate oneself from others, like a Cartesian meditator, for that is just to rely on one's own authority. Cavendish sees reasoning as dialectical through and through. To reason properly means not simply to think from one's armchair, or to perform experiments alone in a lab, but to exchange reasons.

Section 8.3 Mistaking effects for causes

When we attempt to reason from effects to causes, we do not reach knowledge of causes, and must instead content ourselves with '[finding] out many necessary and profitable Arts and Sciences, to benefit the life of man' (PL 4 27). Cavendish includes in this category the motions of the heavens, the causes of eclipses, and the 'vertues and effects of Vegetables and Minerals'. While some of this might sound like knowledge of causes, Cavendish writes that in finding these out, 'the search of a hidden cause' instead 'finds out visible effects' (OEP 15). So even when we use reason to 'penetrate deeper' into finite creatures than our sense perception allows, we are only discovering new 'visible effects'. This reflects that we only have perceptual access to the exterior figures of things and that perceptual access is all the cognitive access we have to creatures.

What about Cavendish's claim that our reason can guess at what is beneath the proverbial surface? There may be some extremely loose sense in which what reason discovers is 'deeper' than the phenomenon whose cause we seek. But given how complex are the causes of a particular phenomenon, there is no real sense in which we can be said to have identified the cause of that phenomenon, rather than just some related effects. At best, 'depth' is evidenced by the amount of control that it gives us over the phenomena, hence Cavendish's claim that this kind of reasoning should be thought of in terms of its benefit to the life of man and not in terms of its discovery of truths. This benefit is perhaps a sign that we have 'chanced upon the truth', but chancing upon truth is very different from coming to see the connections between causes and their effects. This approach is reflected in Cavendish's critiques, in the *Observations*, of the various explanations of creaturely phenomena offered by experimental and other philosophers. These interventions differ in their particulars, but they echo the same basic criticism: they mistake effects for causes.

One way that Cavendish frequently makes this point is by arguing that some proposed cause acts differently in different contexts. For example, 'the sole agitation of air' is not cause of fire because 'then houses that are made of wood…would never fail to be set on fire by the agitation of the air' (OEP 54). Similarly, the pain caused by the sting of nettles cannot 'proceed from a poisonous juice' contained therein because nettles can be eaten without upsetting the stomach (OEP 57). And the fact that different creatures have different perceptions of the same degree of heat and cold means that those perceptions cannot be caused by 'a real entrance of hot and cold particles, into the pores of their bodies' (OEP 98).

We are already familiar with the generalized version of the last argument from Chapter 6, where we saw Cavendish argue that objects do not cause perceptions of them because our perceptions of them are very different. And as we also saw there, several readers have suggested that passages like this indicate that Cavendish accepts Hobbes's understanding of a cause as *causa integra*, or entire cause, defined as 'the aggregate of all the accidents both of the agents how many soever they be, and of the patient, put together: which when they are all supposed to be present, it cannot be understood that the effect is produced at the same instant' (Hobbes 1656: IX 3). It is true that part of what is going on in these cases is that a cause must determine its effect. But this comparison is potentially misleading. In identifying something like poison as a cause, Cavendish does not just think that we are incompletely identifying the entire cause. She thinks that we are identifying the wrong kind of thing as a cause entirely. Consider the alternative that she proposes to explain nettle stings:

> The truth is, I find that stings are of such kind of figures as fire is, and fire of such a kind of figure as stings are; but although they be all of one general kind, nevertheless they are different in their particular kinds; for, as animal kind contains many several and different particular kinds or sorts of animals; so the like do vegetables, and other kinds of creatures.
>
> (OEP 57)

Why should describing stings as different species of related figures explain why nettles do not always and everywhere sting? After all, that suggests that the nettle's poison is still one kind of thing. The point is that nettles contribute to stinging in virtue of their figures, and figures can interact in complex ways with other figures to produce different effects. In contrast, poison, as Cavendish construes it, is an occult quality: it tells us that the sting must be caused by a stingy substance. In that way, Cavendish thinks, we are projecting our knowledge of the effect onto the cause and assuming it must be like the cause.

Similarly, Cavendish argues that given the diversity of thermal phenomena, it is 'impossible to reduce them to one certain cause or principle, or confine them to one sort of motions.' Instead, she writes, 'the several figurative corporeal motions, which make all things in nature, do also make several sorts of heat and cold, in several sorts of creatures' (OEP 98; see also OEP 112). The point is not that the *causa integra* must include all the particulars that contribute to a change in a creature. Rather, it is that these changes are not caused by other creatures but by corporeal figurative motions that underlie what appear to us as the apparent cause and the apparent effect. It is not just a mistake as to which creaturely things are causes, but a mistake as to the very nature of causes themselves. When Cavendish complains that it is an 'absurdity' to imagine that some *primum frigidum* is the common principle of natural heat and cold, that is not because there are many *prima frigida* but because this makes a 'universal cause, of a particular effect' (OEP 114).[3]

Section 8.4 Variety and induction

Cavendish is very impressed by the great variety of nature's creatures. She warns against trying to reduce these creatures to particular kinds, to imagine that there is only one kind of motion or mode of production, and to project our observations about the creatures in our little corner of the world onto nature as a whole. In fact, Cavendish writes, 'there's not anything that has, and doth still delude most men's understandings more, than that they do not enough consider the variety of nature's actions' (OEP 99).

Induction was an important tool in the arsenal of experimental philosophers, by which knowledge could be gained from particular

---

3 As we will see in the next chapter, this can 'in some manner' be called a cause.

observations and experiments. Cavendish is very critical of their reliance on induction:

> I see, that in this present age, learned men are full of art, and artificial trials; and when they have found out something by them, they presently judge that all natural actions are made in the same way: As for example, when they find by art that salt will make snow congeal into ice, they instantly conclude from thence, that all natural congelations, are made by saline particles; and that the primum frigidum, or the principal cause of all natural cold, must needs be salt.
>
> (OEP 100)[4]

The problem here is not simple overgeneralization. That would suggest that salt did in fact cause this particular congelation, but not all congelations. In fact, while we might have discovered a useful association between the presence of salt and congelation, we have not identified any causes. So after Cavendish writes that 'the variety of nature, is a stumbling block to most men, at which they break their heads of understanding,' she continues that this is because 'they consider not so much the interior natures of several creatures, as their exterior figures and phenomena' and thereby, 'supposing that sense and art can only lead them to the knowledge of truth', they 'delude their judgments, instead of informing them' (OEP 99). The problem is that we mistake exterior figures for interior figures. This is connected to our tendency to underestimate variety because that is also a tendency to underestimate the complexity of any given phenomena. We attempt to abstract the superficial features of things that concern us and assume that those give us some idea of what is operative at a deeper level. But in fact we are only identifying some more 'visible effects' of self-moving matter.

This is important because while Cavendish emphasizes the irreducible variety of creatures, that does not imply an irreducible variety of causes. 'Although Nature delights in variety,' she writes, 'yet

---

4   While this passage mentions artificial trials, that is not really what is at stake here—after all, they might have seen salt turn snow into ice by 'natural' observation. We will return to artifice in the next section.

she is constant in her groundworks' (OEP 203). In other words, nature has an irreducible variety of parts and actions, but these arise from very simple principles. And we cannot arrive at knowledge of those principles by generalizing from particular effects.

Section 8.5   Experimental and speculative philosophy

How can we avoid these pitfalls? Well, Cavendish tells us that the proper method of discovery is sense guided by reason. This sounds a lot like the goal of experimental philosophers, who sought to use our rational faculties to improve the observations of our senses. Cavendish also shares her probabilism with experimental philosophers, and she is engaged alongside them in trying to offer explanations of creaturely phenomena like fire, freezing, various kinds of generation, and respiration. She had a small home laboratory with microscopes, and she visited the Royal Society, the headquarters of experimental philosophy, with interest.

And yet, Cavendish is extremely critical of experimental philosophers. There are two big reasons for this. The first, which we will discuss in this section, is that they think they are seeking and identifying causes when they are not. The second is that they rely too much upon artifice. We'll consider her first complaint in this section and the second in the next.

Cavendish is happy to endorse an ideal version of the experimental philosophy, which would do just what observation of particular effects should do: get us probable knowledge of how to improve our lives by developing experience in manipulating the things that matter to us. The best experimentalists would be the people with the most experience in that realm, which is to say, the ladies:

> for they most commonly take pleasure in the making of sweetmeats, possets, several sorts of pies, puddings, and the like…and it may be, they would prove good experimental philosophers, and inform the world how to make artificial snow, by their creams, or possets beaten into froth: and ice, by their clear, candied, or crusted quiddities, or conserves of fruits: and frost, by their candied herbs and flowers: and hail, by their small comfits made of water and sugar, with whites of eggs: And many other the like figures, which resemble beasts, birds,

vegetables, minerals, etc. But the men should study the causes of those experiments: and by this society, the commonwealth would find a great benefit.

(OEP 106)

It is women who know how to make our lives better, which includes discovering 'pretty toys to employ idle time' (OEP 105). But this has nothing to do with discovering causes.

Cavendish's insistence that real men discover causes suggests that she thinks that there is, after all, some way to do that. This complicates the suggestions that we saw earlier that natural philosophers in general can only more or less probably make visible more effects. It turns out that while this is true of reasoning from effects to causes, there is a another option: speculative philosophy, which 'ought to be preferred before the experimental' (OEP 42).

In late 17th-century Britain, natural philosophy was divided into two branches: the speculative and the experimental. Experimental philosophy was strongly associated with the Royal Society, especially Robert Boyle, Robert Hooke, Henry Power—and Francis Bacon, an important influence on those men as well as on Cavendish. The experimental philosophers contrasted their approach to natural philosophy, which was led by experiment and observation, with speculative philosophers, who they saw as pretending to knowledge of principles and systems based merely on contemplation. Here is the difference between the two, as characterized by John Sargeant:

> The Methods which I pitch upon to examine, shall be of two sorts, viz. that of Speculative, and that of Experimental Philosophers; The Former of which pretend to proceed by Reason and Principles; the later by Induction; and both of them aim at advancing Science.
>
> (As cited in Anstey 2005: 219)

As the association of experimental philosophy with induction and of speculative philosophy with reason and principles indicates, by endorsing speculative philosophy over experimental, Cavendish holds that reason gives us some independent access to principles. Responding to her interlocutors' claim in the *Letters* that 'The cause cannot be better known then by its effect; for the knowledge of the effect, leads us to knowledge of the cause', Cavendish answers:

> it is more easie, in my opinion, to know the various effects in Nature by studying the Prime cause, then by the uncertain study of the inconstant effects to arrive to the true knowledg of the prime cause; truly it is much easier to walk in a Labyrinth without a Guide, then to gain a certain knowledg in any one art or natural effect, without Nature her self be the guide, for Nature is the onely Mistress and cause of all.
>
> (PL 3 13)

The prime cause, of course, is self-moving matter, which causes all creaturely phenomenon by her various corporeal figurative motions.

This makes sense of the alternative explanations that Cavendish proposes of the phenomena discussed in the *Observations*. In those examples, she mostly points out that the phenomenon in question is more complex than the proposed cause suggests, and that this complexity results from the fact that both apparent cause and effect involve many interacting corporeal figurative motions. Occasionally Cavendish goes further and tells us something a little more specific, like that the interior figure of water involves 'circle lines'. But her presentation of these theories is perfectly consistent with her claims that such speculations are merely probable guesses.

Though 'contemplative philosophy is the best tutoress' (OEP 241), Cavendish writes, still, 'experimental philosophy is not to be rejected' (OEP 42), because the 'experimental and speculative philosophy do give the surest informations, when they are joined or united together' (OEP 42). But 'reason must first consider the cause, and then sense may better perceive the effects' (OEP 210). In keeping with Cavendish's identification of sense and reason as the grounds of nature as well as of knowledge, this relationship between speculative philosophy and experimental philosophy is reflected in the fact that rational matter 'directs' the sensitive (PL 4 24). Of course, we would still like to know how we can have speculative knowledge of the 'prime cause'. We will return to that in Section 8.9.

Section 8.6 Experimental philosophy and artifice

Cavendish does not just think that experimental philosophers abdicate the search for causes (which would make them, I guess, merely womanly but not in error). She criticizes them for mistakenly believing, as Hooke does, that in contrast to natural history, experimental philosophy does in fact seek the 'Causes and Reasons' of what we observe (Hooke 1665: 49). Now, the experimental philosophers do not see themselves, as Cavendish sometimes characterizes them, as blindly following their senses. On the contrary, they take themselves to be using reason to guide their observations and experiments, which sounds amenable enough to Cavendish's method.

As we saw in the last section, however, for Cavendish, to guide our sense by reason means to bring to bear the independent knowledge that we have of principles to interpret our sense experience: to consider the cause before perceiving the effects. Now, this is not *not* something that experimental philosophers do. After all, many experimentalists were engaged in finding evidence for the mechanical or corpuscular philosophy, which at least some admitted was a hypothesis (e.g. Boyle 1666: 1). However, another sense in which the experimentalists used reason to guide sense was by ameliorating or purifying sense itself. But sense perception, for Cavendish, does what it is naturally supposed to do—it is limited, but it is not lacking. And the experimental philosophers' attempts to rectify and improve sense is an attempt to rectify and improve nature.

Cavendish diagnoses this attempt as artifice, a cudgel that she wields against experimental philosophers as well as other philosophers. The core of Cavendish's problem with artifice is perhaps most clearly seen from her complaints about chymists. Chymists purport to create new forms and reproduce existing natural forms, which Cavendish sees as an attempt to understand and control causes: something that we cannot do. (She attacks Boyle's claim that experimental philosophers have introduced new artificial forms, too (OEP 237).)

When Cavendish writes that we cannot introduce new forms into nature, she does not mean that there is some stock of natural forms, no matter how big, to which human beings cannot contribute. Rather, she means that human beings cannot operate at the level of the causes of things, which is just to say that nature can 'according to the mixture of composition and division of parts…produce what figures they please; but by a new creation, but only a change or alteration of their own parts' (OEP 238). While human beings can influence what happens in nature, we are not causes. This reflects Cavendish's judgment that chymists would do better if they 'did but study well the corporeal motions or actions of Natures substantial body' (PL 3 14).

As Chapter 5 suggested, the problem with artifice is not that there is something particularly bad about it; it is simply that chymistry, like any art, is 'but an effect of Nature' (PL 3 13) and as such cannot 'inform us of Nature' (PL 3 13). Natural philosophers' reliance upon art is that it is a special case of what we have already seen is the source of most errors: it mistakes effects for causes. Specifically, it mistakes *these effects* [gesturing at ourselves] for causes. As Cavendish writes:

> though Art proceeds from Nature, yet Nature doth not proceed from Art, for the Cause cannot proceed from the Effect, although the Effect proceeds from the Cause, neither can Art the Effect of Nature comprehend Nature, for Nature is so far beyond or above Art, as Art is Lost and Confounded in the Search of Nature, for Nature being Infinite, and Art Finite, they cannot Equalize each other.
>
> (PPO2 Preface)

In contrast, Cavendish makes 'sense and reason…the ground of my philosophy, and no particular natural effects, nor artificial instruments' (OEP 100).

Consider how this applies to Hooke's claims that the 'mistakes of human actions' proceed from errors of the senses and the understanding, and that the 'the real, the mechanical, the experimental philosophy' can improve power over natural causes and effects' (Hooke 1665, as cited in OEP 48–49). Cavendish replies: 'I do not understand…what they mean by our power over natural causes and effects: for we have no power at all over natural causes and effects; but only one particular effect may have some power over another, which are natural actions' (OEP 49). 'Those that employ their time in artificial experiment,' she writes, 'consider only nature's sporting or playing actions' and her 'bastards or changelings' (OEP 105). This does not mean that art is something different than nature's other actions, but rather that these are mere particular effects and are 'not to be compared to her wise and fundamental actions'. Experimental philosophers think that they are penetrating nature, but they are just poking her, causing her to produce new effects. These 'artificial effects can no more be excluded from nature, than any ordinary effect or creature of nature', Cavendish writes, but they do not reflect the actions of 'nature in general' (OEP 197). Hence Cavendish's conclusion that experimental philosophers find 'at best superficial wonders' and are merely 'boys that play with watery bubbles or fling dust into each other's eyes' (OEP 51–52).

The experimental philosophers rely on artifice in a number of ways. The most obvious way is that they believe that by using artificial instruments, they can improve upon our natural sense faculties. As we saw in Chapter 6, Cavendish does not think that microscopes and other lens-based technologies allow us to peer any further into the natures of things than our natural senses do, nor do they give us a more accurate view of the exterior figures of things. Cavendish does not deny that such instruments are never useful. They may, she thinks, allow us to chance upon some new effects. In a number of places, Cavendish complains that the microscopists are not using microscopes this way, however, writing for example that 'the inspection of a bee, through a microscope, will bring him no more honey' (OEP 9). When artifice and experiment are beneficial, it is not because they have uncovered causes, improved upon our natural faculties, or achieved a better, deeper, or more accurate view of creatures than we could with our unaided vision. We have simply chanced upon some positive new effects. This pragmatic perspective helps Cavendish avoid the objection that surely microscopes do help us see better and more truly. While she can admit that sometimes microscopes improve our abilities, in the day-to-day, it is obviously best to rely upon our natural sense faculties.

Besides overreliance on artifice in their techniques, Cavendish takes experimental philosophers to project the artificial onto the natural to the extent that they are guided by versions of the mechanical hypothesis. Cavendish explicitly targets Henry Power's claim that 'all natural effects may be called artificial, nay, that nature herself may be called the "art of God"' (OEP 198, see also 21). As Cavendish sometimes assimilates the mechanical with the experimental philosophy (e.g. OEP 196), she criticizes Descartes alongside Hooke for projecting anthropomorphic characteristics onto nature, targeting his account of vortices on the ground that 'he conceived, that nature, or the God of nature, did produce the world after a mechanical way, and according as we see turners, and such kind of artificers work' (OEP 74).

Yet another way that experimentalists rely on artifice is by their use of what we might call intellectual artifacts, which include applied mathematics and 'artificial Logick'. It is not only experimental philosophers who fall prey to this. Because we are always naturally tempted by the siren song of anthropomorphism and anthropocentrism, Cavendish diagnoses the errors of a variety of schools of philosophy as caused by artifice, including chymists and speculative philosophers.

Section 8.7 Intellectual artifacts

Among epistemic artifacts that 'disorder men's understandings more than it rectifies them' (BW 58), Cavendish includes not only instruments like microscopes but also intellectual artifacts like pure and applied mathematics, induction, and logical and syllogistic reasoning.

Cavendish is very critical of both pure and applied mathematics. Pure mathematics, she thinks, is the study of non-beings, and as she tells the spider-men who represent mathematicians in the *Blazing World*, 'I can neither spare time from other affairs to busy my self in your profession; nor, if I could, do I think I should ever be able to understand your imaginary points, lines and figures, because they are non-beings' (BW 55). Applied mathematics, on the other hand, purports to understand nature in terms of these imaginary and artificial beings:

> mathematical rules, measures, and demonstrations, cannot rule, measure, nor demonstrate Nature...
>
> (PL 3 27)

> Mathematicians...endeavour to inchant Nature with Circles, and bind her with lines so hard, as if she were so mad, that she would do some mischief, when left at liberty. Geometricians weigh Nature to an Atome, and measure her so exactly, as less

then a hairs breadth; besides, they do press and squeeze her so hard and close, as they almost stifle her.

(PL 4 19, see also 2 15)

These critiques, along with Cavendish's claim that points, lines, and geometrical figures are non-beings, offer further evidence that when she speaks of the figures of natural things, she is not speaking of geometrical figures.[5]

Cavendish rejects logic along similar lines. The syllogistic forms of logicians put our 'brain on the rack' and 'spoil all natural wit' (BW 58; see also PL 2 15). 'I have had enough,' Cavendish tells the representatives of logicians, 'of your chopped logic, and will hear no more of your syllogisms; for it disorders my reason, and puts my brain on the rack; your formal argumentations are able to spoil all natural wit.' She specifically attacks their failure to realize that 'art does not make reason, but reason makes art', and so 'natural rational discourse to be preferred before an artificial: for art is, for the most part irregular, and disorders men's understandings more than it rectifies them' (BW 58). Similarly, in the *Letters*, Cavendish writes of both the 'ancient and Modern Philosophers' that

I do not understand their sophistical Logick, as to perswade with arguments that black is white, and white is black; and that fire is not hot, nor water wet, and other such things; for the glory in Logick is rather to make doubts, then to find truth; indeed, that Art now is like thick, dark clouds, which darken the light of truth.

(PL 4 18)

She diagnoses logic more specifically with the attempt to make regular nature where nature is not (BW 59).

As Chapter 3 showed, Cavendish also rejects the speculative tendency to make too many distinctions:

I am not of your opinion, That nice distinctions and Logistical arguments discover truth, dissolve doubts, and clear the understanding; but I say, they rather make doubts of truth, and

---

5 For more about Cavendish's critiques of applied mathematics, see Peterman (2019a).

blind-fold the understanding; Indeed, nice distinctions and sophistical arguments, are very pernicious both in Schools, Church, and State.

(PL 4 20)

Cavendish even thinks of philosophical and scientific language as artifice, seemingly cutting off attempts to coin or clarify concepts using language. She does not seem to connect language to any distinctly human thought or rationality, arguing that reasoning 'may very well be done without speech or language' (OEP 14). We speak just because we are the only animal that has an 'upright and straight Shape' (GNP 5 3; see also PPO2 2 7); birds are the next 'most apt for Speech; by reason they are more of an upright Shape' (GNP 5 3). (Indeed, Cavendish here attributes the more general fact that man '*seems* as Lord and Sovereign of other Animal Creatures' (my italics) not to any cognitive capacities but to the fact that he is 'fit and proper for more several sorts of exterior actions'.) In fact, man's ability to express his thought in words 'doth not declare by it his excellency and supremacy above all other Creatures, but for the most part more folly, for a talking man is not so wise as a contemplating man' (PL 1 36).

In general, Cavendish writes,

Wherefore though other Creatures have not the speech, nor Mathematical rules and demonstrations, with other Arts and Sciences, as Men; yet may their perceptions and observations be as wise as Men's, and they may have as much intelligence and commerce betwixt each other, after their own manner and way, as men have after theirs: To which I leave them, and Man to his conceited prerogative and excellence, resting.

(PL 1 36)

Human intelligence is simply not a function of our development of any of these intellectual artifacts; if anything, Cavendish thinks, it is impeded by them, and so 'the best Natural Philosophes, are those, that have the Clearest Natural Observation, and the Least Artificial Learning' (PPO2 Preface).[6]

---

6   This section goes some way toward explaining what Cavendish means when she writes that we should reason with 'facility' and 'ease'. But I think the question of what that means for her is worth further investigation.

Section 8.8 The Council-Chamber

So reason should guide us, not by artificially attempting to improve our natural faculties in what they are supposed to do, but by doing what it is supposed to do, which is give us independent knowledge of causes, and especially of the 'prime cause'. We already know what that principle is, or those principles are, but consider Cavendish's explicit answer to the question heading up a section: 'Whether there Be any Prime or Principal Figure in Nature; and of the True Principles of Nature' (OEP 204). The answer to the first part is, of course, 'no': there are no prime figures because figures are creatures or effects of nature. As for the second part,

> the principles of nature, out of which all other creatures are made or produced…is but one, viz. matterwhich is a mixture of animate and inanimate matter to make one self-moving body… divided into infinite figures or parts.
>
> (OEP 205–207)

Cavendish asks us to compare these principles with those proposed by atomists, Descartes, Van Helmont, and others and to consider whether her opinion

> contains not as much probability as the opinion of those whose principles are either whirlpools, insensible minima, *gas*, *blas* and *archeus*, dusty atoms, thrusting backwards and forwards, which they call reason, and the like, or of those that make artificial experiments the ground and foundation of the knowledge of nature, and prefer art before reason.
>
> (OEP 207–208)

Here again the reader is invited to determine for herself the probability of Cavendish's opinion. And this is far from the only place that Cavendish assesses, as more or less probable, claims of reason about the very deepest principles. Besides the probabilism of the Argumental Discourse, she characterizes as probable her opinions about the eternity of nature (OEP 44), for example, and the claim that all creatures are knowing (OEP 139). The former she describes as 'more probable to regular reason', which means that she associates probability with the highest kind of knowledge that she admits:

regular reason. Similarly, she writes that natural philosophers should investigate 'Prime Causes' rather than effects, but she continues to state that 'the Cause cannot be throughly Known, yet it may by much Contemplation and Observation be found out Better than it is, at least some Probability thereof' (PPO2 Another Epistle).

So while Cavendish is sympathetic to speculative philosophy, she does not purport to have anything like the level of certainty of her principles that some speculative philosophers claimed to have (like, say, Descartes) and that experimental philosophers complained about. And as we foreshadowed in Section 8.2, when it comes to speculative matters, Cavendish often frames them as, properly, matters of ongoing debate. Cavendish often describes reasoning or speculation or cogitation as a conversation, debate, or dispute among parts, as when she identifies 'Human Contemplation' with 'a Conversation amongst some of the Rational Parts of the Human Mind' (GNP 160). She frequently characterizes her own philosophizing in the same terms, as in the Epistle to the Reader that introduces the 1663 edition of her *Opinions*, wherein Cavendish writes that while she was writing it,

> my Brain was like a University, Senate, or Council-Chamber, wherein all my Conceptions, Imaginations, Observations, Wit, and Judgment did meet, to Dispute, Argue, Contrive, and Judge, for Sense, Reason, and Truth.
>
> (PPO 1663 XIV)

The debates between Cavendish's former and latter thoughts or her major and minor thoughts are not pathological, or merely incidental, or mere rhetorical devices. These dialogues are not aimed at establishing the dominance of one particular side. Rather, such conversations between parts are essential to proper philosophizing. Cavendish assimilates reason understood as 'rational enquiry into the causes of natural effects' with 'an arguing of the mind...for discourse is as much reasoning with ourselves' (OEP 14). And this makes perfect sense, given that Cavendish conceptualizes not just the human being but the human mind as a society of parts.

Finally, Cavendish seems to connect the fact that speculative philosophy is essentially probabilistic and discursive to an inability to have any certainty in it. Addressing Van Helmont's claim to have demonstrated that there are three and not four elements, Cavendish writes that

> it is too great a presumption in any man, to feign himself so much above the rest, as to accuse all others of ignorance, and that none but he alone hath the true knowledg of all things as infallible and undeniable and that so many Learned, Wise and Ingenious Men in so many ages have been blinded with errors; for certainly, no particular Creature in Nature can have any exact or perfect knowledg of Natural things, and therefore opinions cannot be infallible truths, although they may seem probable; for how is it possible that a single finite Creature should know the numberless varieties and hidden actions of Nature?
>
> (PL 3 3)

The best we can do, Cavendish continues, is listen to other philosophers and assess competing probabilities.

Section 8.9 The principles

We have argued that Cavendish holds that, through reason, we can come to have probable knowledge of the 'Prime Cause' in nature. As the last chapter showed, 'reason' is complex, for Cavendish. It is not always clear whether it is a mental activity like musing or imagining, an inference or a judgment, or rational perception, which is direct perception of some deeper, nonsensory facts.

Despite all this, it is just still not obvious exactly how Cavendish thinks that we know that her principles are true. If it is by some kind of reasoning, what are our starting points, if not natural effects? If it is rational perception, how do we come to perceive something about infinite nature, when Cavendish tells us repeatedly that we cannot perceive the infinite? And more generally, how does Cavendish's naturalized epistemology allow that 'by the help of Philosophy our minds are raised above our selves, into the knowledg of the Causes of all natural effects' (PL 4 1)? What could it possibly mean, for Cavendish, for us to be raised above ourselves?

I don't know the answer to these questions, but I will close with three general points, which hopefully relieve some of the tension that these questions raise.

First, as we have seen, Cavendish presents her arguments about principles as merely probable. For her, that means that they are part of an ongoing conversation with herself and with others. And from one perspective (though not every perspective), she does seem to regard herself first as participating in this conversation and only after as moving toward truth.

Second, let us accept Cavendish's invitation to compare her principles with vortices, atoms, archeus, and gas. Cavendish takes all of these proposals to be of a very different kind from her own proposal. As we have seen, matter is not a kind of thing; it is simply being, period. All the kinds of things there are in existence are corporeal figurative motions, and matter is the principle of those. In contrast, Cavendish sees atoms and other principles as attempts to make creatures into principles, and so just another way of mistaking effects for causes. We argued that Cavendish formulated her principles by considering the most minimal posit to account for why nature and creatures are the way they are. Her principles had to explain that something exists, that there is variety and coherence, and that there is change. From one perspective, matter and self-motion, the principles of being and change, are barely characterized positively. The lesson here is that Cavendish does not think that reason is so powerful that it can intuit very much. This by no means answers the question of what it is and how it can raise us above ourselves, but it makes it a little less vexing.

Third, and much more speculatively if not more satisfyingly, we might draw on Cavendish's assimilation of knowledge and being to understand why we have knowledge of these principles. We know other parts of nature because we are joined with them. We have perfect self-knowledge as a metaphysical fact, but because we are composite and joined with other things, that does not mean that we know anything about how we are constructed or about our parts. But what all of our parts have in common, and what we have in common with everything else, is that we are composite, self-moving matter.

This invites a comparison with Spinoza, a contemporary of Cavendish. The two did not know of one another, but they share striking similarities, at the heart of which is their naturalism, especially about human beings. Like Cavendish, Spinoza holds that our knowledge of particulars is limited because we are finite and that our experience of those particulars is not of them in themselves but rather of how they affect our bodies. From this, Spinoza concludes that all our perceptual knowledge is inadequate. However, because certain things are common to parts of our bodies and to the things we interact with, Spinoza argues, our ideas of those things are adequate.

I don't find this very convincing as an account of how we come to have anything like propositional knowledge about the basic features of nature. But the idea is not so much that we perceive what is everywhere adequately but that we know something adequately by being that thing. This fits nicely with Cavendish's assimilation view of knowledge, and it makes more sense alongside the minimal metaphysics. To know nature is to be part of it, and part of being part of it is being made of the same stuff as it.

Section 8.10 Conclusion

When Cavendish tells us that her method is regular sense and reason, she means a number of specific things. First, we need to rely on our sense perception, and other kinds of perception, to learn about the world around us; this is the only way we can learn about particulars. Second, we need reason to tell us about causes. Reason must have independent insight into causes, because it cannot infer causes from particulars. It is not perfectly clear how either rational perception or rational conception allow us to peer into the natures of things, but Cavendish also does not require reason to do quite as much as other speculative philosophers do, and she does not invest it with the same degree of certainty. I think it is a still open and interesting question exactly how Cavendish's philosophy of mind and the foundations of her epistemology, on which to know something is to be it or be joined with it, provide us with the knowledge of nature that she takes us to have. The resultant method, however, encourages us to dwell in our wonder and humility at the infinite variety of ways that creatures are produced, but not to mystify nature at the fundamental level. Infinite and eternal matter's ability to generate all that variety is 'miraculous', but that does not mean that the principles themselves are miracles.

Further reading

Clucas, Stephen. 2003. 'Variation, Irregularity, and Probabilism: Margaret Cavendish and Natural Philosophy as Rhetoric.' Pp. 199–209 in *A Princely Brave Woman: Essays on Margaret Cavendish, Duchess of Newcastle.*New York: Routledge.

Clucas, Stephen. 2011. 'Margaret Cavendish's Materialist Critique of van Helmontian Chymistry.' *Ambix* 58(1): 1–12.

Cunning, David. 2016. Chapter 1. *Cavendish.* New York: Routledge.

Garber, Daniel. 2020. 'Margaret Cavendish among the Baconians.' *Journal of Early Modern Studies* 9(2): 53–84.

Lascano, Marcy P. 2021. 'Margaret Cavendish and the New Science: "Boys That Play with Watery Bubbles or Fling Dust into Each Other's Eyes, or Make a Hobbyhorse of Snow."' Pp. 28–40 in *The Routledge Handbook of Feminist Philosophy of Science.* New York: Routledge.

Sarasohn, Lisa T. 2010. *The Natural Philosophy of Margaret Cavendish: Reason and Fancy during the Scientific Revolution.* Baltimore: Johns Hopkins University Press.

Wilkins, Emma. 2014. 'Margaret Cavendish and the Royal Society.' *Notes and Records: The Royal Society Journal of the History of Science* 68(3): 245–260.

Nine
Order

Man:
Nature gives no such knowledge to mankind,
But strong desires to torment the mind,
And senses, which like hounds do run about,
Yet never can the perfect truth find out.
O Nature—Nature!—cruel to mankind,
Gives knowledge none, but misery to find.

Nature:
Why doth mankind complain and make such moan?
May not I work my will with what's my own?
(P&F A Dialogue betwixt Man and Nature)

We live, according to Cavendish, in a 'well-ordered universe' (OEP 8). What does this mean? It is clear enough that what is ordered are the effective parts of nature, that they are ordered into 'Only and Infinite' nature, and that order concerns how these parts relate to one another. But what makes those relationships orderly?

Cavendish consistently characterizes nature's order as the product of nature's wisdom, and she describes the parts of nature as free to submit to that wisdom. 'Infinite natural wisdom', Cavendish writes, 'is the cause of her orderly government in all particular productions, changes and dissolutions, so that all creatures in their particular kinds, do move and work as nature pleases, orders and directs' (OEP 109). This is often interpreted to mean that nature's order is irreducibly the product of one or more agent-like things. Moreover, nature's order is the main reason Cavendish gives that all creatures must be perceptive and knowing. So if you think that perception and

DOI: 10.4324/9781003107255-10

knowledge require thoughtful agency, then this is a further reason for thinking that order depends on a mind-like thing or things.

Predictably, I do not think that any intentional agency is necessary to explain natural order. I argue for that in this chapter, and develop an alternative interpretation of Cavendishian order which—predictably again—starts with composition and division. Cavendish takes it to be a manifest fact about nature that it contains a great and irreducible variety of things, which hang together. This is the result of the fact that nature is composite, with many parts. That is order, for Cavendish: the fact that nature strikes a 'poise and balance' between composition and division, so that there are individuals, but those individuals are related to each other. As we will see, order is distinct from regularity, another concept that Cavendish frequently uses and one that is sometimes assimilated with order by her readers. While there is no disorder in nature, there are irregularities. Motions are as a matter of fact regular or irregular, though only relative to a particular creature.

To talk about the way that the finite parts of nature hang together is to invite the question of influence among creatures. We have already seen the reasons that Cavendish denies that there is full-fledged causation between creatures, the most important one being that the only true causes are the corporeal figurative motions of nature. That said, Cavendish allows that one creature, or effect, can influence another, and that 'some Effects producing other Effects is in some sort or manner, a Cause' (GNP 5 16). This influence, like the related concepts of perception and sympathy, is ultimately explained by self-motion, facilitated by participation of two parts in one composite.

Section 9.1 Order as unity

Cavendish tells us that 'Nature hath but One Law, which is a wise Law, viz., to keep Infinite Matter in Order' (PL 2 5). What sort of thing might 'order' be? An initial reply to this question might be: why expect that we can answer it? Even if we deny that nature literally has a mind. When Cavendish writes that nature has one wise law, she is presumably at least in part pointing to the inaccessibility to us of nature's principle(s) of order.

That said, to begin to understand order, for Cavendish, we might identify two minimum requirements for something to be orderly.

First, order requires some kind of complexity. A perfectly simple unit might not be disorderly, but it doesn't seem right to call it orderly. Order requires that multiple things are ordered.

Second, for some things to be ordered means at minimum for them to be related. We can ask, further, what kinds of relations must obtain, but totally unrelated things are not ordered.

One conception of order familiar among Cavendish's contemporaries is also familiar to us: that of law-like regularity, according to which things, events, properties, or actions may be subsumed under general or universal laws. But as we have seen, Cavendish calls it a 'very wild and extravagant conceit, to measure the infinite actions of nature according to the rule of one particular sort of motions' (OEP 72)—a conceit which Cavendish thinks that Descartes, for example, is guilty of with his theory of vortices (Descartes 1985: 204). The infinite variety of nature's effects manifests an infinite variety of actions or motions, and 'those who doth confine nature but to one way of acting or moving, had better to deprive her of all motion; for Nature being infinite, has also infinite ways of acting in her particulars' (OEP 68). This critique of generalizing extends to attempts to explain order in terms of law-like regularities. Criticizing Henry More's talk of laws of motion, and implicitly Descartes, whom More draws on, Cavendish writes that she does 'not know what [they] mean by Laws' and that 'Nature hath but One Law, which is a wise Law, viz., to keep Infinite Matter in Order' (PL 2 5). Generalizing, we may say that Cavendish rejects conceptions of order that appeal to regularity in the sense of the repeatability or generalizability of kinds, laws, essences, or any other ontological category.

What might order be if it does not unite disparate motions, things, properties, or events under some laws or kinds? Sticking with the idea that order should involve a unification of some kind: what if things are ordered to be unified not under kinds or regularities but by being parts of one individual?

There is indeed an alternative conception of order in the early modern period, self-consciously opposed to the law-governed conception of order, that sees order as a coherence among parts that is not underwritten by laws. This alternative is often signaled by talk of harmony, coherence, or coordination among nature's parts.[1] It is inspired by the observation that individuals in nature seem to respond to each other as if they could perceive and communicate with one another. They make small adjustments in their motions based on differences in the states of a wide variety of other bodies, accommodating and harmonizing with one another, often at a distance. It is not obvious that what explains law-like regularities is also what explains this kind of coherence.

It should not be surprising by now that this latter conception is closer to Cavendish's conception of order. Cavendish writes at the very beginning of the *Grounds* that 'where Unity is not, Order cannot be' (GNP 1 4). It is also evident from Cavendish's critique of atomism. The things in nature can only be related if they are parts of nature's body, which is why, as we have seen, a world of atoms can never be ordered.

So we know that for Cavendish order requires that nature's parts be united into her body. But two questions remain.

First, are the parts of nature ordered just in virtue of being composed? Or must they be composed in some particular to count as ordered?

Second, whatever order turns out to be, does its achievement require that nature and/or her parts have intentional agency to pursue it?

Before we address these questions, we can eliminate one possibility: that for nature's parts to be ordered is simply for them to be whatever nature wants them to be. Even if it turns out that nature must intentionally order her parts, by identifying her as wise, Cavendish signals that she is what we might call an intellectualist about nature's power. I borrow this label from intellectual historians who use it to describe the position that God's intellect is prior to God's will in creation. Intellectualists about God hold that, in creating nature, God looks to certain facts, norms, or truths, like eternal truths or immutable essences or mathematical forms or some

---

1   For more about these two notions of order and especially the latter, see Peterman (2021).

standard of absolute goodness or harmony. In contrast, voluntarists about God hold that God's will is entirely unconstrained, and God creates according to God's whim.[2]

Cavendish is an intellectualist about nature: the fact that nature is guided by her wisdom implies that she is not guided by her mere whims. If nature's parts are arranged the way that nature wants them to be, that does not alone ground order. So even if nature's ordering does involve taking intentional actions or proscribing norms to her creatures, we can still ask what order is.

Section 9.2 Regularity

Before we tackle this question, we must address a concept that Cavendish uses even more frequently, especially in the *Observations*: 'regularity'. Order and regularity (as well as disorder and irregularity) are sometimes assimilated by readers of Cavendish, but they are not the same.[3]

Cavendish describes as regular and irregular the figures and motions of creatures. The examples that Cavendish gives of regular and irregular motions, along with what she tells us about regularity and irregularity in general, indicate that what is regular is what conduces to the preservation of a creature, and what is irregular is what does not. 'All those motions that belong to the particular nature and consistence of any figure', Cavendish writes, 'they call regular, and those which are contrary to them, they call irregular' (PL 3 23).

---

2   Boyle (2018: 113) asks this about God, for Cavendish. If the laws of nature are normative, are they so because God dictated them, or is there 'some other standard or goal to which the source of norms (God) is responding in deciding how the parts of Nature ought to behave'?

3   Boyle (2018: 8) argues that, while free, creatures tend to act in 'regular, predictable ways', and Cavendish interprets irregular motions as 'those motions which move not after the ordinary, common, or usually way or manner' (Boyle 2018: 23, citing OEP 64). As the last section argued, I do not think that Cavendish associates regularity with predictability. For one, it certainly can't be important for her that things are predictable for us. Second, predictability (as opposed to determinism, on which see Section 9.9) usually involves law-like generalities, which is not, I think, how Cavendish understands regularity.

Accordingly, irregular motions are 'nothing but an opposition or strife between parts' (OEP 144) without which 'there would be no... pain or sickness, nor the dissolution of any natural figure' (OEP 145).

As this passage reflects, the preservation of a creature is its continued composition, so regularity is what conduces to continued composition and irregularity to dissolution. Some irregularities contribute directly to a creature's demise, as in the case of dissolving and putrefaction: 'corruption or putrefaction, is nothing but irregular dissolving motions; whenas freezing or congelation is made by regular, contracting and condensing motions' (OEP 123). Other irregularities are less direct but can still be understood in terms of their impact on a creature's survival. For example, Cavendish describes as irregularities perceptual anomalies like the vision of a damaged eye and the sense of taste of a sick man, which are not directly decomposing but may lead an animal to decomposing actions.

Some dissolutions may count as regular because they are involved in the continued composition of whatever creature we are focused on, which is why Cavendish is able to describe some dissolutions as well as compositions as regular (e.g. OEP 145). As this indicates, regularity and irregularity do not have respect to fundamental composing and dissolving motions, only creaturely ones. For one, although we can think about dividing and composing in the abstract as principles, as we did in Chapter 3 and 4, there are not really more or less fundamental dividings and composings in nature. All dividings and composings involve creatures with parts and who are parts of other creatures. For another, if we do focus on dividing and composing in the abstract, Cavendish gives no indication that the former is regular and the latter irregular.

Especially since regularity and irregularity pertain only to creatures, this interpretation is consistent with an association between regularity and conformity to kinds and sorts. As we have seen, Cavendish does think that creatures fall into kinds and that these kinds run medium-deep, though they do not play a role in fundamental explanations. Most of the time, an individual can ensure its survival by doing what is good for things of its kind. So regular motions are almost always those that are proper to a species. This explains the passages that Lascano (2023) and Detlefsen (2007) rely on to argue that regularity is fundamentally a matter of conformity with kinds and sorts, such as Cavendish's description of irregular motions as 'those motions which move not after the ordinary, common or usual way' (PL 3 29). But regularity is not fundamentally such a conformity. Bread-eating and bread-digesting motions are regular for humans but irregular for someone with celiac disease. And bread-digesting motions are always irregular for the bread even as they are regular for the non-celiac human.

Cunning (2006) has argued that there are no true irregular-ities, pointing to passages where Cavendish describes 'respect to particulars, and to our conceptions' (PL 3 29) and claims that that 'properly there is no such thing as Irregularity in Nature' (PL 4 33). Such passages are very important, but what they tell us is not that there are no true irregularities.

First, it is true that irregularities have 'respect to particulars.' Bread-digesting motions really do contribute to my preservation, and really are decomposing for the bread, so they really are regular for me and irregular for the bread. That a motion is regular or irregular only relative to particular creatures does not mean that they are any less real; they are just not absolute. Sadly, believing that an irregular motion is regular does not make it so.

Second, we tend to focus on what is regular and irregular for us and the things that are meaningful to us, and so we more commonly label as irregular the things that are irregular for us. This explains why Cavendish sometimes suggests that regularity is a matter of labeling, like when she writes that 'all those Motions that belong to the particular nature and consistence of any figure, [men] call regular, and those which are contrary to them, they call irregular' (PL 3 23). This does not mean that regularity and irregularity are determined by which labels we apply.

Third and finally, in the passages where it sounds like regularity and irregularity are matters of perception or labeling, Cavendish is usually trying to emphasize that regular and irregular motions, including pain and death, are just so many corporeal figurative motions.[4] When she writes that 'what we call irregularities in nature, are really nothing but a variety of nature's motions' (OEP 71) or that

---

4   As far as I understand Cunning's view of irregularity, it is close to the one I have developed here. However, he seems to interpret whether something is good or bad as something in the mind of a creature and so not really in nature.

'health and diseases are nothing else but the regularity or irregularity of sensitive corporeal Motions' (PL 3 26), Cavendish is not telling us that there is no fact of the matter as to whether something is regular or irregular, in the sense of being conducive to a creature's survival or not. She is telling us that there is no fact of the matter as to whether those things are *bad*. In these passages, Cavendish is trying to tell us that irregularity does not have a fundamental normative dimension. Consider another passage of this kind:

> But, to conclude, there is no such thing as corruption, sickness, or death, properly in Nature, for they are made by natural actions, and are onely varieties in Nature, but not obstructions or destructions of Nature, or annihilations of particular Creatures.
> (PL 3 26)

Cavendish acknowledges here that corruption, sickness, and death are real natural actions. When she says that there is no such thing, she means that there is no such thing if we understand those terms (as we almost always do) to be fundamentally (negatively) normative. While regularity and irregularity is a source of normativity for us, it is not a source of absolute normativity.[5]

This is reflected in the fact that regularity and irregularity are relative to creatures. Can we identify some absolute regularity or irregularity? We have already said that Cavendish does not describe the fundamental action of dividing as irregular or composing as regular. We might still ask whether there is absolute regularity or irregularity in another sense: is nature as a whole regular or irregular? The answer is no. As we will see in the next section, nature poises and balances regularity and irregularity, and cannot be said to be regular or irregular herself.

---

5 Cavendish also writes in one place that we call irregularities not just anything that conduces to dissolution but what conduces to 'untimely dissolutions' (PL 3 26). I think we can explain this in the same way: what we focus on and label as irregularity is what we care about.

Section 9.3 Order

Sometimes Cavendish seems to assimilate order and disorder with regularity and irregularity. In the *Grounds* as well as in both editions of the *Opinions*, Cavendish identifies irregularity with disorder (e.g. GNP 5 4, 6 8, 9 5), describes parts as 'ordering' themselves into figures (GNP 12 20), and labels as 'disorders' examples of what look like irregularities as described above. In the *Observations*, however, she only occasionally identifies order and regularity, and only occasionally describes particular creaturely motions as ordered or disordered. And in stark contrast with the *Grounds*, she uses the word 'disorder' there only three times: once, where she denies it of nature, and two other times, where it is not synonymous with 'irregularity.'

Moreover, Cavendish sometimes characterizes order in a way that entails that it is not synonymous with regularity. Specifically, she describes order as involving a 'poise and balance' of something or another, including a poise and balance of regularity and irregularity themselves:

> Although Nature be Infinite, yet all her Actions seem to be poysed, or balanced, by Opposition; as for example, As Nature hath dividing, so composing actions: Also, as Nature hath regular, so irregular actions; as Nature hath dilating, so contracting actions.
> (GNP 1 14, see also GNP 6 12, 8 1)

As McNulty (2018) has argued, order, unlike regularity, involves opposition as well as agreement and dividing as well as composing. At least in the *Observations*, Cavendish mostly uses 'order' to describe nature's actions in general, or at least more general states of affairs, as opposed to creaturely motions.[6] And it does not seem creature-relative the way that regularity is. McNulty highlights as well the importance of 'poise and balance' for understanding Cavendish's conception of order. But we may ask, further: what is this poise and

---

6 Cavendish seems more frequently to identify irregular and disorder in the *Grounds*, which might seem like evidence that this is her 'mature' position. But as I have suggested, it matters that the *Grounds* is presented as a revision of the previous *Opinions*—perhaps she did not update her terminology.

balance *of*? While Cavendish does indeed attribute all kinds of poises and balances of all kinds of elements, one is fundamental: the poise and balance between composition and division, which is also to say between regularity and irregularity.

In the passage above, Cavendish focuses on poise and balance between dividing and composing and regular and irregular actions. She goes on in the same paragraph to describe other kinds of poise and balance but concludes that they are all made by 'the Corporeal Figurative Motions of Nature' (GNP 1 4) which, we have argued, are dividing and composing. Consider also this passage:

> [W]ithout any opposition of parts, there could be not a union or composition of so many several parts and creatures, nor no change or variety in nature; for if all the parts did unanimously conspire and agree in their motions, and move all but one way, there would be but one act or kind of motion in nature; whenas an opposition of some parts, and a mutual agreement of others, is not only the cause of the miraculous variety in nature, but it poises and balances, as it were the corporeal figurative motions, which is the cause that nature is steady and fixt in herself, although her parts be in a perpetual motion.
>
> (OEP 199)

Here, Cavendish identifies 'union' with 'composition' and with the agreement of parts, which is just composition. And she writes that it is 'an opposition of some parts, and a mutual agreement of others' that is 'the cause of the miraculous variety in nature' (OEP 199). If she imagined that there were all kinds of oppositions and agreements besides simple divisions and compositions, why would the variety that results from that be 'miraculous'? No, what is miraculous is nature's production of such a variety from such an austere source: self-moving matter. And it does so by poising and balancing its corporeal figurative motions, which is to say its dividings and composings.

We have seen that the ordering of nature's parts is the achievement of a poise and balance between composition and division. But is the poise and balance between composition and division simply the fact that nature contains both variety and coherence? Or is it something further, something about how the parts divide and cohere, or which parts do, or when, or how many? Is it sufficient to order herself that nature simply does have both parts and coherence, or must something else be 'right' about that compositional structure?

I think that there is good reason to think that the poise and balance between variety and unity is simply the fact that nature is both composed and divided, and not some further way in which it is composed and divided. Cavendish identifies 'ordering' with 'changing' as well as 'dissolving and composing' when she writes that nature is always 'dissolving and composing, changing and ordering her self-moving parts as she pleases' (OEP 55). Compare Cavendish's claim that nature divides and composes her parts 'as she pleases' with the intellectualist considerations presented in Section 9.2 above. 'As she pleases' suggests that it is indifferent *how* nature is divided and composed, whereas it is not indifferent *that* it is divided and composed.[7] This provides further support for the claim that when nature orders her parts, she does not aim at dividing and composing them in some particular way. Nature doesn't have to order her parts in some specific way in order to create whatever fine balance achieves her continued survival because she cannot but survive.

Another reason to hold that ordering simply is dividing and composing is Cavendish's insistence that order involves divisions, oppositions, and variety just as much as compositions, agreements, and unity. Nature makes 'orderly and regular compositions' as well as 'dissolutions' (OEP 145, see also 167). (Here, Cavendish uses both 'orderly' and 'regular' to mean what she usually means by 'orderly', unlike in the *Grounds*, where she often uses both terms to mean 'regular'.) Cavendish tells us that 'several sorts, kinds, and differences of Particulars, causes Order'—not because it unifies, but because it 'causes Distinctions: for, if all Creatures were alike, it would cause a Confusion' (GNP 2 10). Differences, oppositions, and varieties are as much a part of order as compositions and agreements; nature

---

7 This interpretation of order is, I think, at least compatible if not the same as the one in Georgescu (2021: 623–624): 'when Cavendish says that there would be no order in Nature without self-knowledge and perception…she is saying that the fundamental grounds for an orderly world are the individuality of parts and their connection with other parts.'

is as pleased with variety as it is with unity and coherence. There is no sense in which order is more aimed at unity than at variety. The beauty is in the varieties, the differences, the oppositions, and the irregularities as much as in the coherence, the similarities, the agreements, and the regularities. There is as much order in death as in birth.

I suspect that, strictly speaking, Cavendish would not claim that we know for certain that order is simply this. There is something right in the thought that we are very far from 'understanding nature's wisdom'. That is not because whimsical ladies are impossible to understand, but because the true order of nature is beyond our capacity to glean. However, on the interpretation developed, Cavendish should be wary of suggesting that there are any further principles, including norms, in nature, than the ones we have posited, and it is hard to see how a further conception of order might be achieved without that.

Section 9.4 Is nature a fish?

Cavendish sometimes describes order as the peace and unity of the whole of nature, emphasizing that this is consistent with the oppositions within it. Given that regular motions are those that conduce to the preservation (that is, the continued composition) of some particular creature, we might have interpreted this peace and unity as the continuous composition of all the parts of nature, and we might have concluded that order is regularity relative to the whole of nature. But Cavendish's insistence that order involves division, opposition, and irregularity as much as composition, agreement, and regularity should give us pause. And after all, what could irregular motions with respect to nature possibly be? It is *impossible* for nature to dissolve, because matter is eternal. And Cavendish's resistance to characterizing nature as a whole in terms of regularity or irregularity is an acknowledgement of that.

But this raises a question. Sure, there is nothing outside nature that can annihilate it (except for God, but don't worry about that). That means that there are no irregular motions relative to nature that are analogous to, say, the irregularity of a bird's digestion for a worm. But Cavendish seems to admit that there can be motions internal to a thing that lead to its destruction. So why can't nature become disordered and fall apart from the inside?

Here is one answer that Cavendish gives to that question:

> Every particular motion or action of nature is balanced and poised by its opposite, which hinders a running into infinite in nature's particulars, and causes a variety of natural figures; for although infinite matter in itself, and its own essence, is simple and 'homogeneous', as the learned call it, or of the same kind and nature, and consequently is at peace with itself; yet there is a perpetual opposition and war between the parts of nature.
>
> (OEP 199)

Here, Cavendish tells us nature's peace is a consequence of the fact that 'infinite matter in itself, and its own essence, is simple and "homogeneous,"' that is, 'of the same kind and nature'. In a number of places in this book, I have suggested that when it comes to creatures, Cavendish attributes their relationships to facts about their composition rather than similarities of kinds, especially in the *Observations*. Does Cavendish's claim that nature's order is ultimately a consequence of its homogeneity undermine this? Is she telling us that nature's unity is, after all, grounded in sameness of kind?

Well, yes and no. As we glimpsed in Chapter 3, Cavendish connects nature's homogeneity with the fact that it is a concrete individual. It is because every part is made of matter and is thereby dividable and composable that every part can divide and compose with other parts. So nature's order is not identical with the fact that everything is the same kind of thing. It is rather the fact that because all the parts of nature are made of dividable and composable stuff, they can be divided and composed *with each other*. Note how this differs from other ways that one might understand the relationship between homogeneity and unity. It is not because all the parts have the same nature or properties and can thereby be united under laws. It is not because all matter occupies the same spatiotemporal realm. And it is not because, as it (sometimes) seems for Descartes, matter's homogeneity, and hence its continuity, means that at rest it is not actually divided.

Just because nature's order involves the division and composition of everything with everything else does not mean that nature's order means that everything is composed as part of a single composition or whole. Does Cavendish hold that nature, in addition to being ordered by being one dividable and composable matter, is also one body in the way that an animal is?

Cavendish asks something like this question in the *Letters*, following Harvey (as identified by Duncan), '*Whether this World or Universe be the biggest Creature?*' She answers that 'it is not possible to be known, unless Man could perfectly know its dimension or extension, or whether there be more Worlds then one: But, to speak properly, there is no such thing as biggest or least in Nature' (PL 4 15). Cavendish speaks here of the 'world or universe', and we know that our world, at least, is not the biggest creature, since there are (likely) many others. But Cavendish seems also to be entertaining the question, perhaps under the auspices of asking about the universe, whether nature herself is the biggest creature. Intentional or not, her agnosticism, as well as her reminder that there is 'no such thing as the biggest or least in Nature', should make us suspicious of the notion that nature is one big creature.

It is true that Cavendish often tells us that the parts of nature are 'joined in one body' (OEP 30, see also 25). On the other hand, however, this seems to be undermined by some of the considerations of the last section. For to identify nature's order with the preservation of a single unified creature would seem to privilege regularity and composition over irregularity and division.

There is also the issue of the relationship between nature's oneness and its infinity. As we saw in Chapter 2, in earlier work, Cavendish denies that nature has a figure because nature is infinite. Her reason there is that to have a figure is to be bound in a sense in which it is impossible for infinity to be bound. Moreover, to have a figure is to have *one* figure, and the infinite cannot be numbered, even if that number is one. As we have seen, Leibniz, writing several decades after Cavendish, holds that everything in nature is fundamentally organic in a sense similar to Cavendish: nature is full of nested self-moving composed systems. He is, however, extremely concerned to refute what would seem to be the natural conclusion that the entire universe is one organism. He compares the cosmos instead to a pond full of fish, which is not 'an animated body, although the fish are' (Leibniz et al. 1989: 87, 89). One of his many arguments against such a view is that unlike creatures, the world cannot be one organism because it is infinite: 'if the world were infinite in magnitude, it would not be one whole...such a world would not be one body, nor could it be regarded as an animal, and so it would have only a verbal unity' (Leibniz 2007: 33).[8]

As we saw in Chapter 2, Cavendish eventually comes to hold that nature, being matter, has a figure in the same sense that creatures do. We interpreted this as a sign that she was moving towards a compositional account of matter, on which the whole is not prior to the parts and on which infinite matter, just like finite creatures, has a compositional structure. And she continues to deny that it has what she calls a 'limited and circumscribed figure' (OEP 32):

> [I]nfinite is what has no terms, bounds or limits, and therefore it cannot be circumscribed; and if it cannot be circumscribed as a finite body, it cannot have an exterior magnitude and figure, as a finite body; and consequently, no measure. Nevertheless, it is no contradiction to say, it has an infinite magnitude and figure: for, although infinite nature cannot have anything without, or beyond itself, yet it may have magnitude and figure within itself, because it is a body: and by this the magnitude and figure of infinite nature is distinguished from the magnitude and figure of its finite parts; for these have each their exterior and circumscribed figure, which nature has not.
>
> (OEP 130–131)

It is plausible to interpret this passage to indicate that while nature has a compositional structure, it is not composed into one body, with one overall compositional structure. The poise and balance between parts and wholes is not the achievement of some *ratio* or proportion among the parts that poises them into a whole, as Cavendish's former thoughts express here:

> Well, replied my latter thoughts, if there be such oppositions between the parts of nature, then I pray inform us, whether

---

8 Recall, however, that for Leibniz a unified creature requires a more robust principle of unification than it does for Cavendish, who takes composition to account for a creature's unification. For this reason, too, while both allow for nested creatures, Cavendish holds that there are overlapping creatures and Leibniz does not.

they be all equally and exactly poised and balanced? To which the former answered, that though it was most certain that there was a poise and balance of nature's corporeal actions; yet no particular creature was able to know the exactness of the proportion that is between them, because they are infinite.

(OEP 36)

While former thoughts say that we cannot know this proportion, I suspect that they mean that no such proportion is knowable, because there is none, and nature 'cannot be circumscribed as a finite body'.

So nature is not a fish. That does not mean that it is a Leibnizian pond—that would look suspiciously like an atomistic world to Cavendish, with all the fish separated by water as atoms are self-contained little worlds separated by space.[9] Nature is an infinite composition of overlapping fish. This in fact brings infinite nature again back to some analogy with finite things. For while we have sometimes talked about a thing's 'figure' as if a creature is one composition with all its parts, we have seen that the identity conditions of the things we call creatures are in fact vague, and dependent upon the things around it. A human mind is many disputing parts, a human being is all kinds of perceptive processes that connect her to the world around her. A finite thing is limited where infinite nature is not because there are things around it. But it is like nature in that it is not a single part with a single figure.

Section 9.5 Perception, knowledge, and order

We are finally in a position to understand Cavendish's claim that natural order requires that all creatures are perceptive and knowing.

As we saw in Chapter 7, Cavendish calls the principle of composition of matter 'self-knowledge', and she calls the ground of the relationship between matter's parts in virtue of that self-knowledge 'perception'. Perception is the relationship between two distinct

---

9   That does not mean that Leibniz is an atomist—he is not, at least not in any sense we have discussed here. But he does seem to countenance something like relations (which are grounded in individual intrinsic perceptions) that are between creatures but not between parts of a creature.

parts of matter in virtue of the fact that they are also one composite. So perception and (self-)knowledge are simply what matter has because it has compositional structure. When Cavendish tells us that order requires that all creatures perceive each other, she means that they must be parts composed with one another. And to say that every creature must be knowing for there to be order is to say that self-knowledge must compose those parts.

On this interpretation of natural order, the parts of nature are ordered simply because they are composed in this way. Cavendish takes composition to ground the fact that anything is related to anything else at all. Just as two things that are not composed cannot perceive each other, two things that are entirely distinct cannot be related. Recognizing this alone goes some way towards undermining a certain easy interpretation of Cavendish's claim that order requires perception. On that kind of reading, two creatures are conceived as two completely distinct things, and so perception is necessary as a kind of communication of information between them. This relies implicitly on over-analogizing all perception with patterning and imagining that for parts to order themselves requires representing each other and nature's dictates. In perception, two parts know each other because, despite the fact that they are distinct parts, they are one composition. In a sense, this is all there is to their knowledge of one another: they are acquainted. This point is again anticipated by Georgescu, who writes that

> when Cavendish says that there would be no order in Nature without self knowledge and perception, she should not be understood to be talking about the particular information required for appropriate action; rather, she is saying that the fundamental grounds for an orderly world are the individuality of parts and their connection with other parts.
>
> (2021: 623)

Similarly, as we have seen, we do not need mentalistic knowledge for bodies to know what to do.

Section 9.6 Wisdom

While we have identified a standard of order, we have not yet addressed whether achievement of this standard of order requires that nature intentionally pursue it. But it does open the way to an account of order that does not appeal to such intentional action on nature's part. That is because we already know how nature divides and composes simply in virtue of its self-motion: that is just the 'chief and general action of Nature'. So we are not faced with identifying the mechanism of action of a new principle. And we do not need a new place for a new norm to live, like the mind of nature, or a force of organization, like intentional action toward that norm.

In a section of the *Observations* entitled 'Of the Providence of Nature, and of Some Opinions Concerning Motion', Cavendish writes that 'if there be any providence in nature, then certainly nature has knowledge and wisdom; and if she hath knowledge and wisdom, then she has sense and reason; and if sense and reason, then she has self-motion' (OEP 72). The rest of the section goes on to focus entirely on self-motion, arguing that without it there would not be the order that we see in nature. This flowchart of conditionals takes us from providence to self-motion. While this does not entail that self-motion is all there is to sense and reason, and sense and reason is all there is to knowledge, and knowledge is all there is to providence, why this flowchart of entailments? On the interpretation I've offered, it makes perfect sense: self-motion yields sensitive and rational matter, which yields knowledge, which yields providence. It is not the only way of making sense of the flowchart, but other interpretations, to make sense of it, need to explain the reason for each entailment.

In another place, Cavendish attributes the very same ordering wisdom not to Lady Nature but simply to self-moving matter:

> Self-moving matter…does act and govern wisely, orderly and easily, poising or balancing extremes with proper and fit oppositions, which could not be done by immaterials, they being not capable of natural compositions and divisions; neither of dividing matter, nor of being divided.
>
> (OEP 35)

It is matter, dividing and composing itself, that poises and balances itself.

Cavendish immediately follows up her description of nature as a 'wise and provident lady' who 'governs her parts very wisely, methodically, and orderly' by further specifying that nature 'is very industrious, and hates to be idle, which makes her employ her time as a good housewife does, in brewing, baking, churning, spinning, sowing, etc.' (OEP 105). Should we take that description of nature literally? Of course not: Cavendish is reminding us that nature is the source of all productions and works in a variety of ways. And Cavendish goes on to clarify that she has these 'numerous employments' because nature, 'being infinitely self-moving, never wants work' (OEP 105). Again we see explanations bottom out in self-motion. Later in this paragraph, Cavendish uses this analogy to argue that women are best fitted to understand nature and 'would prove good experimental philosophers' (OEP 105–106). So the fact that she chooses this analogy can be at least partly explained by her desire to make a practical point.

There are other reasons, too, for Cavendish to choose anthropomorphic idiom in her descriptions of nature. One, as we have seen, is that it is unavoidable. We are human beings, and we engage with the world around us in human ways. We cannot abstract away from that experience to achieve a perfectly general and objective description of nature and its parts. We know that in order for our behavior to be orderly, we need knowledge and perception. While one kind of knowledge and perception is cognitive, Cavendish thinks that we often over-focus on that kind, forgetting about all the wisdom and sensitivity in all the other parts of our bodies that is necessary for us to live orderly lives. But to avoid it entirely would be to transcend our particular human natures, which we cannot do, and a philosopher who pretends that she can will just end up relying on anthropomorphism unawares.

Moreover, just like knowledge, Cavendish analyses even human wisdom in terms of composition. After evaluating the position of some skeptics, she proposes that

> it is best, in my judgment, for sceptics and dogmatists to agree in their different opinions; and whereas now they express their wit by division, to show their wisdom by composition; for thus they will make an harmonious consort and union in the truth of nature.

> (OEP 214)

Here, Cavendish analyses a substantive philosophical dispute in terms of division and composition and identifies philosophical wisdom as a kind of composition.

Even more strikingly, it is not clear that wisdom, strictly speaking, applies to humans at all. Between the *Observations* and the *Grounds*, Cavendish only describes as 'wisdom' something that nature possesses, except for one place, in a list of activities of the mind, where she writes that man names 'wisdom' 'when all the Parts of the Mind move regularly, and sympathetically' (GNP 6 2). Obviously, this is not possible for a finite mind. Similarly, we saw in the last chapter that Cavendish to some extent eschews method as applied to human beings, dismissing many aspects of it as artificial. But she does seem to associate nature's wisdom with nature's method, writing now that nature 'governs her parts very wisely, methodically, and orderly' (OEP 105, see also 158, 207). This is by now a familiar dialectic. Cavendish identifies ways in which we take ourselves (effects) as principles, tells us that in fact it is nature that serves those functions, but ultimately shows that the way that nature serves those functions is not to be understood in human terms.

Another reason that Cavendish characterizes the cause of nature's order as nature's wisdom is to point to the fact that it is not God's wisdom. In one place, Cavendish uses the claim that nature acts freely to justify our natural philosophical investigation into 'the hidden causes of natural effects' against the objections of the church; there, the claim that nature acts freely is best understood as the claim that nature acts by her own power (viz. self-motion) and not by God's decree. So we can have insight into those hidden causes rather than attributing them to God's mysterious designs (PL 2 30). In the following passage, Cavendish might seem to say just the opposite:

Nature is neither absolutely necessitated, nor has an absolute free will: for, she is so much necessitated, that she depends upon the all-powerful God, and cannot work beyond herself, or beyond her own nature; and yet hath so much liberty, that in her particulars she works as she pleaseth, and as God has given her power; but she being wise, acts according to her infinite natural wisdom, which is the cause of her orderly government in all particular productions, changes and dissolutions; so that all creatures in their particular kinds, do move and work as nature pleases, orders and directs: And therefore, as it is impossible for nature to go beyond herself; so it is likewise impossible, that any particular body should extend beyond itself, or its natural figure.

(OEP 109)

This passage is important because it also connects nature's ordering wisdom to free will and to necessitation, which we will consider in the next sections. Here is how it should be read, I think. As we saw in Chapter 2, to say that nature depends upon God is to say that she is not self-created and does not give herself her own nature, and so she 'cannot work beyond herself, or beyond her own nature'. To say that she has free will and liberty is to say that she works according to her own nature and power, which is to cause 'orderly…changes and dissolutions'. It is not to say that she has thoughtful agency to represent and choose her ends or to say that those ends are not determined by her nature. Nature can be called both necessitated and free because she genuinely acts, but according to her nature, which is not within her own power.

Section 9.7 Creatures' freedom

Just as it is 'impossible for nature to go beyond herself', it is 'likewise impossible that any particular body should extend beyond itself, or its natural figure' (OEP 109). The actions of a body are determined by its own figure as well as by the figures of other things, through its perceptions. At the same time, Cavendish frequently describes finite creatures as having freedom or free will to conform to nature's wisdom, writing, for example, that 'every Self-moving Part, or Corporeal Motion, have free will to move after what manner they please' (GNP 1 6).

Detlefsen (2007) and Boyle (2018) interpret such claims to mean that the parts of matter, or creatures, have a robust kind of free agency that allows them to choose, in a fully agential and libertarian sense, what they do. Furthermore, they trace Cavendish's conception of irregularity and ultimately of normativity to the failure of the parts to do so; as Detlefsen writes, the freedom of matter 'allows choices to agree or dissent from the good' (2007: 181).

We have just seen how to understand Cavendish's claims that nature is free without requiring that it make choices like an agent. There are, similarly, plenty of textual reasons to read the freedom of finite creatures in the same way.

Cavendish uses freedom in a number of senses. In one sense of 'free', it simply means 'self-moving' (GNP 5 16) which, of course, does not entail that any parts or creatures are agents. In another sense, as we saw in Chapter 7, Cavendish uses 'freedom' and 'free will' to pick out specifically cognitive-type figurings that are not patternings (OEP 19–20, 35, 97, 127, 170; GNP 5 16, 2 12). By this, she means to isolate figurings that are not perceptions of objects outside of an animal's body. That does not mean that such figurings are not responsive to and occasioned by other figures and actions: they can be occasioned by figures and actions inside the body. (In one place, Cavendish seems explicitly to characterize the voluntariness of cognitions as opposed to perceptions as 'inwardness' (GNP 7 1)). So such motions can still be explained in terms of internal and external structural facts and do not require spontaneous agential will.

In yet another sense, 'free' indicates motions that are less encumbered by inanimate parts. This is the sense in which rational matter is freer than sensitive matter, which is more burdened by inanimate matter (e.g. PPO 2 3 17; OEP 152; GNP 1 9). And in still yet another sense, Cavendish calls something free when it is not 'bound to any particular Action' (GNP 12 2). But by this Cavendish means that, as we have seen, no bit of matter is always tied to a particular figure or motion. It does not mean that a bit of matter can choose whatever particular figure or motion it wants at any time. All of these usages imply a certain lack of constraint, restriction, burden, or bound, but I do not think that Cavendish identifies a core conception of freedom as either a lack of some particular privileged kind of constraint, or a total lack of determination or influence. Nor do any of these senses entail that the actions concerned require thoughtful agency.

Moreover, Cavendish tell us that the question of human free will is beyond the purview of natural philosophy. So whatever sense she means by this is not the sense that she invests 'freedom' with when she calls natural bodies free, for that is within the purview of natural philosophy. To the extent that this question can be addressed by natural philosophy (which treats man as a natural creature), she is at best agnostic about it:

> I do not say, That man hath an absolute Free-will, or power to move, according to his desire; for it is not conceived, that a part can have an absolute power: nevertheless his motion both of body and mind is a free and self-motion, and such a self-motion hath every thing in Nature according to its figure or shape; for motion and figure, being inherent in matter, matter moves figuratively. Yet do I not say, That there is no hindrance, obstruction and opposition in nature; but as there is no particular Creature, that hath an absolute power of self-moving; so that Creature which hath the advantage of strength, subtilty, or policy, shape, or figure, and the like, may oppose and over-power another which is inferior to it, in all this; yet this hinderance and opposition doth not take away self-motion. But I perceive your *Author* is much for necessitation, and against free-will, which I leave to Moral Philosophers and Divines.
>
> (PL 1 29)

Here, Cavendish explicitly contrasts the sense that should be left to divinity with the sense of freedom that concerns natural philosophers, which, from this paragraph, has nothing to do with whether human beings, say, could do otherwise and what that means for whether we are free.

Section 9.8 Occasional causation

An important motivation for those who read freedom in the way that entails thoughtful teleology is that they take it to form part of Cavendish's explanation of the fact that creatures can influence one another's behavior. It might be a surprise that we are only getting to such a seemingly foundational topic now. That is because we needed to see how Cavendish thinks of a number of other things, including self-motion, perception, and order, to grapple with this question. Now that we know what those are, we can see that explaining occasional causation requires nothing beyond these things.

As we have seen, Cavendish holds that there is 'but one Cause, which is self-moving matter' (PL 1 5) and that self-moving matter is 'the prime and only cause of all natural effects' (OEP 116, see also 118, 127, 138). She denies the coherence of one thing's acting on another. And yet, she allows that one creature may 'influence' or have 'power' over another:

> For we have no power at all over natural causes and effects; but only one particular effect may have some power over another, which are natural actions: but neither can natural causes nor effects be overpowered by man so, as if man was a degree above nature, but they must be as nature is pleased to order them; for man is but a small part, and his powers are but particular actions of nature.
>
> (OEP 49)

Cavendish sometimes describes one creature as an 'occasion' or 'occasional cause' of some change in another creature. For example, a hand tossing a ball is the occasion of that ball's flight (PL 445), another hand pulling a rope 'doth occasion the rope to move in such a manner' (PL 1 5), and a watchmaker is the occasion of the figure of a watch (PL 1 23). Cavendish distinguishes between occasional causes (or 'occasions')[10] and 'Prime or Principal causes' (PL 1 23, PL 1 30), arguing that confusing these two is one of the most important sources of error in natural philosophy. At the same time, it is 'to be noted' that 'some Effects producing other Effects is in some sort or manner, a Cause' (GNP 5 16) and that an effect depends counterfactually on its occasional cause (PL 447).

The question, then, is what sort or manner this is, and how is it to be distinguished from a prime or principal cause (and also from an 'immediate efficient cause' (PL 3 9)).[11] To start, let us consider an example. Wind will

---

10 As Boyle (n.d.: 23) points out, in some places, Cavendish distinguishes occasions from causes.

11 There have been a variety of interesting accounts of Cavendishian causes; see especially Detlefsen (2007), O'Neill (2013), Boyle (2018 and n.d.), and Lascano (2023). Eileen O'Neill (2013) has provided a careful account of Cavendishian occasioning, tracing it to the Stoic conception of antecedent triggering causes

occasion the air to be either hot or cold, according to their own temper, but also animals and vegetables, and other sorts of creatures: for, the sensitive, corporeal motions in several kinds of creatures, do often imitate and figure out the motions of exterior objects, some more, some less; some regularly, and some irregularly; and some not at all, according to the nature of their own perceptions. By which we may observe, that the agent, which is the external object, has only an occasional power; and the patient, which is the sentient, works chiefly the effect by virtue of the perceptive, figurative motions in its own sensitive organs or parts.
(OEP 120–121)

In this passage, Cavendish describes occasional causation in a way that sounds almost exactly like perception, and as all interpreters have noted, there is clearly a tight connection between the two. A perception is an action of a perceiver in response to an external object that does not strictly cause that action (but influences it); here, a change in a 'patient' is in fact an action of that 'patient' in response to an external object that does not cause that action (but influences it). The comparison is reaffirmed by the fact that even though Cavendish denies that we have reason to believe that non-animals perceive by patterning, she suggests that the air is warmed or cooled by imitating or figuring the wind.

Continuing to walk the (very) fine interpretive line around perception that I drew in Chapter 6, I will argue that this shows that Cavendish assimilates perceiving with being occasioned but also that it should not make us reconsider whether patterns are anything close to copies of external forms that can be abstracted from and replicated in various media. For one thing, I don't think it is insignificant that Cavendish writes that the air can imitate and figure but stops short of claiming that it patterns. While she surely sometimes treats these as

---

via Van Helmont's *Oriatrike*. Lascano resists Detlefsen's and Boyle's claims that creatures must have bodily free will to account for occasional causation and rightly emphasizes that the only prime or principal cause of natural effects is self-moving matter. Boyle (n.d.) traces Cavendish's distinction between an immediate and occasional cause to Van Helmont's *Oriatrike* (which text, we argued in Chapter 4, was an influence on her account of the mixture of the triumvirate).

synonymous, they each have a different emphasis, and 'patterning' is the one that Cavendish really associates with animal sense perception. As I argued, 'imitating' does not obviously involve producing copies, and 'figuring' does not entail patterning (although 'figuring out' is admittedly less clear). For another thing, Cavendish stresses here, twice and as always, that the 'patient' figures 'according to its own perceptions'. And in the rest of the paragraph, she makes clear that the very different effects of wind on different creatures is an important motivation for her account of occasional causation, just as it is for her account of perception. Given that we defined perception as an action responsive to an external thing, it makes sense to conclude for something to act responsively to an occasion is just the same as for it to perceive something.[12]

As we saw, perception is a direct relationship with another part in virtue of a thing's being composed with that part. Cavendish's critiques of atomism made clear that there can be no influence between single parts. So an occasion and the creature in which a change is occasioned must be parts of one composite as well. We can think of the influenced creature as partaking in the self-motion of the occasion inasmuch as they are one self-moving object (though they are also two parts). And as we have amply seen, Cavendish attributes their ability to compose and divide from one another to the fact that they are all made of matter, so that

> Certainly, there is an Influence amongst all Creatures, for All Creatures being made of the Only and Infinite matter, and there being a Union in its Nature, the Creatures of this Only matter must necessarily have an Influence upon each other.
>
> (PPO2 3 7; see also GNP 1 16 and 2 3)

---

12 We sometimes differentiated in Chapter 6 between a thing's being occasioned by X and a thing's perceiving X. But that is only if we are not being precise. A hallucination might be occasioned by a certain mushroom (or by something I encounter after eating said mushroom), which is not a perception of the mushroom or the thing encountered. But we have argued that this perceptual situation is quite complex and relies not only on the external environment but on other goings-on in the animal. So this is not a problem for the identification of being occasioned with perceiving.

However, this is not a complete analysis. As we saw in the last chapter, when we try to isolate the cause of some particular phenomenon, we frequently fall into the trap of mistaking effects for causes. I think it would be an example of such an error to imagine that there is a relationship that one single creature has with another single creature, which is responsible for it changing the way that it does. The right way to think about occasional causation is not in terms of a single occasion and a single change that it occasions. Rather, the counterfactual relationship between an occasioning creature and an occasioned creature results from the combination of the corporeal figurative motions that underlie both, which include their own motions as well as those of many other parts. While it is certainly true that the motions underlying, say, a ball's movement and the hand that tosses it together contribute to the motion of the ball, this is possible only because the motions underlying the hand, ball, surrounding environment, and all the changes therein are together the causes of the effects that we experience. This is obscured if we think of occasioning as requiring some kind of communication between distinct entities, just as it is if we think of perception that way. On this interpretation, occasional causation is not a new kind of influence but a manifestation of the deeper causes that we already knew were at work. We may contrast this with O'Neill's (Introduction to OEP; xxxiv) and Detlefsen's (2007: 178) claims that Cavendish provides no mechanism for occasional causation.

Consider, for example, that Cavendish sometimes identifies an occasioned action as one that is 'forced' rather than voluntary. She explains:

> When I say, *A thing is forced*, I do not mean that the forced body receives strength without Matter; but that some Corporeal Motions joyn with other Corporeal Motions, and so double the strength by joyning their parts, or are at least an occasion to make other parts more industrious.
>
> (PL 4 33)

The influence of the one forcing body on the forced body is the result of their matter being joined and, as a result, their motions having joint effect.

Cavendish's explanation of contagion also illustrates this analysis. Cavendish rejects Kircher's (OEP: 245, ed. n. 161) proposal that the plague is caused by swarms of tiny animals entering into the body, proposing instead that the plague and other diseases are 'produced several manners or ways' and 'generally do all proceed from the irregularities of corporeal natural motions' (OEP 246). Cavendish makes the same move here that she did in response to other examples in the *Observations*: the cause of the phenomenon is, properly speaking, not some creature external to the phenomena but certain 'corporeal natural motions' that involve the figures and motions of both things, as well as other parts.

Finally, Cavendish's account of what is going on when fire burns wood provides an even clearer example. She writes that fire is 'but a different figure, which being mixt with the parts of the wood, is an occasion that the wood turns into ashes' (OEP 228). She does not tell us that the occasion of the change in the fire is an external object but rather the *combination* of the two (or more) figurative motions of the fire and the wood. This passage is even more explicitly suggestive that apparent transeunt causation in fact involves the combination of the corporeal figurative motions that underlie our identifications of agent and patient.[13]

Section 9.9 Necessitarianism and determinism

A number of aspects of Cavendish's system, as we have interpreted it so far, suggest that she is inclined to determinism and even necessitarianism. For one thing, Cavendish denies that there is true chance in nature, which is to say that there is nothing that happens without a cause or reason: there is 'no such thing as a motion by chance' for 'wherever there is reason, there can be no chance' (OEP 264). What seems to us to be chance is nothing but an effect of 'some hidden Cause' (GNP 1 16), in other words, some cause of which we are ignorant (OEP 264). Therefore, Cavendish writes, infinite nature 'knows of no chance...nor is this visible world, or any part of her, made by chance' (OEP 264).

---

13 There is some consonance here with Mary Shepherd's claim that an effect is a new nature that arises from the combination of other natures.

Cavendish *could* count libertarian free will as a kind of cause, which would make her denial of chance compatible with a denial of determinism. But this would not be in keeping with the spirit of the historical denials of chance that influenced her, either rhetorically or substantively. For example, Cavendish contrasts her denial of chance with Epicurus, who allowed that there was chance in order to avoid fatalism. In contrast, the Stoics, like Cavendish, denied chance and embraced determinism and fatalism.

Cavendish relates her denial of chance to the claim that what happens in nature happens 'out of that preexistent matter that was from all eternity' (OEP 264). This reminds us of Cavendish's frequent claims that not just matter is eternal, but every motion and figure is eternally in matter. In Chapter 3, we interpreted this to mean that self-moving matter, simply by being self-moving matter, always has the potential to make and remake any natural figure. This is true, but it does not quite explain Cavendish's frequent and passionate insistence that neither matter, nor figure, nor motion can perish (e.g. OEP 261). She acknowledges, of course, that everything in nature can change, but at least rhetorically, her insistence that there can be nothing new in nature suggests that everything that happens in nature is just an unfolding of predetermined potentialities.

As we have also seen, Cavendish embraces the notion that a total cause is one that is both necessary and sufficient for its effect, writing that 'the conjunction of sufficient Causes, doth produce such or such Effects; which Effects could not be produced, if any of those Causes were wanting' (GNP 1 16, see also PPO2 3 11) and that 'all Effects are in the power of the Cause' (GNP 5 16). As Cunning argues, passages like this suggest that all causes necessitate their effects, making Cavendish a causal determinist (2016: 205) and even a necessitarian, so that 'bodies cannot do otherwise than what they do' (213).[14] Lascano (2023), in agreement with Cunning, argues that a full set of causes guarantees their effects (153).

---

14 Cunning interprets this determinism as a result of the fact that every body is forced by other bodies to move in certain ways (2016: 157). While, as I have argued, there are counterfactual relations between the different creatures that we identify as individual bodies, this is a result, ultimately, of the fact that all effects are in the power of self-moving matter.

Along with Detlefsen (2007), Boyle argues that since creatures have libertarian freedom, their actions are not determined, and they can genuinely do otherwise (though Boyle (n.d.) argues that how some bodies act is fixed if they decide to act in response to an occasional cause.) Both Boyle (11) and Cunning (2016: 214) genially acknowledge that there are passages that support both deterministic and nondeterministic interpretations. This is true, and I suspect one's choice depends, again, on the deeper question of how anthropomorphic a thinker one takes Cavendish to be. The arguments in favor of indeterministic readings are motivated largely by taking bodies to have libertarian freedom.

In contrast, the deterministic reading squares better with Cavendish's commitment to nature's fundamental rationality. That does not mean that nature is mind-like, but that there is an order to it that is quite independent of our finite knowledge of it. This makes Cavendish interesting to compare with Leibniz and Spinoza, who are closely associated with the principle of sufficient reason. They hold that, for somewhat different reasons from each other and from Cavendish, reason is baked into what is real and that explanatory rational connections that are recognizable by us mirror, at least in principle, the explanatory causal connections that order nature. But as this book argues, when Cavendish writes that 'nature is full of reason' (OEP 264), she does not mean that it is full of anything like what seems reasonable or rational to a human finite mind.

Spinoza is driven not only to determinism by his commitment to the principle of sufficient reason and to rationalism but also to necessitarianism; Leibniz famously courts necessitarianism despite descrying it, and his attempts to circumvent it can often seem unsatisfying. Is Cavendish a necessitarian? That would require not only that causes determine their effects but that everything that happens could not have been otherwise, which means that the ultimate causes of things could not have been otherwise.

We saw in Chapter 2 that the main significance of Cavendish's argument that nature depends on God is that nature could not have its existence and its self-moving power by chance (OEP 220). This suggests that she holds that there must be some explanation of those facts. She does not, however, think that 'it was God' is a satisfying explanation; rather, her arguments indicate that we do not have an explanation, that it is appropriate to expect that there is one, but that we will not know it because it is outside of nature and therefore inaccessible to us.

It is a matter of natural necessity that nature is only matter, that matter is self-moving, and that there are many parts to nature's one body. But it seems that there are many possible ways that creatures could have been, given all of that. We argued in Chapter 2 that Cavendish's account of worlds may be an attempt to think through whether nature would have been otherwise in its particulars (that is to say, whether it could have been made of self-moving matter but manifest an entirely different suite of creatures). Perhaps she is tempted by the notion that all possible creaturely worlds are realized in nature, but I do not think that she takes this to be something we can know.

Section 9.10 Normativity

Detlefsen and Boyle hold that Cavendish 'conceives of order and regularity as the highest goods—in human society as well as in Nature as a whole' (Boyle 2018: 6), and that Cavendish's concern with order is fundamentally normative and 'unabashedly teleological' (Boyle 2018: 8). As Boyle puts it,

> As Cavendish puts it in *Worlds Olio*, 'Nature hath made every thing Good, if it be rightly placed'. This 'rightful placement'—of parts of matter, of rulers and subjects, of men and women, of plants, and animals, and minerals—is what is needed for order, and, Cavendish claims, order is the 'One Law' of Nature.
>
> (Boyle 2018: 8)

On the flip side, Detlefsen holds that there are true irregularities (and disorders) and that 'there are some effects in nature that Cavendish holds to be truly disharmonious, and perhaps even evil' (Detlefsen 2007: 175; see also Boyle 2018). According to both, order is normative not just for nature and the bodies in it but for human life and society as well. Both human and non-human bodies have appropriate roles; it is good when they follow them, and it is not when they don't.

This has the virtue of continuity, in that it acknowledges the fact that human beings are just so many bodies, as are societies.

If normativity were not widespread in nature, one might be worried about explaining its emergence in humans and other animals just as a panpsychist is worried about explaining the emergence of the psychic or mental.

But I do not think that Cavendish is worried about these things. Explaining normativity, like mentality, is important because it is an important part of human life. But I see no reason to doubt that Cavendish thinks that it can be explained in terms of principles that are not fundamentally normative. As I argued in Section 9.2, Cavendish's comments about regularity and irregularity suggest the view that they are real inasmuch as they are certain kinds of motions but not inasmuch as they have fundamental normative significance.

It is undeniable that the language that Cavendish uses to describe nature is normative through and through. And it is completely understandable that some readers are inclined to take this language literally. At the same time, I hope to have given enough reason to hesitate. It is tempting, and not entirely wrong, to describe this as a reductionist interpretation, inasmuch as Cavendish thinks that normative phenomena, like mental phenomena, can be described fully in terms of corporeal figurative motions. But that term threatens to obscure as much as it illuminates. Cavendish holds that these are important human phenomena, that we do indeed experience the world as shot through with normativity and intention, and that it is very difficult if not impossible for us to avoid doing so. She thinks that there are corporeal figurative phenomena that are equally important to other creatures, equally complex and equally mysterious to us. Reductionism can sometimes be associated with an overconfidence in our own understanding of the world, and in particular the explanatory abilities of science, which overconfidence Cavendish does not share. Cavendish holds that everything can be explained with a few principles, but she does not think that we have a complete and certain understanding of those principles, any more than we have a complete and certain understanding of how the great variety of creaturely phenomena are caused by them.

Like perception, Cavendish seems to take normativity to result from the fact that finite creatures have perspectives. The order of nature as a whole is not something at which nature, or anything else, can aim; it is a feature of nature that results from the fact that it is made of matter. That, along with the fact that we are matter and parts of nature, is a precondition of all our interactions with nature, all the knowledge we can have of it, and all the meaning we can make of it.[15]

All this said, a virtue of Boyle's and Detlefsen's work is that the connection that they draw between the human and the social, on the one hand, and the rest of the natural world, on the other, motivates them to give careful philosophical attention to Cavendish's ethics and her political commitments. Because they take more literally the analogy between, say, the roles of the three degrees of matter and the roles of architects and laborers in society, they give sensitive and interesting readings of Cavendish's social views. Such readings also tend to consider the connection between Cavendish's natural philosophy and her eventful life at the center of an eventful time in Europe, relating, for example, her interest in order with her royalist commitments and her reaction to the violence of war, the execution of her loved ones, and the destabilization of exile. Finally, some readers of Cavendish, in taking seriously social and ethical metaphors, see a role for Cavendish's views on gender and sometimes her gender itself in coming to understand aspects of her natural philosophy.

This book does not grapple with these topics, but not because they are uninteresting or unimportant. It is because these are not properly subjects of natural philosophy, and natural philosophy is a reasonable scope for this study. I encourage anyone interested in these topics to visit the suggested reading for this chapter, which lists selected works about Cavendish's ethics and politics.[16]

Section 9.11 Conclusion

In this final chapter, I have tried to disassociate order, for Cavendish, from orderliness for any finite creature, and particularly from orderliness for any mind-like creature, like us. We are able to provide

---

15 Cunning (2016) takes a similar view, arguing that it is 'difficult to locate' normativity in Cavendish's system.

16 Boyle (2018), Chapter 8, contains a useful account of the places where Cavendish suggests that human beings are, after all, exceptional among other natural creatures.

an account of what Cavendish takes natural order to be, along with a mechanism for its preservation, without appealing to nature's plans, to the intentional action of creatures, or to the exchange of representational information by creatures. As perception does not require that bodies communicate about their states or desires, neither does occasional causation. Both perception and occasioning are manifestations of complex figurative motions, some of which involve relationships between two things and some of which are the ultimate causes of all natural effects.

Furthermore, this did not involve the attribution of absolute or fundamental norms to nature. We need not see orderliness as something that nature aims at, certainly not something that nature aims at because it is good. Rather, nature is orderly because everything is both divided and composed, and therefore everything is related. This is ensured by the unity of matter both in the sense of homogeneity and in the sense of compositional unity.

Further reading

Battigelli, Anna. 2021. *Margaret Cavendish and the Exiles of the Mind.* University Press of Kentucky.

Blake, Liza. 2022. 'Margaret Cavendish's Forms: Literary Formalism and the Figures of Cavendish's Atom Poems.' Pp. 38–55 in *Feminist Formalisms*, edited by L. Dodds and M. M. Dowd. Lincoln, NE: University of Nebraska Press.

Boyle, Deborah. 2006. 'Fame, Virtue, and Government: Margaret Cavendish on Ethics and Politics.' *Journal of the History of Ideas* 67(2): 251–289.

Boyle, Deborah. 2012. 'Margaret Cavendish on Gender, Nature, and Freedom.' *Hypatia* 28(3): 516–32.

Boyle, Deborah. (2018), Chapters 1 and 6–8. *The Well-Ordered Universe: The Philosophy of Margaret Cavendish.* New York, NY: Oxford University Press.

Boyle, Deborah. n.d. 'Reason, Freedom, and Occasionalism in Cavendish's Metaphysics.'

Clucas, Stephen. 2003. *A Princely Brave Woman.* New York: Routledge.

Cunning, David. (2016). Chapter 6. *Cavendish.* New York: Routledge.

Detlefsen, Karen. 2007. 'Reason and Freedom: Margaret Cavendish on the Order and Disorder of Nature.' *Archiv für Geschichte der Philosophie* 89(2): 157–191.

Detlefsen, Karen. 2018. 'Margaret Cavendish on laws and order.' In *Early Modern Women on Metaphysics.* Edited by Emily Thomas. New York: Cambridge University Press.

Lascano, Marcy P. 2021. 'Cavendish and Hobbes on Causation.' Pp. 413–30 in *A Companion to Hobbes.* Hoboken, NJ: John Wiley & Sons, Inc.

McNulty, Michael Bennett. 2018. 'Margaret Cavendish on the Order and Infinitude of Nature.' *History of Philosophy Quarterly* 35(3): 219–40. doi: https://doi.org/10.2307/48563633.

Rees, Emma L.E. 2003. *Margaret Cavendish : Gender, Genre, Exile.* Manchester, UK; New York: Manchester University Press.

Siegfried, Brandie R., and Lisa T. Sarasohn. 2016. *God and Nature in the Thought of Margaret Cavendish.* New York: Routledge.

Walters, Lisa. 2014. *Margaret Cavendish : Gender, Science and Politics.* Cambridge, UK: Cambridge University Press.

Conclusion

Each of the other volumes in this series ends with a chapter about the legacy of the philosopher who is the focus of that volume. It's a series about the Greats, after all, and what is a Great without a legacy? The thought that the canonization of a philosopher must at least somewhat track the value of their philosophy is an extremely difficult one to dislodge. Even if one in principle recognizes that the reception of a philosopher is historically contingent in countless respects, it is hard not to revert to wondering: how can centuries of thinkers be wrong? It's the kind of thing that causes someone to confidently declare a philosopher 'not very good' without thinking too hard about it.

Luckily, and exceptionally, Cavendish matches this confidence— or, at least, her writer's persona does. Cavendish's hope that her philosophy would be resurrected by later generations is not just prescient but remarkable: who would even think about the possibility that, after being ignored by her contemporaries and by generations after, later philosophers would discover that she was, after all, really very good? Cavendish's attitude acknowledges both the historical contingency and the importance of a legacy without accepting that it determines the worth of her work. It is tremendously fun to think about who she fantasized would be judging her work more justly and when and how she thought it might happen. Whatever she imagined, her faith in us, living three and a half centuries later, endears her to us and brings her philosophy alive.

Aside from the stubbornness of the association of a legacy with philosophical interestingness, we sometimes encounter a very different assessment of the importance of a canon, coming from a perspective that recognizes and emphasizes its historical contingency.

DOI: 10.4324/9781003107255-11

The thought is that a philosopher's importance is independent of the intrinsic 'goodness' of their work, and that the importance of a canon is to give us a shared cultural and intellectual inheritance, offering us insight into why we think the way that we do. So while Cavendish might be a good philosopher, someone might argue, she is not really an important one since she did not influence other philosophers the way that, say, Plato, Descartes, and Hegel did.

Hopefully no one actually holds this view as so flat-footedly described, but in any case, if part of the importance of the canon is to give us insight into the development of our philosophical questions, concepts, and frameworks, Cavendish gives us this in spades. Not only is she a unique and perceptive critic of both the history of philosophy and the most important developments in philosophy in her time, but her development of her own views draws on these traditions in a way that distils, clarifies, radicalizes, and challenges them all at once. The result is a system that is as novel as it gets but invites us to reexamine our understanding of the early modern period in European philosophy, and—given the influence of that period on subsequent philosophers—our own.

Here are the central ways in which it has done so. There are two, equally deep, polestars of Cavendish's natural philosophy. The first is that nature is full of variety. Cavendish celebrates variety: in how people look and in creatures and their behavior; in the perspective and opinions that people have; in conversation, in dresses, and in speeches, plays, and storylines; in our memories, passions, and perceptions. Cavendish advocates an attitude of wonder that resists our easy, everyday habituation to the world around us. Every bee is a special bee, every fern a special fern.

The second is that there is a deep coherence among things that binds them together as parts of nature and renders our fates inextricable from the fates of the things around us. The explanation of this is that all creatures are both effects and parts of a common principle: self-moving matter. There is infinite complexity involved in the generation of any particular creature by self-moving matter, a complexity that is infinitely beyond our ability to limn it. And yet, Cavendish holds that our reason can provide us a glimpse—just a glimpse!—of what the cause of this great variety must be.

By thinking about what is absolutely essential to the relationship between variety and unity, Cavendish concludes that the being of nature must be the being of something dividable and composable, a principle that captures both coherence and variety with the most minimal of ontological posits. It avoids proliferating kinds of things, kinds of distinctions, kinds of relations—kinds of any kind, really, at least at the fundamental level. Instead, Cavendish argues, the great variety in nature is generated by the infinite potential of structure and activity. It is precisely because matter is not bound to any particular nature or action that it can manifest the infinite variety of forms; the fact that nature is diverse beyond our imagining is best explained if natural principles are maximally simple. This way of resolving variety and unity also refuses to identify one or the other as prior. We need not choose between Parmenides and Heraclitus when it comes to the one and the many. And Cavendish's claim that matter is a complete mixture of the animate and inanimate means we need not choose between them when it comes to the primary of permanence or change.

Cavendish begins with this ontology and with her account of the human mind and of our knowledge of nature that is derived from it. We are just one kind of creature among others, no better or worse than they are, with no special connection to the divine (at least, not in respect of our natural lives). A central claim of this book has been that this anti-anthropocentrism is linked to anti-anthropomorphism and not, as Cavendish is sometimes read, to anthropomorphism. And this has some pretty radical implications for how we think about the mind and about our knowledge of the world.

Cavendish sees the activities and states that we call mental or cognitive as, first and foremost, corporeal figurative motions of bodies with certain structures, just like digestion, photosynthesis, and the freezing of water into ice. This entails that human minds and human persons are much less unified than most of Cavendish's contemporaries thought and more than most philosophers nowadays think. Cavendish takes seriously the question of why, despite this continuity, human and animal sense perception and cognition seem to have such unique characteristics: in particular, she is concerned to explain why these particular kinds of perception and knowledge seem to allow us, despite the very nature of knowledge as being, to peer into other creatures. Her answer is that it cannot, not exactly. We are able to perceive other creatures only to the extent that we are united with them, and to the extent that we are at the same time distinct from them, we are ignorant. In this way, perception grounds the responsiveness of one body to another, and indeed for the fact that creatures are related to each other at all. Sense perception is just one way that some animals do it.

Cavendish's account of perception explains why we have something like internal states that reflect, to some extent, the nature of things outside of us. It is more difficult to see how states and motions that are not perceptions can tell us about anything outside of us and indeed anything at all. We saw that Cavendish is strongly tempted by the view that they do only insofar as they are connected with perceptions, and this explains the vast majority of what she says about our mental lives and about epistemology. The states and activities of our bodies allow us to 'probably guess' at motions beyond our immediate perceptions, which results, at best, in an ameliorated understanding of effects that is practical for life but which does not provide us with insight into causes.

Finally, despite all this, Cavendish seems to think that reason can, in some form or another, allow us to have insight into nature's true causes, without inferring that from effects and creatures. This is how we know that there is one principle, which is (dividable and composable) self-moving matter. It is also by reason, presumably, that we know some of Cavendish's other central claims: that all things are ordered, that all creatures are perceptive and knowing, and that matter is full of sense and reason. But, guided by Cavendish's warning against mistaking effects and creatures for principles and thereby proliferating principles, we have interpreted these claims in ways that do not require adding further principles to dividable and composable self-moving matter.

Cavendish's resistance to mystifying, on the one hand, and her extremely critical attitude toward human hubris, on the other, make her a unique and fascinating presence in the pantheon of early modern philosophers. To inquire into nature requires taking seriously the prospects of intelligibility. But to take those seriously is not to dissect nature, manipulate her, or project our own designs and frameworks onto her. To practice natural philosophy does not mean to place ourselves above nature, but to recognize ourselves as parts of nature, which is both the source of our understanding and of our ignorance. Cavendish's careful attention to the challenge of seeking intelligibility without falling prey to human exceptionalism guides her inquiry. The result is a system of natural philosophy, and a brand of naturalism, that is all Cavendish's own—an unexpected orchid on the forest floor.

There are many different kinds of definitions, and the question of what they are, what definition in general is, and how different kinds of definition can be used in philosophy are themselves philosophical questions. There are dictionary definitions, which clarify a lesser-known word with better-known ones, there are stipulative definitions, which dictate what a word will mean in a certain context, there are real definitions which, if they exist, tell us the essence of the thing defined. These are all represented below, and probably a number of other kinds of definitions. Some of the definitions are specific to Cavendish's usage, some are not; some are anodyne, and some are controversial. For some, I include some philosophical explication. In short, this list is not coherent, and certainly not complete, but hopefully it is helpful.

Active: containing a principle of change.
Agreement (of parts): composition.
Animate matter: matter that is self-moving.
Anthropocentric: attributing special importance to human beings or human characteristics as compared to other creatures.
Anthropomorphic: attributing human characteristics to a non-human creature.
Artificial: per Aristotle, the product of the 'wise contrivance' of a human being.
Atomism: the view that what is fundamental in nature are atoms, or (naturally or metaphysically) indivisible bits of matter, which travel through and interact in empty space.
Brute: fundamental.

Chance: the absence of a cause.

Clayeyness: an example of a creaturely way that things are. Matter isn't clayey.

Composition and division: the fundamental structure of matter. It is cumulative and dissective, nonhierarchical, and basic.

Corporeal: relating to body.

Creature: an effective part of nature that has further parts. Creatures include human beings, other animals, plants, planets, rocks, minerals, elements, and (controversially) artifacts.

Divinity (aka theology): the study of the supernatural.

Error: irregular motions, especially if they are kinds that we classify as mental or sense-perceptual.

Experimental philosophy: a school of natural philosophy according to which inquiry into natural causes should be guided by experiments and observations.

Figure: the compositional structure of a creature, including its parts.

Generation: see Production.

God: what nature depends upon, which is immaterial and distinct from nature.

Ignorance: the lack of knowledge between one part and another that is essential to the relationship between two parts.

Infinite: that which lacks limits or boundaries.

Inherence: the relationship of an attribute, mode, or substance to a substance. An inherent entity depends on the subject in which it inheres.

Irregular: conducing to the dissolution of a particular creature (and so relative to that creature)

Knowledge: the corporeal figurative motions that allow a particular creature to act and react. This includes perception, or exterior knowledge, and self-knowledge, which are the internal structures of creatures.

Love: see Sympathy.

Materialism: in general, the position that everything that exists is matter or is material. For Cavendish, materialism is the claim that everything is matter, or stuff.

Matter: what exists, as far as it concerns us. For Cavendish, matter is essentially dividable and composable stuff.

Mechanists (or, mechanical philosophers): a diverse group of natural philosophers related by some family resemblances, including the commitment to explaining natural phenomena in terms of their parts, on analogy with machines, or in terms of 'mechanical' affections including size, shape, and motion.

Mind: all the corporeal figurative motions that ground what we recognize as mental activities, like thoughts, conceptions, memories, and dreams. Cavendish does not usually include sense perceptions in this. The mind, for Cavendish, is not an immaterial substance as it is for Descartes, and it lacks any special kind of unity that cannot be attributed to other creatures.

Mixture: canonically, the combination of distinct substances with distinct properties into a new substance with new properties. Cavendish argues that natural matter is a complete mixture of the three degrees of matter, but she does not think that they are distinct substances (or that they have properties).

Motion: change. For Cavendish, fundamental natural motion is division and composition, or changes in compositional structure. There are also a variety of creaturely motions that depend upon division and composition.

Natural necessity: necessary, given the basic features of nature. Those are that nature is made of matter, is divided but composed, and is self-moving.

Natural philosophy: the study of the causes of natural phenomena.

Nature: all of continuous infinite matter; everything that there is, as far as it can possibly concern us.

Normativity: relating to some norm, such as goodness, justification, correctness, justice.

Occasional causation: a counterfactual relationship between changes in one creature and changes in another.

Order: the fact that there are many parts of nature that nonetheless are related to one another.

Panpsychism: the view that mentality (in some form) is (in some form) ubiquitous in nature.

Parsimony: simplicity. Ontological or metaphysical parsimony minimizes the kinds of entities, distinctions, structures, and relations that there are.

Patterning: the response of certain creatures upon perceiving another, which involves a reaction to and—to some extent and because of their structures—an imitation of the other in some respects.

Perception: knowledge of exterior parts and actions.

Plenism: the denial of a vacuum and the affirmation of the continuity of matter.

Principles: the most fundamental things, or those things 'out of which all other creatures are made or produced' (OEP 205). Cavendish usually says that she holds that there is one principle, which is self-moving matter.

Principle of sufficient reason: the principle that everything must have a reason or cause.

Production: matter's making new creaturely phenomena.

Rational matter: the freest and subtlest degree of matter, because it is the least burdened by inanimate matter.

Regular: conducing to the survival of a particular creature (and so relative to that creature).

Self-motion: matter's power to cause changes in itself, or the changes that are caused by that power. For Cavendish, this is nature's dividing and composing itself.

Sense perception: knowledge of exterior parts and actions that comes by the five animal sense organs. This is distinct from 'sensitive perceptions', which are more burdened perceptions that reflect the burdens of sensitive matter.

Sensitive matter: animate matter that is more burdened with inanimate matter than is rational matter.

Society: a composition of parts.

Speculative philosophy: this was coined a bit as an epithet by experimental philosophers, much like 'Spinozist' or 'Epicurean'. It picked out those who carve out a significant role for reason prior to observation and experiment.

Structural: features of a creature that depend upon the relationships between its parts, or changes in relationships between its parts. All features of creatures are structural, for Cavendish.

Substance: in Aristotelianism, and in European philosophy much more generally, this refers to what exists, in the 'primary sense'. For Cavendish, everything that exists, exists in the primary sense.

Sympathy: a tendency toward similarity or union in virtue of a similarity or union.

Teleological: an explanation of a phenomenon in terms of its purpose, aim, or goal.

Vacuum: space without matter. Cavendish denies the possibility of a vacuum.

Wisdom: see Order.

World: a part of nature, distinguished from others by the kinds of creatures that is contains.

Bibliography

Adams, Marcus P. 2016. 'Visual Perception as Patterning: Cavendish against Hobbes on Sensation.' *History of Philosophy Quarterly* 33(26): 193–214.

Adams, Marcus P. 2021. 'Motion as an Accident of Matter: Margaret Cavendish and Thomas Hobbes on Motion and Rest.' *The Southern Journal of Philosophy* 59(4): 495–522.

Allen, Keith. 2019. 'Cavendish and Boyle on Color and Experimental Philosophy.' Pp. 58–80 in *Experiment, Speculation and Religion in Early Modern Philosophy*, edited by P. Ansley and A. Vanzo. New York: Routledge.

Anstey, P.R. 2005. 'Experimental Versus Speculative Natural Philosophy.' In *The Science of Nature in the Seventeenth Century*. Studies in History and Philosophy of Science, vol 19. Edited by P.R. Anstey and J.A. Schuster. Springer, Dordrecht. https://doi.org/10.1007/1-4020-3703-1_9

Aristotle. *Metaphysics*. Trans. W.D. Ross. https://archive.org/details/aristotlesmetaph0001aris

Aristotle. *On generation and Corruption*. Trans. J.J. Joachim. https://classics.mit.edu/Aristotle/gener_corr.html

Aristotle. *Physics*. Trans. R.P. Hardie and R.K. Gaye. https://classics.mit.edu/Aristotle/physics.html

Azzouni, Jody. 2020. *Attributing Knowledge: What it Means to Know Something*. Oxford: Oxford University Press.

Bacon, Francis. [1620] 2000. *The New Organon*, edited by L. Jardine, trans. M. Silverthorne. Cambridge University Press.

Bacon, Francis. 1627. *Sylva Sylvarum: or A Naturall Historie in Ten Centuries*. London: W. Lee.

Baptiste, Jean, John Chandler, and van Baron. 1662. *Oriatrike; Or, Physick Refined*. Trans. John Chandler. London: Lodowick Lloyd.

Battigelli, Anna. 2021. *Margaret Cavendish and the Exiles of the Mind*. Lexington, KY: University Press of Kentucky.

Bennett, Jonathan. 1986. 'Spinoza on Error.' *Philosophical Papers* 15(1): 59–73.

Bigelow, John, Brian Ellis, and Caroline Lierse. 1992. 'The World as One of a Kind: Natural Necessity and Laws of Nature.' *The British Journal for the Philosophy of Science* 43(3): 371–388.

Blake, Liza. 2022. 'Margaret Cavendish's Forms: Literary Formalism and the Figures of Cavendish's Atom Poems.' Pp. 38–55 in *Feminist Formalisms*, edited by L. Dodds and M. M. Dowd. Lincoln, NE: University of Nebraska Press.

Borscherding, Julia. 2021. '"I Wish My Speech Were like a Loadstone": Cavendish on Love and Self-Love.' *Proceedings of the Aristotelian Society* 121(23): 381–409.

Boyle, Deborah. n.d. 'Freedom, Necessity, and Occasional Causation in Cavendish's Metaphysics.' Unpublished MS.

Boyle, Deborah. 2006. 'Fame, Virtue, and Government: Margaret Cavendish on Ethics and Politics.' *Journal of the History of Ideas* 67(2): 251–289.

Boyle, Deborah. 2012. 'Margaret Cavendish on Gender, Nature, and Freedom.' *Hypatia* 28(3): 516–532.

Boyle, Deborah. 2015. 'Margaret Cavendish on Perception, Self-Knowledge, and Probable Opinion.' *Philosophy Compass* 10: 438–450.

Boyle, Deborah. 2018. *The Well-Ordered Universe: The Philosophy of Margaret Cavendish*. New York, NY: Oxford University Press.

Boyle, Robert. 1666. *The Origine of Forms and Qualities, (According to the Corpuscular Philosophy) Illustrated by Considerations and Experiments*. Oxford: H. Hall. https://quod.lib.umich. edu/e/eebo/A29017.0001.001?view=toc

Boyle, Robert. 1669. *Certain Physiological Essays and Other Tracts, Written at Distant Times and on Several Occasions by the Honourable Robert Boyle. The Second Edition, Wherein Some of the Tracts Are Enlarged by Experiments, and the Work Is Increased by the Addition of a Discourse about the Absolute Rest in Bodies*.

Boyle, Robert. [1649] 2000. 'Of the Study of the Book of Nature.' In *Collected Works of Robert Boyle: Vol. 13*, edited by E. Davis and M. Hunter. London: Pickering & Chatto.

Broad, Jacqueline. 2007. 'Margaret Cavendish and Joseph Glanvill: Science, Religion, and Witchcraft.' *Studies in History and Philosophy of Science Part A* 38(3): 493–505.

Burge, Tyler. 1977. 'A Theory of Aggregates.' *Noûs* 11(2): 97

Cavendish, Margaret, Edward 1838–1910 Jenkins, and William Cavendish. [1872] 2016. *Cavalier & His Lady*. Wentworth Press.

Chamberlain, Colin. 2019. 'Color in a Material World: Margaret Cavendish against the Early Modern Mechanists.' *The Philosophical Review* 128(3): 293–336.

Chamberlain, Colin. 2024a. 'Duchess of Disunity: Margaret Cavendish on the Materiality of the Mind.' *Philosophers' Imprint* 24(1): 1–18.

Chamberlain, Colin. 2024b. 'Move Your Body! Margaret Cavendish on Self-Motion.' In *Powers and Abilities in Early Modern Philosophy*, edited by S. Bender and D. Perler. New York: Routledge.

Chao, Tien-yi. 2012. '"Between Nature and Art"—The Alchemical Underpinnings of Margaret Cavendish's Observations upon Experimental Philosophy and The Blazing World.' *EurAmerica* 42(1): 45–82.

Charleton, Walter. 1654. *Physiologia Epicuro-Gassendo-Charltoniana; Or, a Fabrick of Science Natural*. London: Tho. Newcomb for Thomas Heath. https://quod.lib.umich. edu/e/eebo/A32712.0001.001?view=toc

Clarke, Samuel. 1731. 'A Letter to Mr. Dodwell.' *Clarke-Collins Correpsondence*. London: Knapton.

Clucas, Stephen. 1994. 'The Atomism of the Cavendish Circle: A Reappraisal.' *The Seventeenth Century* 9(2): 247–273.

Clucas, Stephen. 2003a. *A Princely Brave Woman: Essays on Margaret Cavendish, Duchess of Newcastle*. New York: Routledge.

Clucas, Stephen. 2003b. 'Variation, Irregularity, and Probabilism: Margaret Cavendish and Natural Philosophy as Rhetoric.' Pp. 199–209 in *A Princely Brave Woman: Essays on Margaret Cavendish, Duchess of Newcastle*. New York: Routledge.

Clucas, Stephen. 2011. 'Margaret Cavendish's Materialist Critique of van Helmontian Chymistry.' *Ambix* 58(1): 1–12.

Conway, Anne. 1930. *The Conway Letters*, edited by Marjorie Hope Nicolson. New Haven: Yale University Press.

Coope, Ursula. 2015. 'Self-Motion as Other-Motion in Aristotle's Physics.' Pp. 245–264 in *Aristotle's Physics: A Critical Guide*, edited by M. Leunissen. Cambridge: Cambridge University Press.

Crasnow, Sharon, and Kristen Intemann. 2020. *The Routledge Handbook of Feminist Philosophy of Science*. Milton: Taylor & Francis Group.

Cudworth, Ralph. 1678. *The True Intellectual System of the Universe. The First Part Wherein all the Reason and Philosophy of Atheism Is Confuted and its Impossibility Demonstrated*. London: Richard Royston. https://quod.lib.umich.edu/e/eebo/A35345.0001.001?view=toc

Cunning, David. 2006. 'Cavendish on the Intelligibility of the Prospect of Thinking Matter.' *History of Philosophy Quarterly* 23(2): 117–136.

Cunning, David. 2016. *Cavendish*. New York: Routledge.

Cunning, David. 2023. 'Cavendish and Strawson on Emergence, Mind, and Self.' Pp. 369–398 in *Oxford Studies in Philosophy of Mind 3*, edited by Uriah Kriegel. Oxford Academic.

de Harven, Vanessa. 2022. 'The Metaphysics of Stoic Corporealism.' *Apeiron* 55(2): 219–245.

Dea, Shannon, Julie Walsh, and Thomas Lennon. 2018. 'Continental Rationalism.' *Stanford Encyclopedia of Philosophy*. https://plato.stanford.edu/cgi-bin/encyclopedia/archinfo.cgi?entry=continental-rationalism

Dea, Shannon, Julie Walsh, and Thomas M. Lennon. 2017. 'Continental Rationalism.' *Stanford Encyclopedia of Philosophy*. https://plato.stanford.edu/entries/continental-rationalism/

Della Rocca, Michael. 2020. *The Parmenidean Ascent*. New York: Oxford University Press.

Descartes, Réne. 1984. *The Philosophical Writings of Descartes*, Volume II. Trans. John Cottingham, Robert Stoothoff, and Dugald Murdoch. Cambridge: Cambridge University Press.

Descartes, Réne. 1985. *The Philosophical Writings of Descartes*, Volume I. Trans. John Cottingham, Robert Stoothoff, and Dugald Murdoch. Cambridge: Cambridge University Press.

Descartes, Réne. 1991. *The Philosophical Writings of Descartes*, Volume III. Trans. John Cottingham, Robert Stoothoff, Duglad Murdoch, Anthony and Anthony Kenny. Cambridge: Cambridge University Press.

Detlefsen, Karen. 2007. 'Reason and Freedom: Margaret Cavendish on the Order and Disorder of Nature.' *Archiv für Geschichte der Philosophie* 89(2): 157–191.

Detlefsen, Karen. 2009. 'Margaret Cavendish on the Relation between God and World.' *Philosophy Compass* 4(3): 421–438.

Detlefsen, Karen. 2018. 'Margaret Cavendish on Laws and Order.' In *Early Modern Women on Metaphysics*, edited by Emily Thomas. New York: Cambridge University Press.

Deutsch, Harry. 1990. 'Real Possibility.' *Noûs* 24(5): 751.

Digby, Kenelm. 1644. *Two Treatises: In the One of which the Nature of Bodies, in the Other, the Nature of Mans Soule Is Looked into in Way of Discovery of the Immortality of Reasonable Soules*. Pari: Gilles Blaizot.

Diogenes Laertius. 1925. Tr. Robert Drew Hicks. *Lives of the Eminent Philosophers, Volume 2*. Cambridge: Harvard University Press.

Duncan, Stewart. 2012. 'Debating Materialism: Cavendish, Hobbes, and More.' *History of Philosophy Quarterly* 29(4): 391–409.

Duncan, Stewart. 2022. *Materialism from Hobbes to Locke*. Oxford: Oxford University Press.

Evelyn, John. 1906. *Diary and Correspondence of John Evelyn*. Edited by William Bray. London: G. Routledge & Sons.

Figdor, Carrie. 2018. 'The Fallacy of the Homuncular Fallacy.' *Belgrade Philosophical Annual* (31): 41–56.

Fine, Kit. 2002. 'Varieties of Necessity.' Pp. 253–281 in *Conceivability and Possibility*, edited by T. Szabo Gendler and J. Hawthorne. Oxford: Oxford University Press.

Garber, Daniel. 2020. 'Margaret Cavendish among the Baconians.' *Journal of Early Modern Studies* 9(2): 53–84.

Georgescu, Laura. n.d. 'Infinities within Infinity: Cavendish on Infinities and Finitude.' Unpublished MS.

Georgescu, Laura. 2021. 'Self-Knowledge, Perception, and Margaret Cavendish's Metaphysics of the Individual.' *Early Science and Medicine* 25(6): 618–639.

Georgescu, Laura. 2022. 'Bodies and Their Potential Parts.' In *The Philosophy of Kenelm Digby*, edited by L. Georgescu. Cham: Springer.

Georgescu, Laura. 2023. 'Cavendish on Life.' *Notes and Records of the Royal Society of London* 77: 697–715.

Gibson, James J. 1979. *The Ecological Approach to Visual Perception*. New York; Hove, England: Psychology Press.

Grant, Edward. 2010. *Much Ado about Nothing: Theories of Space and Vacuum from the Middle Ages to the Scientific Revolution*. Cambridge: Cambridge University Press.

Hobbes, Thomas. 1651. *Leviathan*. https://www.gutenberg.org/files/3207/3207-h/3207-h.htm

Hobbes, Thomas. 1656. *Elements of Philosophy, the First Section, Concerning Body.* London: R. & W. Leybourn.

Hooke, Robert. 1665. *Micrographia.* London: Martyn and Allestry. https://quod.lib. umich.edu/cgi/t/text/text-idx?c=eebo;idno=A44323.0001.001

Hübner, Karolina. 2022. *Human: A History.* New York: Oxford University Press.

Hutchins, Barnaby R. 2015. 'Descartes, Corpuscles and Reductionism: Mechanism and Systems in Descartes' Physiology.' *The Philosophical Quarterly* 65(261): 669–689.

Hutton, Sarah. 1997. 'In Dialogue with Thomas Hobbes: Margaret Cavendish's Natural Philosophy.' *Women's Writing* 4(3): 421–432.

Jalobeanu, Dana. 2021. 'Francis Bacon's "Perceptive" Instruments.' *Early Science and Medicine* 25(6): 594–617.

James, Susan. 1999. 'The Philosophical Innovations of Margaret Cavendish.' *British Journal for the History of Philosophy* 7(2): 219–244.

James, Susan. 2018. 'Hermaphroditical Mixtures: Margaret Cavendish on Nature and Art.' In *Early Modern Women on Metaphysics*, edited by E. Thomas. Cambridge: Cambridge University Press.

Kment, Boris. 2014. *Modality and Explanatory Reasoning.* Oxford: Oxford University Press.

Lascano, Marcy. 2020. 'Margaret Cavendish and the New Science.' In *Routledge Handbook to Feminist Philosophy of Science*, edited by S. Crasnow. Milton: Taylor & Francis Group.

Lascano, Marcy P. 2021a. 'Cavendish and Hobbes on Causation.' Pp. 413–430 in *A Companion to Hobbes.* Hoboken, NJ: John Wiley & Sons, Inc.

Lascano, Marcy P. 2021b. 'Margaret Cavendish and the New Science: "Boys That Play with Watery Bubbles or Fling Dust into Each Other's Eyes, or Make a Hobbyhorse of Snow."' Pp. 28–40 in *The Routledge Handbook of Feminist Philosophy of Science.* New York: Routledge.

Lascano, Marcy P. 2023. *The Metaphysics of Margaret Cavendish and Anne Conway.* New York: Oxford University Press.

Leeuwen, Henry G. van [1970] 2013. *The Problem of Certainty in English Thought 1630–1690.* New York: Springer.

Leibniz, G. W. 2007. *The Leibniz–Des Bosses Correspondence.* New Haven: Yale University Press.

Leibniz, G. W., Roger Ariew, and Daniel Garber. 1989. *Philosophical Essays.* Indianapolis: Hackett Publishing Company.

Leibniz, G. W. 2006. *Leibniz's 'New System' and Associated Contemporary Texts*, edited by R. S. Woolhouse and R. Francks. Oxford: Clarendon Press.

Lennox, James G. 2012. 'The Comparative Study of Animal Generation: William Harvey's Aristotelianism.' In *The Problem of Animal Generation in Early Modern Philosophy*, edited by J. E. H. Smith. Cambridge: Cambridge University Press.

Letters and Poems in Honor of the Incomparable Princess, Margaret, Dutchess of Newcastle. 1676. Thomas Newcombe, London. https://quod.lib.umich.edu/cgi/t/text/text-idx? c=eebo;idno=A48252.0001.001

Lewis, David. 1991. *Parts of Classes.* Oxford: Basil Blackwell.

LoLordo, Antonia. 2011. 'Epicureanism and Early Modern Naturalism.' *British Journal for the History of Philosophy* 19(4): 647–664.

MacCarthy, B. G. 1994. *The Female Pen: Women Writers and Novelists, 1621–1818.* New York: New York University Press.

Makin, Bathsua. 1673. 'An Essay to Revive the Antient Education of Gentlewomen in Religion, Manners, Arts & Tongues with an Answer to the Objections against this Way of Education.' London. https://quod.lib.umich.edu/e/eebo2/A51611.0001.001?view=toc

Markosian, Ned. 1998. 'Brutal Composition.' *Philosophical Studies* 92: 211–249.

Martinich, Alyosius. 2009. *Hobbes: A Biography.* Cambridge: Cambridge University Press.

McNulty, Michael Bennett. 2018. 'Margaret Cavendish on the Order and Infinitude of Nature.' *History of Philosophy Quarterly* 35(3): 219–240.

Melamed, Yitzhak Y. 2016. *Eternity.* New York: Oxford University Press.

Michaelian, Kourken. 2009. 'Margaret Cavendish's Epistemology.' *British Journal for the History of Philosophy* 17(1): 31–53.

Millikan, Ruth Garrett. 1995. *White Queen Psychology and Other Essays for Alice.* Cambridge, Mass: MIT Press.

Mueller, Janel (ed.). 2018. *John Donne: Selected Writings.* New York: Oxford University Press.

Newman, William Royall and Lawrence M. Principe. 2005. *Alchemy Tried in the Fire: Starkey, Boyle, and the Fate of Helmontian Chemistry.* Chicago: University of Chicago Press.

Newton, Isaac. [1687] 1729. *Philosophiæ Naturalis Principia Mathematica.* Trans. Andrew Mott as *The Mathematical Principles of Natural Philosophy.* London: Benjamin Mott.

O'Neill, Eileen. 2013. 'Margaret Cavendish, Stoic Antecedent Causes, and Early Modern Occasional Causes.' *Revue Philosophique de la France et de l'étranger* 138(3): 311–326.

Osborne, Dorothy. 1912. *The Letters from Dorothy Osborne to Sir William Temple,* edited by Edward Abbott Parry. London and New York: J.M. Dent & Sons.

Pasnau, Robert. 2013. *Metaphysical Themes 1274–1671.* New York: Oxford University Press.

Paul, L. A. 2017. 'A One Category Ontology.' In *Being, Freedom, and Method: Themes in the Philosophy of Peter Van Inwagen,* edited by J. A. Keller. Oxford: Oxford University Press.

Peterman, Alison. 2019a. 'Empress vs. Spider-Man: Margaret Cavendish on Pure and Applied Mathematics.' *Synthese (Dordrecht)* 196: 3527–3549.

Peterman, Alison. 2019b. 'Margaret Cavendish on Motion and Mereology.' *Journal of the History of Philosophy* 57(3): 471–499.

Peterman, Alison. 2021. 'The World Soul in Early Modern Philosophy.' In *Oxford Philosophical Concepts: The World Soul,* edited by J. Wilberding. Oxford: Oxford University Press.

Peterman, Alison. 2023. '"Actions of a Body Sentient": Cavendish on the Mind (and against Panpsychism).' *Oxford Studies in Philosophy of Mind* (3): 399–431.

Peterman, Alison. 2025. 'Cavendish on Materialism and Metaphysical Structure.' *Oxford Studies in Early Modern Philosophy.* Volume XII. (forthcoming).

Price, Huw. 2004. 'Naturalism without Representationalism.' Pp. 71–88 in *Naturalism in Question,* edited by D. Macarthur. Cambridge: Harvard University Press.

Rees, Emma L. E. 2003. *Margaret Cavendish: Gender, Genre, Exile.* Manchester, UK; New York: Manchester University Press.

Rescher, Nicholas. 2000. *Kant and the Reach of Reason: Studies in Kant's Theory of Rational Systematization.* Cambridge: Cambridge University Press.

Rovelli, C. 2021. 'Relations and Panpsychism.' *Journal of Consciousness Studies* 28(9): 32–35.

Rozemond, Marleen. 2014. 'Pasnau on the Matieral–Immaterial Divide in Early Modern Philosophy.' *Philosophical Studies* 171(1): 3–16.

Rozemond, Marleen, and Alison Simmons. 2023. 'It's All Alive! Cavendish and Conway against Dualism.' In *The Routledge Handbook of Women and Early Modern European Philosophy,* edited by K. Detlefsen and L. Shapiro. New York: Routledge.

Sarasohn, Lisa T. 2010. *The Natural Philosophy of Margaret Cavendish: Reason and Fancy during the Scientific Revolution.* Baltimore: Johns Hopkins University Press.

Schliesser, Eric. 2015. *Sympathy: A History.* Oxford; New York: Oxford University Press.

Schliesser, Eric, and Marcy Lascano. 2022. 'Margaret Cavendish on Human Beings.' Pp. 168–195 in *Human Beings,* edited by K. Hübner. Oxford: Oxford University Press.

Shaheen, Jonathan L. 2019. 'Part of Nature and Division in Margaret Cavendish's Materialism.' *Synthese* 196(9): 3551–3575.

Shaheen, Jonathan L. 2021. 'The Life of the Thrice Sensitive, Rational and Wise Animate Matter: Cavendish's Animism.' *HOPOS* 11(2): 621–641.

Shaheen, Jonathan L. 2022. 'A Vitalist Shoal in the Mechanist Tide: Art, Nature, and 17th-Century Science.' *Philosophies* 7(111).

Shapiro, Barbara J. 1983. *Probability and Certainty in Seventeenth-Century England.* Princeton, NJ: Princeton University Press.

Sharp, Brooke Willow. 2024. 'Veil of Light: The Role of Light in Cavendish's Visual Perception.' *Ergo* 10: 1471–1494.

Sider, Ted. 2018. *Crash Course on Natural Necessity.* https://tedsider.org/teaching/structuralism_18/crash_course_on_natural_necessity.pdf

Siegfried, Brandie R. and Lisa T. Sarasohn. 2016. *God and Nature in the Thought of Margaret Cavendish.* New York: Routledge.

Skrbina, David. 2017. *Panpsychism in the West.* Cambridge, Mass: The MIT Press.

Smith, Justin E. H. 2012. *The Problem of Animal Generation in Early Modern Philosophy.* Cambridge: Cambridge University Press.

Spiegel, Thomas J., Simon Schüz, and Daniel Kaplan. 2023. 'Introduction to Naturalism: Challenges and New Perspectives.' *Topoi: Special Issue.* 42: 671–674.

Stanley, Thomas. 1656. *The History of Philosophy, in Eight Parts.* London: Humphrey Mosely and Thomas Dring. https://quod.lib.umich.edu/e/eebo/A61287.0001.001?view=toc

Stoljar, Daniel. 2001. 'Physicalism.' *Stanford Encyclopedia of Philosophy*. https://plato.
stanford.edu/entries/physicalism/

Thomas, Emily. 2018. *Early Modern Women on Metaphysics*. Cambridge, UK; New York:
Cambridge University Press.

Van Helmont, Jan Baptist. 1662. *Oriatrike, or Physick Refined*. London: Lodewick
Lloyd. https://archive.org/details/bim_early-english-books-1641-1700_oriatrike-
or-physick-re_helmont-jean-baptiste-v_1662

van Inwagen, Peter. 2011. 'Relations vs. Constituent Ontologies.' *Philosophical Perspectives*
25(1): 389–405.

Walters, Lisa. 2014. *Margaret Cavendish: Gender, Science and Politics*. Cambridge: Cambridge
University Press.

West, Peter. 2022. 'Margaret Cavendish on Conceivability, Possibility, and the Case of
Colors.' *British Journal for the History of Philosophy* 30(3): 456–476.

Whitaker, Katie. 2002. *Mad Madge*. New York: Basic Books.

Whiting, Daniel. 2024. 'Is Margaret Cavendish a Naïve Realist?' *European Journal of
Philosophy* 32: 321–341.

Wilkins, Emma. 2014. 'Margaret Cavendish and the Royal Society.' *Notes and Records: The
Royal Society Journal of the History of Science* 68(3): 245–260.

Winegar, Reed. 2018. *Infinity in Early Modern Philosophy*, edited by O. Nachtomy. New
York: Springer.

Wolfe, Charles T. 2016. *Materialism: A Historico-Philosophical Introduction*. Switzerland:
Springer.

Wolfe, Charles. 2017. 'Materialism and "the Soft Substance of the Brain": Diderot
and Plasticity'. *British Journal for the History of Philosophy* 24(5): 963–982.

Wolfe, Charles T. 2023. 'The Life of Matter: Early Modern Vital Matter Theories.' *Notes
and Records the Royal Society Journal of the History of Science* 77(4): 673–675.

Woolf, Virginia. 2015. *A Room of One's Own*, edited by David Bradshaw and Stuart
Nelson Clarke. Chichester; Malden: Wiley Blackwell.

Woolf, Virginia. 2022. *The Common Reader – First and Second Series – Complete Edition*.
Redditch, UK: Read Books Ltd.

Index

For Product Safety Concerns and Information please contact our
EU representative GPSR@taylorandfrancis.com Taylor & Francis
Verlag GmbH, Kaufingerstraße 24, 80331 München, Germany